# CLINT
# EASTWOOD
## BILLION DOLLAR MAN

### DOUGLAS THOMPSON

JOHN BLAKE

Published by John Blake Publishing Ltd,
3, Bramber Court, 2 Bramber Road,
London W14 9PB, England

www.blake.co.uk

First published in hardback in 2005

ISBN 1 85782 572 1

British Library Cataloguing-in-Publication Data:

A catalogue record for this book is available from the British Library.

Design by www.envydesign.co.uk

Printed & Bound in Great Britain by Creative Print & Design (Wales)

1 3 5 7 9 10 8 6 4 2

Papers used by John Blake Publishing are natural, recyclable products made from
wood grown in sustainable forests. The manufacturing processes conform to the
environmental regulations of the country of origin.

Every attempt has been made to contact the relevant copyright-holders,
but some were unobtainable. We would be grateful if the appropriate people
could contact us.

Pictures reproduced by kind permission of Pictorial Press, Rex Features,
Universal City, Warner Bros.

For Lesley, always

# CLINT
## EASTWOOD
### BILLION DOLLAR MAN

# ACKNOWLEDGEMENTS

There are scores of people to thank for their help over a disquieting number of years and most of them appear in what follows. Those who don't include James Ravenscroft at John Blake Publishing, for his help and enthusiasm, and my agent Robert Smith, who originated the project and believed in a truly popular 21st-century biography of Clint Eastwood.

I first encountered Clint in 1974. He was a gentleman then and has been ever since, on movie sets, at Hollywood studios, at grand events and in his home town of Carmel, California, which has always been his anchor, his antidote to the worldwide acclaim he has achieved in a unique movie-making career. He's always been generous with his time.

As have a myriad of his co-stars and film-making collaborators, friends, family and lovers. Richard Burton told me Clint was the easiest actor – 'no histrionics whatever' – he ever worked with. He came up with his now famous phrase to describe his *Where Eagles Dare* co-star: Clint, he said, had 'dynamic lethargy'. No one, then or now, had a clue what he meant other than it was intended as a generous compliment. Charlie Bronson, who got hauled into a *Dirty Harry* versus *Death Wish* movies war and had appeared in his early days in *Rawhide*, offered: 'Clint's all class so there's no conflict.' Richard Harris rattled on that he had one of the great experiences of his life co-starring in *Unforgiven*. Among a host of others, Morgan Freeman, Gene Hackman, Sean Penn and Tim Robbins are fans and Oscar beneficiaries of their friend's work.

A Civil Rights supporter and activist actor, Robbins said of his first meeting: 'Clint is not really a Republican, he's a libertarian. I thought I was going to meet "Dirty Harry" but he's a sweet, gentle, decent person. Look at his crew: there are people that have been with him for years and years. He's a loyal, honourable man. That's what's important for all of us.'

Meryl Streep was more intimate: 'I love him.'

Which is something echoed by Hilary Swank from *Million Dollar Baby*, Rene Russo from *In the Line of Fire*, Wanda De Jesus and Anjelica Huston from *Blood Work* and Marcia Gay Harden from *Mystic River*. Eastwood has always brought women into his films for a reason, not as decoration.

He is a family man in a grand, jigsaw-puzzle sense: he has seven children by five different women; in 2005 the eldest, Kimber, was forty-one and the youngest, Morgan, nine. Almost all are open and easy to talk with. Clint is patriarch of an unusual but usually very happy family.

Eastwood is not a superstar corporation but a sharp, individual businessman who knows the balance of box office and integrity, professionalism and privacy and, most of all, understands loyalty. He's been that way since his 1950s television series *Rawhide*. He has worked with the same people for decades, and explains: 'They know the shorthand.'

They also all know Clint. And that is so welcome when you want to discover the inside story of a living legend ...

To all, salutations.

'Dougie Thompson's one of the good guys.
He's been around. He knows the stories.'
CLINT EASTWOOD


'Go on, make my day.'
CLINT EASTWOOD AS HARRY CALLAHAN IN
*SUDDEN IMPACT*, 1983


'Clint's the least disappointing icon in American film.'
SEAN PENN, OSCAR WINNER 2004, FOR THE
EASTWOOD-DIRECTED *MYSTIC RIVER*


'I think this might be the last Oscar I see Clint win,
but then I said the same thing when he won in 1992.'
CLINT EASTWOOD'S MOTHER, RUTH, AGED 96, AT THE
CONCLUSION OF THE 2005 ACADEMY AWARDS

# CONTENTS

# PREFACE

## Baby Love

'I'm just a kid.'

CLINT EASTWOOD, AGED 75 ON 31 MAY 2005, AS HE ACCEPTED
ONE OF THE FOUR OSCARS FOR *MILLION DOLLAR BABY*

BEING Clint Eastwood is a delicate act but he's a master at it. Experience, you could argue.

When he won the evening of 27 February at the 2005 Oscars at the Kodak Theatre in Hollywood with *Million Dollar Baby*, the movie presented with the Academy Awards for Best Film, Best Director, Best Actress and Best Supporting Actor, his co-producers were up on stage with him.

The film-makers were accepting the award for Best Film for *Million Dollar Baby*, which had been over many high hurdles to get made. With such movies we only see the result and, in this case, the glory.

The Oscar broadcast producers are extremely aware of

television time and when winners go on for too long the orchestra is instructed to blast out 'wrap up' music.

Eastwood's co-producer, Tom Rosenberg, who had taken a big financial risk in support of the film, was speaking as the music swelled to drown him out.

If you get out your video of the seventy-seventh annual Academy Awards you'll hear that whisper through the gravel which is Eastwood's voice, telling Rosenberg: 'Don't let 'em run you off.'

Rosenberg didn't. He'd joined the 'good guys'.

Clint Eastwood has never been 'run off'. He's always been his own man.

It's summed up in a singular, grown-up attitude, which he explained a few years ago: 'I've always had the theory that actors who beg their audiences to like them are much worse off than actors who just say: "If you don't like this don't let the door hit you in the ass..."'

# PROLOGUE

## The Numbers Game

'Life? It's all improvisation.'

CLINT EASTWOOD, 2003

AGE? Just a number?

Clint Eastwood was 75 years old on 31 May 2005.

Old?

Yes, by the calendar; no by the attitude.

'I'm just a kid, I've still got a lot of stuff to do,' he said a few weeks earlier, his hands weighed down by the couple of Oscars he clasped like workout weights. You need a little more than daily exercise to be able to deftly handle the Academy Awards, to deal with fame adroitly. Yet, by the look of Clint Eastwood, he could bench-press many more fistfuls of the gold-plated, 13½-inch tall statuettes, which undergo a remarkable metamorphosis when placed in the right hands.

Which he might do in 2006 with his film version of *Flags of Our Fathers*, the hugely praised account by James Bradley detailing the battle of Iwo Jima in the Second World War. He's only going to direct and co-produce that film, not act in it. It should be released in cinemas before his seventy-sixth birthday. Yes, he's still 'got stuff to do'.

Clint, the man renowned for being cool and laconic, slow and easy, liberal with his attitude and judgements, is always in action. Watch his face, his sparkling, bright-green eyes especially, and his interest is everywhere. He's his own software program. He gathers all around him and then logs on to his singular inquisitiveness. Every book, documentary, news event, man, woman, child, local event and turn in the road is an opportunity to tell a story and most surely to write a song or a movie soundtrack. It is, as he always says, all about improvisation. Life, he also insists, is where you are constantly adjusting to everything.

So, as far as he's concerned, numbers, even intimidating ones, don't comprise a large part of the equation. But at the Kodak Theatre in Los Angeles on 27 February 2005, they came into play like the lottery.

Clint and *Million Dollar Baby*, which he called his 'humble movie', were in contention for top honours. The main opposition was two first-class pictures, both biographical: Martin Scorsese's big-budget Howard Hughes saga *The Aviator* and the admirable *Ray* by Helen Mirren's husband Taylor Hackford, the story of music giant Ray Charles. Also in the running at the annual cavalcade of self-acclaim were Mike Leigh's *Vera Drake* and Alexander Payne's amusing, with a hint of boldness, wine-soaked *Sideways*.

The 5,808 Academy of Motion Pictures and Sciences voters made Clint's day. At 74 he became the oldest director to earn the top honours as Best Director. He'd previously won the Best Director trophy for *Unforgiven* in 1992.

Numbers? Interesting ones. With television viewers turning off worldwide, the Oscars producers wanted a younger, hipper image, which was why Chris Rock appeared as the host of the 2005 Awards. Hip? As it turned out, some of the big winners might be candidates for hip replacements.

Eastwood directed his first film three years before Hilary Swank, who was named Best Actress for *Million Dollar Baby*, was born. He displayed both his long-matured cool and his elan when he was named Best Director. The slightly less veteran Martin Scorsese, then 62, lost his fifth nomination for the award in what had been the most hotly contested and watched conflict of the 2005 Oscars. It was the victory of a small, intimate character piece over *The Aviator*, which, true to the extraordinary life and legend of Howard Hughes, was a super-sized, $110-million extravaganza of Hollywood movie-making.

Numbers?

Clint thanked his mother Ruth, then 96, for her 'genes' and pointed out: 'I'm happy to be here and still working.' He then expressed his gratitude to a long list of veteran collaborators, including production designer Henry 'Bummy' Bumstead, aged 90 in 2005 and winner of two Oscars, for *To Kill a Mockingbird* and *The Sting*, whom he described as a member of 'our crack geriatrics team'.

Who, to use the vernacular of *Million Dollar Baby*, were in Clint's corner. The contest between front-runners

Scorsese and Eastwood proved to be the evening's only true nail-biter. These two well-respected men embody different strains of Hollywood film-making: Scorsese, the diminutive, fast-talking Italian New Yorker, was an *enfant terrible* of the 1970s who spearheaded one of the greatest periods in American film with such intensely personal, super-macho stories as *Taxi Driver* and *Raging Bull*. More than 30 years later, when most of his auteur comrades had faded from the scene (with the entertaining exception of Steven Spielberg), Scorsese devotes himself to visually flamboyant historical pageants like *Gangs of New York* and *The Aviator*, both of which featured Leonardo DiCaprio.

In the other corner was 'Dirty Harry', the film star who also became a director in the 1970s with movies like *Play Misty for Me* and *The Outlaw Josey Wales*. At that time Eastwood was largely derided by critics as either a crypto-fascist or a dud; arguably because of the single-minded *New Yorker* critic Pauline Kael, who attacked the original *Dirty Harry* for its 'fascist medievalism' and 'remarkably single-minded attack on liberal values'. This critical contempt for the five furious, Magnum .44-driven Dirty Harry Callahan movies only dissipated, and even then not in all circles, with 1992's Oscar bonanza, *Unforgiven*.

Eastwood, still angered by what he saw as Kael's bigotry, says of the series, films that created their own genre: 'I was playing a part. I'm an actor playing a role and if somebody thinks I'm supposed to be that guy, then great. You have to put yourself in the roles, and if you put yourself into them positively enough, strongly enough, people believe you are this person. It's a fantasy. But it's a fantasy the audience wants to believe.'

Of the now-dead Kael, he was asked if she did him real damage. He softly replied: 'No, no. I'm still here. And she's not.

'Kael was saying I was a product of the Nixon years – that I represented Nixon. But I was doing very well as an actor long before Nixon became President. And I was doing well after Nixon. And somebody else said: "Well, he's an actor of the 1980s." But the 1990s and onwards have been some of my best years, so I don't know where all these experts come from.

'I just went ahead and did my own thing.'

Since *Unforgiven* he has told his stories tersely, with creative economy and increasingly lean budgets. In Scotland's canny capital, Edinburgh, they'd build this fast and frugal man a monument. Clint, who is at his happiest at the piano and loves the blues, wrote and played those films' jazzy, melancholic scores. In the 21st century he is a Hollywood legend, one of the most consistent top attractions in the history of the movies, and on the marque with Clark Gable and Gary Cooper and John Wayne and Paul Newman in terms of star longevity.

Eastwood won this particular Oscar contest. Scorsese is not giving up, and a cinematic rematch is on the way. In 2006, when *Flags of Our Fathers* will be in contention, so will he be with *The Departed*, an Irish gangster story starring DiCaprio, who seems to have taken Robert De Niro's place in his repertory company, and the non-retiring, in every sense, Jack Nicholson.

Nicholson? He's a number too.

In the early 1990s he and Eastwood were playing golf together and they talked about retirement. Eastwood recalls: 'Jack said he was going to do just one more movie, *The Crossing Guard*, and that would be his last. I said I would do *In the Line of Fire* and *A Perfect World* and that would be it. Well, he went on to act in about ten more movies, and I went on to act in or direct six more. They keep saying yes to you, so you keep on going.'

Yet *Million Dollar Baby*, which many prominent people rate as Eastwood's greatest work, was a film the powers that be in Hollywood were not too keen to say yes to. It was one of the hardest 'sells' of his career, and this baby was nearly never born. Especially as an Eastwood film. At an early stage in the film's development, Arnold Schwarzenegger, 2005's Governor of California (a job you could have bet on Clint getting a couple of decades ago), was considered for the role of the boxing trainer played by Eastwood; Sandra Bullock was once the favourite for Swank's part as a boxer in search of a mentor.

In another incarnation it was to be an HBO TV mini-series or an independent film directed by Clint's friend Anjelica Huston. Then, Hollywood happenstance. It happens. *Million Dollar Baby* proves it, along with so many other things. Life, even the movies' version of it, can be changed by serendipity. In this case, both at the same time.

Jerry Boyd, a Hemingway wannabe, was one of life's rejects. His three wives had thrown him out, publishers didn't want his stories, written as Francis Xavier Toole, and he was scuffling a living working in a boxing gym in Los

Angeles. And writing his short stories; his collection *Rope Burns* was finally published in 2000, when he was nearly 70.

Then a dead man gave him a little luck. But just a little. The influential Hollywood producer Al Ruddy had cast the late actor Al Lettieri as Virgil 'The Turk' Sollozzo in *The Godfather* in 1972. Ruddy was asked by Anjelica Huston to meet Boyd to discuss his short stories.

Boyd was a friend of Lettieri's and when he met Al Ruddy he mentioned the name. 'I said: "Let's go and have a drink at the Havana Club,"' recalls Ruddy. 'He said: "I can't, I'm in Alcoholics Anonymous." I said: "So, you'll have a Coke and I'll have a drink." Needless to say, we both drank until 5am.'

But Huston had moved on to work on a project with Mrs Hollywood, Julia Roberts. Nevertheless, Ruddy made Boyd's dream true and bought the rights to his stories, a month before Boyd died from a heart attack in September 2002.

The project went ahead, which is where Paul Haggis, a creator of the television series *Walker, Texas Ranger*, came in. He told Ruddy he would write a movie script for *Million Dollar Baby* – if he could direct it. The script, an adaptation of two of Boyd's stories, was then shown to Tom Rosenberg's Lakeshore Entertainment, who were enthusiastic. Hilary Swank and Morgan Freeman were set up as the stars. Ruddy then showed the script to his old friend Clint, who said he had all but retired from acting. Nevertheless, Clint read the script as a favour to Ruddy and liked it; he was just concerned how it might be directed.

Although he'd sworn he would never again star and direct a film at the same time, he asked Ruddy if he could direct. Haggis, who was nominated at the Oscars for his script, said:

'It was a tough ten minutes for me. I decided, of course, I would let him direct. How often do you get to work with Clint Eastwood?'

But it was no first-round knockout. Warner Brothers, Clint's long-time studio home, initially declined to participate, worried that boxing movies weren't commercially viable. They thought the script 'too dark' and the comparatively modest budget of $30 million 'too high'. The rejection came despite the fact that the Eastwood-directed *Mystic River* was one of 2003's best-reviewed films and a box-office hit for the studio. Lakeshore Entertainment agreed to bankroll *Million Dollar Baby* and, after other studios passed, Warner Brothers relented and agreed to share the film's cost.

Unlike most movies that are put through endless rewrites, Clint filmed the first and only draft of Paul Haggis's script in 37 days, working in and around the vibrant downtown area of Los Angeles to tell the story of cantankerous – is there any other sort? – boxing trainer Frankie Dunn.

And of the 'Million Dollar Baby'. Dunn runs a haven for hopefuls and puts up with the hopeless. Morgan Freeman, as former boxer Eddie 'Scrap Iron' Dupris, helps him with the job, which suddenly includes looking after the fortunes of Maggie Fitzgerald, played by Hilary Swank. Maggie wants to fight her way out of dire straits with self-justifying success in the ever-more popular discipline of women's boxing.

So far, a boxing movie with a twist in that the contender is a woman. But there's more to it than that, which is why Eastwood got involved. 'I'm at an age in life when I'm not trying to do things that I did years ago. I've tried to shoot my persona down so many times. I'm looking for different stories, stories to go with the maturing of the years. I probably would have retired years ago if I hadn't found interesting things to do.'

This was interesting. And it got more so as the Oscars for 2005 approached. There had been Golden Globe awards and many other critical and endorsing honours, but then Clint was accused of being a soft-hearted, left-wing sympathiser.

Hey, this was the man who at the height of anti-Vietnam protest supposedly supported President Richard Nixon. He also backed Ronald Reagan, who borrowed his fellow actor's catchphrase 'Make my day' for a colourful stand-off with the US Congress in 1983. Around the same time Eastwood phoned President Reagan to lobby for White House support to send a team of mercenaries into Laos in search of long-missing POWs. Even after Reagan refused, Clint was said to have helped to fund two such missions.

Left-wing extremist? Yes, according to high-profile right-wing commentators who attacked *Baby* for spreading 'liberal propaganda' behind the smokescreen of a sports drama. Their argument was that the film's downbeat conclusion was an apparent endorsement of mercy killing. Not to Clint: 'I never thought about the political side of this when making this film. How people feel about that is up to them. I'm not a pro-euthanasia person and this is a story about a giant dilemma and how one person had to face that.'

Later he said of the controversy: 'I've had them work me over before.' And of the honours: 'It's very nice. But I just do what I feel like I should be doing and whether you are nominated for something has never been the motivating force for me. It's in the eye of the beholder, and once you finish a film, in a way, it doesn't belong to you any more, it belongs to the audience to interpret it in the way they feel like interpreting it, and that goes for whoever is nominating whatever. You can't make movies thinking about that.'

He calls where he is in life 'the back nine' and he does enjoy his golf, although he qualifies this: 'I like playing golf but I don't want to *have* to play golf. I like work. I'm involved. That challenges me. I like playing golf as an avocation – but while I'm good at it, I'm not talented at it. And I keep getting offered things. There's always a new hurdle.

'I love the spirit of acting, I love to watch actors, I love to direct them. I probably, in my mind somewhere, could have retired from acting a long time ago if somebody had said: "OK, that's what you should do." But then, you know, there's always some fool out there who wants you.'

He also likes doing his business deals with the help of his agent-business manager Leonard Hirshan, who first began representing him in 1961. Many years later, in 2005, they were both happy with a scheme to use Clint's image on gambling machines to be set up in Las Vegas. The name?

'They wanted to make one called "A Fistful of Dollars", which is a great title for a slot machine,' says Eastwood. 'And then there's "A Few Dollars More". You get the picture. They already got a Marilyn and a Bogart.

'Maybe I'm the only one alive, though.'

And kicking.

# ONE

## FAMILY MATTERS

'He believes a bug has as much right
to be on this earth as anybody else.'
DINA EASTWOOD ON HER HUSBAND, 2003

THE secret may be in the numbers. Or the diet. Clint's always had a way of surviving but he is very much of a generation that likes to look after itself. 'I worked for every crust of bread I ever ate.' It is an attitude which has driven his life and his work. He despises waste, especially of time. He's a pioneer who has always wanted to put down roots. 'I never bought any real estate I didn't really like. I like land, the land out here.'

The Bay area of northern California, especially the exceptional town of Carmel on the Monterey Peninsula, of which he owns several thousand acres, is his home. Carmel was nicknamed 'Clintville' in 1986 when the man who, in worldwide votes, remains the world's most respected and popular star, was elected mayor.

Yet he was born in the Bohemia of America itself, San Francisco, on 31 May 1930. On that date in 2005 many, including tourists on the Golden Gate Bridge and the others and residents sipping Starbucks in Washington Square and all the other city hangouts – in Tadich Grill with the good guys and maybe even the ghosts of Alcatraz out there on the water with the Hollywood accountants – raised a glass to celebrate his seventy-fifth birthday.

He is part of our imagination of that photogenic city for *Dirty Harry* and *Magnum Force*, as much as the cable cars and Steve McQueen in *Bullitt*, as the rolling fog, as Bogart as Sam Spade in *The Maltese Falcon*. He didn't stray too much for a location for classic movies like his first job as a director, *Play Misty for Me*, set in Steinbeck's Monterey, or try to *Escape from Alcatraz*.

Eastwood is so like the most European of American cities, laconic, laid-back, full of surprises but locked into loyalty, and, for all the tolerance and counterculture, determined to get things done – his way.

He is only one of a trio – Charlie Chaplin and Woody Allen are the others – of independent film-makers who have totally controlled their own pictures. Even a faint acquaintance with the machinations of control-freak Hollywood reveals what an achievement that is.

Many grew up watching him as Rowdy Yates, the number-two trail boss on the TV series *Rawhide*. He went on to the 'spaghetti Westerns' as the Man with No Name, a role which provoked so much interest. But it wasn't until *Dirty Harry* in 1971 that the phenomenal impact Eastwood would have on popular culture first became evident. Everyone from President Nixon to Muhammad Ali wanted Eastwood to say his trademark 'Make my day' for them. Lots of people he meets still do. He lives in Pebble Beach with his second wife, Dina, a former television journalist at KSBW, Salinas, California, whom he met – she was 27 then – when she interviewed him in 1992 following the success of *Unforgiven* and whom he married after filming 1995's *The Bridges of Madison County*. That story of found and lost love had a major impact on him.

That was most apparent in Paris, for when he talked of Dina Ruiz he did not sound like the Clint of the past. The message from *The Bridges of Madison County* was, he said, 'Don't let anything pass.'

During his European promotional tour for that movie he was asked about love. Clint Eastwood? Love? He answered: 'It's much stronger when one meets in the second half of one's life.'

Eastwood, who has had a long, eventful and complex love life – he was a true sexual cowboy – had finally settled down. He and Dina have a daughter, Morgan, who was nine in 2005; that year they shared their home with a well-fed black and white rat, Whiskers, who keeps having litters by an older rat they call Norbert, three chickens, a black and pink pig, Penelope, and Paco, a very politically correct green lady parrot with a yellow nape who only ever says, 'I Love You' or 'Happy Birthday.'

Which, given Eastwood's extended family, should possibly be patented as an energy-saving device. For everybody from his previous marriage and relationships is in touch and involved with one other. In January 2005 he and his sister Jeanne hosted a surprise party for their mother's ninety-sixth birthday.

He's in contact with 'Mumsy' every day: no matter where he is he talks to her on the phone every evening. He's acutely aware of age, and respectful of it. When he was making *Piano Blues*, one section of a seven-part television documentary on the blues in 2003 – call it happenstance again, for it was produced for America's Public Broadcasting System by Martin Scorsese – he worked with legendary musician Joe Willie 'Pinetop' Perkins.

He was told: 'Pinetop looks good; he's 89, you know.'

Clint: 'Eighty-nine? Wonder what he eats.'

The numbers, the age issue, is there more in his personal than his professional life. When he collects Morgan from school he's the oldest dad around and aware of it. That the mothers might swoon over him doesn't make him less conscious of the situation.

It's an issue that is apparent and no matter how strong or disciplined or in charge you are, there is nothing that can be done about it. The clock does not tick the other way.

Clint, a lean six foot four with the healthy cheeks of someone who looks after himself, just gets on with it. Life, remember, is an improvisation. You can help it along. His tall frame is still rangy from his daily runs and workouts on his black Universal exercise machine, with its parallel bars, weights, slantboards and two punching bags, which allows him to do sit-ups, back lifts, bench-presses and boxing routines to Bach or jazz from a Sony tape deck.

Asked about cosmetic surgery – self-improvisation if you like – in 2002, he said: 'I have no choice but to look the way I am, because they don't make enough shoe polish for my hair and they don't have a sander for my face. What the hell, when you get to a certain age you've just got to make fun of it. I've never considered myself a matinee idol anyway. I always felt I was a character actor. At some point you have to say: "This is who I am."'

Yet, a couple of years later, when he collected an award in February 2004 at the Beverly Hilton Hotel in Los Angeles, he looked considerably less lined, fresher face to face. Later one of his close, lifetime associates confided: 'Clint's had some work done.'

Possibly. Understandably. Possibly not. He looks good, energetic and youthful, maybe not such a crinkly, thanks to whatever, be it the surgeon or the gym and the fruit smoothies he blends fresh for himself and his family every morning.

This he does in the kitchen of his one-storey Spanish hacienda in Pebble Beach. He designed his home, built out of native redwoods and Douglas fir and circled by Monterey cypresses on the Peninsula, with spectacular views of the jagged, ragged coast and out to the Pacific as far as his olive-green squint can see. Across and down the Peninsula and along Ocean Trail you run into Carmel-by-the-Sea, one of California's most popular tourist resorts. And one of America's richest and quaintest communities. Clint's house has a superb gym, eight rooms and two pianos which he is always content to be with. The courtyard entrance is given shade by a huge oak tree and a squadron of eucalyptus and palm trees. It's a gathering place for his family.

Clint married his first wife, the former Maggie Johnson, a model, when he was 23. They were divorced 30 years later; they have two children, Kyle, a talented musician who was best man at his father's second wedding, and Alison, who is an actress. In 2005 they were aged 37 and 33 respectively. His daughter Kimber, from his affair with actress Roxanne Tunis, was 41. He has two children, Scott, 19, and Kathryn Ann, 17, with former air stewardess Jacelyn Reeves. Then there's his 12-year-old daughter Francesca with actress Frances Fisher.

And now Morgan with his Dina.

He is in regular contact with all his children and their mothers. 'I enjoy it. And I give credit to my wife, who is great. She brought everybody together. She's terrific, she brings all the mothers in, everybody, my mother, she's brilliant.

'With my youngest kids I spend a lot of time with them at school events and all that sort of thing so I'm kinda going through at this stage of my life a lot of what people do when they're maybe much younger. Maybe that helps keep you young. I don't know. I think that the sad trick of nature is that people propagate at a rather early age when they really enjoy it at a later age. I really enjoy kids. I love their honest, curiosity. It's always fascinating to me and to watch them grow and see what they are going to become. I like them now as much as I ever have in my life, maybe more so. I don't know if I feel vulnerable; I feel very happy.

'I think as you mature you have seen a lot of relationships

come and go; you have a lot of things to draw upon within your soul.

'Dina is everything I ever wanted and never found anywhere before. I'm very lucky. I've got a great girl. She's completely unselfish. It was a wonderful romance. We went together four or five months. Then I knew I could get married again. Instinctively, I knew she was the right person.

'I was never a guy on a white horse. She's a self-feeder. Dina is a tremendous person and she had to embrace a lot of different elements from my past and she has done it so gracefully.

'We're a great family. We come from a lot of different directions, but everybody loves each other and that is my greatest enjoyment. I try to spend as much time as I can with all my children and grandchildren. Because I have had children at an older age, I have had to learn patience that I didn't have in my earlier life when I was more ambitious. I now try to do less, but try to do what I do properly.'

As well as younger children, he has a much younger – by 35 years – wife; one of their family games is for her to list famous people and see if Clint knew them. 'Once in a while when she gets in the mood she'll say: "Did you know Elvis?" and I'll say: "Yep, sure." "And James Dean?" "Yep." And then it will be: "How about Bobby Darin?" and I'll go: "Oh, yeah."

'We were all hanging around at the same time in the 1950s, we were all in town struggling in some way – well, not Elvis – but I was doing *Rawhide* and those guys would be on various stages around the studio. There was a kind of camaraderie around the younger group of people.'

He's happy to indulge his wife in her quizzes. He screened *Dirty Harry* for her – she'd never seen it – after her friends told her she couldn't be married to Clint without knowing the movie. He recalled: 'She watched it on DVD and she said: "Oh, I get it now."

'It's the only film I've revisited other than *Play Misty for Me*, which they had a screening for in Carmel to celebrate the thirtieth anniversary. I had to sit through it with the audience. Any time I look at myself I get somewhat embarrassed. It was interesting seeing myself with long sideburns, a lot more hair, and dark hair. I've got a little blonder since then. And wearing these horrible bell-bottom pants.'

He's much more touchy-feely in 2005, more relaxed than in the *Play Misty for Me* era. Is it the wife?

'Let me say this: she's a very, very fine woman and she's having me at a much better period of time than I was 30 years ago. I think the world of her. Is she jealous of me? No. If I flirt with other women it's not because I'm going anywhere. I'm very happy where I am.

'I think that I'm a better person now than before I met her and you like to think that every year you're a better person. I certainly know more at my age; you like to think you're improving as a person. I think she and I have met at the proper time in life.

'I'm much older than my wife but I feel as young as she does – at least I think I do. Mentally I do and if she lets me think that then that's great. My only advice [on the age issue] is that if you're any mellower as an older person, you're going to be a better person to get along with. I think that's my case.

'But then she may someday have to take care of me. When I was campaigning for mayor [of Carmel] in the mid-1980s I went to visit a lady who was 102 years old. She'd heard I was dating a woman who was maybe ten years younger than me. She said to me: "Clint, you must get yourself a much younger woman. You need somebody to be nice to you and take care of you."

'I said: "You mean, like a nurse?"

'It was kinda humorous coming from a woman of that age. I think age is all in people's minds. If you feel young and you think young and you look young it should be great.

'Dina keeps me on my toes, let's put it that way. We both enjoy family a lot, we both enjoy pets and we love to play golf. To me, as I said, life is like the back nine in golf.

'Sometimes you play better on the back nine.

'You may not be stronger, but hopefully you're wiser.'

# TWO

# CLINTVILLE, CALIFORNIA

> 'When he was four, we discovered he was
> allergic to dogs and cats, so he collected snakes.
> One time, he had 13 snakes. I guess he's kind
> of a supernatural person.'
> CLINT EASTWOOD'S MOTHER, RUTH, 2003

EVERYWHERE Clint goes people nod their recognition
and mostly don't bother him. He moves in his own space
without fuss or the attention magnet of bodyguards
and entourage.

He has never been known as one to chew the fat. He chews
tobacco. Or gently barbecued swordfish without the lemon
sauce. Or marinated chicken steamed with vegetables and
washed down with a chilled, always nursed, glass of Anchor
Steam beer. He's not a big drinker and sticks to beer and
wine. He's smoked – but only on screen.

As an actor he shoots straight. As a director he has a formidable reputation for bringing projects in ahead of schedule and below budget. For many years his private life was his private life but in later years he has become considerably more open. Yet he rarely gives interviews and then almost always to help his films at the box office. Even when he does, his low-profile attitude makes his words soft, slow and lean. Remember, he didn't make his name talking.

He accomplished that, and began a billion-dollar film dynasty, by forgetting to shave for a couple of days, mumbling if spoken to and shooting 42 people in 93 minutes. In 1964 he was paid a straight $15,000 for *A Fistful of Dollars*. By 2005 his films had earned close to $3 billion. His success over the years had been increased by his calculated underexposure; by making his every appearance a celebration for his worldwide audience. Less known is his remarkable second career as a Casanova. Possibly that explained why, for decades, he was intimidating in his reluctance to become involved in publicity unless he was controlling the format.

Yet he's also affable. He certainly was to visitors to the restaurant, the Hog's Breath Inn, he co-owned in Carmel. Even the menu and the entranceway were Eastwood-style. There are Dirty Harry (cheese) hamburgers, Magnum Force (hot pepper) omelettes and Eastwood's favourite, Gauntlet (boysenberry) cheesecake. The alley was a gunmetal colour. Once I took a chance on meeting him there for an interview. He had not been pre-warned. Sixteen steps took me down into the restaurant's patio with its crowd of customers and roaring fire. There was a redwood bar and above it one of those *High Noon*-style clocks which tick on and on with no sight of 'the Man'.

Then, out of the shadows, he arrived, striding into view in his Nike running shoes, Levi jeans and shirt and shoulder jacket. When he glanced around, his eyes narrow like blinds being drawn on a private room. I suggested we might talk and suddenly his hand went to his side. He pulled out a fistful of dollars and said: 'Well, I better buy you a beer.'

He sat and leaned back by the fire. At first he was reluctant: 'I don't usually talk business in any form here. I'm partners with two other guys and we modelled this like an English pub – a place for folks to have a drink and enjoy themselves. Look, you see me relaxing. But everybody has to have an edge and my edge is instinct. There are always people telling me what to do, but I've always done what I felt like doing.'

He was just another customer as far as the Hog's Breath regulars were concerned. Tourists would pull out cameras and ask for autographs. He never seemed concerned. 'I don't have much respect for people who look down on the public as somebody who gets in the way. After all you've just asked for it, you fought to get where you are. You just don't – you can't look down. On the other hand you want privacy too, because otherwise your central nervous system goes berserk.'

It was a younger Eastwood. Not the happily married man you meet in 2005. Then he was very much on the lookout. Yes, he agreed we would talk. But in a moment. He had something to arrange first. Eastwood took his beer and his charm across the patio to join a small group. One of them is a tall, stunning-looking blonde in her early 30s. The *other* Eastwood – the sexual cowboy – went into action. When he returned to talk, a smile played on his lips and there was a twinkle in his eye. He has made his 'arrangements'. He has always been a ladies' man. In his early army days he would moonlight at other jobs to earn enough cash to take dates out to drive-in movies.

He could afford much, much more than that when his regular film editor, Ferris Webster, introduced him to a female colleague at a sound laboratory at Burbank Studios in 1978.

'Clint, I want you to meet a girl who works with me. Sally meet Clint.'

Apparently, Eastwood soared to his feet with: 'How do?'

'I just wanted to say hello,' said Sally, then: 'Well, I have to get back.'

'Come back anytime,' said Eastwood. 'You an editor?'

'No. Accounting.'

'No. I was just about to say you had a job editing...'

Webster showed his colleague out and when he returned to the room he complimented her figure. Eastwood acted upset with him: 'I didn't even notice her body. I was just looking ... straight into her eyes.'

Another film editor made a remark and Eastwood responded: 'A nice girl for those of you who like girls. Me, I'm just a poor, unfortunate ... asexual.'

'Sure,' said a soundman. 'He just likes fast cars.'

Eastwood got a moony grin on his face at that moment and said casually: 'Fast cars and fast women.'

Paul Lippman, a former partner of his at the Hog's Breath, has talked of his charm and style with women – girls he calls Eastwood's 'hip-pocket-rockets'. Some of them took off as remarkably as Clint's career. He was an original Hollywood 'hunk', a contract player who posed bare-chested for publicity pictures. Usually not with one, but two girls.

For many years, it seemed we knew all about him, but we didn't know anything about him. Eastwood is a charmer.

When he was elected mayor of Carmel in 1986, a gift shop there cashed in on the name 'Clintville' and the business that having an international movie star as the civic leader led to. They sold Eastwood T-shirts and hats and all manner of bric-a-brac and paraphernalia that could remotely be linked to the celebrity mayor. Anything, really, they could stick his name or image on. One big seller was 'Make My Night' panties. It seemed the locals knew more about their mayor and local resident than his movie fans.

He fell in love with Carmel the first time he saw it. It has been the pivotal place in his life. It looks like a film set – the impossibly sweeping ocean views, the ice plant and the Monterey cypresses. Eastwood was an army private stationed close to the town at Fort Ord in 1951. It was a Saturday night when he and some friends finished too late to make the trip to the bright lights of San Francisco. 'One guy had a car and we drove to Monterey, hit a few pubs, then came over the hill to Carmel. I said to myself: if I ever have any dough, I'd like to live in this place. I fell for it in a big way: beautiful green mountains, well-timbered, coming right down to the shoreline and some clean white beaches. If I ever made a few bucks...'

He's always been passionate about what he wants. But he always seems to be calm and in control of his emotions, sending the message that the screen image is also reality; he admits there is a price to pay for that: 'You do pay – sometimes it's better to get things off your chest because people get relief from that. It's like going out and yelling obscenities in the middle of the highway. You come back and say "Aaah." I'm not afraid of showing emotions, but there are certain things I just don't enjoy sharing with everybody else.

'There are certain thoughts – I don't feel compelled to tell every thought that is in my mind. I know a lot of people get a catharsis, they get a release, from that and that's why psychiatrists make so much money. They can sit down and really unload, but to me I've never felt that. I don't particularly want to unload on anybody else. I always felt I could go out and walk through a field and look at the flowers and just unload to myself.'

The field and the flowers are on the outskirts of Carmel. If you live there, you must die to get out of town. There is no cemetery. There is also no mail delivery, for the residents refuse to put up house numbers. The post office is where they meet for a gossip.

Originally, around a century ago, artists boosted the population of the modern Carmel, which was discovered in 1602 by a Carmelite friar, Sebastian Vizcaino, and named for his patron saint, Our Lady of Carmel. In the 1920s city ordinances were introduced banning street lights, pavements and traffic lights, and today it's still against the law to wear high heels without a licence. The artists of the past frowned on business but there are now 67 art galleries, 31 real-estate brokerages and restaurants and bars lining every street of the tiny village, which sits on a slope above Monterey Bay 120 miles south of San Francisco. This is Eastwood's 'Heaven can wait' place.

In 1930 Carmel might have been 120 light years away for Clinton Eastwood, his wife Ruth, daughter Jeanne and newborn son Clinton Junior. The boy had been born on 31 May that year and there wasn't much in the bank – certainly not for trips to quaint seaside communities. 'It was my parents, my sister and me,' Clint recalls. And any trips that were made were out of necessity. There were many as he was growing up – another job for his father, another school for him. 'Once we moved from Sacramento to Pacific Palisades [450 miles, from central California to the outskirts of Los Angeles] so that my dad could start work as a gas station attendant. It was the only job open.'

His father sold stocks and bonds, but there wasn't much business in the early 1930s. Eastwood is particularly proud of his parents and especially his father's work ethic. It's reflected in his life today, for although one of the world's richest movie stars, he never stops work for more than a short break. He admits to being a workaholic and at one time was averaging a new film every ten months; in one 30-month period he made six films, two of which he directed.

And if you look with hindsight at his work, it is easy to recognise the Depression-era hardship and humour in films like 1982's *Honkytonk Man*. But he and his sister did better than many during the bad days.

'I can't remember us being poor or suffering as children. Maybe my father did have his worries but neither Jeanne nor I ever knew about them. When I look back I know Dad had to think pretty fast at times because there were a lot of people out of work in America around the time I was born. He often moved from one stocks and bonds company to another to try and better himself. That's why although I was born in San Francisco, my earliest memories are of living in Oakland. But it seems to me now we didn't live much in houses at all – we lived in cars. I can remember only a few of the places like Oakland and San Francisco and Sacramento – twice – and Seattle. The frustrating thing about moving around like this as a kid is that you're constantly having to make adjustments. My grandmother had a small farm where I stayed as a boy. Sometimes when you move a lot as a little kid, animals are your best friends. Animals just like you for you.

'Just as soon as I'd get to make friends in a place and start making progress at my studies, we'd be on the move again. I was alone a good portion of the time. I lived in my imagination. It gave me a taste for living all right, but I never got those feelings of security a kid most probably needs. I was always feeling left out of things. I'd walk into a fresh school and find the standards were different or they were on different phases of a subject. So although it wasn't that I wasn't bright I was never out front. I always seemed to be running to catch up.

'The traumas of childhood? I was raised in the height of he Depression but I didn't know the difference; you only know what you know. As long as somebody fed you, your toys could be a stick or a rock or something and that seemed to suit at the time.

'I was kind of an introverted kid. I was born left-handed but because of inkwells you couldn't write, you'd smear the ink; this was before ballpoint pens, so you smeared the ink, so they changed you to right-handed, so consequently my writing today still stinks. I blame it on that.

'I could have sat down and probably worked it out and studied and become a little better at penmanship and things like that. All of a sudden, instead of using the right side of my brain to work the left, I was using the left side to work the right and it made me ambidextrous as far as throwing a ball but did nothing for anything else.

'I've always felt maybe I was slightly dyslexic or one of those things they have so many names for now. We didn't have any of that. It was just: "He's a dummy." Or: "He's a smart guy." One or the other.

'I was a mediocre student and because of all that I think I grew more interested in things in life. Edward Teller, the famous physicist, says a genius is someone who does well at things he hates, so I was no genius. If I didn't like a subject I had a tough time passing it.

'I became interested in music only because when I sat down at the piano at a party the girls at the party would come around. I could play a few numbers. I learned a few off listening to records and things that were popular at that era. I thought this was all right, so I went home and practised when my mother couldn't get me to practise.

'So it sort of dovetails. You sort of become the sum of what your whole existence is and finally you find a subject you're interested in. Mine was films and I got into films thinking: This may last a couple of weeks.

'I got that wrong.

'The feeling that I was always trying to catch up has sort of stuck with me and maybe it has something to do with making me a loner – why I like driving fast and riding motorcycles fast. Since I was always the new boy on the block, I often played alone and in that situation your imagination becomes very active. You create little mythologies in your own mind. I suppose it was the best thing that happened in my youth.

'I was a constant daydreamer. When I wasn't going crazy trying to catch up on the lessons I'd missed, I'd sit there dreamy-eyed looking out of the window. I dreamed of being a great air pilot. I rescued a lot of people from drowning. I was the world's greatest surfer. And I guess I saved more people on the operating table than any surgeon who ever lived.

'You name it, I thought of it. I was pretty much bottled up in those days.

'I suppose my parents guessed the way I felt at times. My father was a big man physically and had been good at [American] football and track. He was fond of the outdoors and he took me hunting and fishing. He also taught me to swim well.

'I remember when my father died I went through a terrible guilt period where I wished I'd asked him to play golf more often.

'I was a young guy trying to make it as an actor and doing pretty well and busy with my life, so I never took enough time. I wish I could have said: "Let's hang out" or "I love you" or whatever.

'When we lived in Redding and Sacramento the Sierra Nevada Mountains were nearby and Jeanne and I were pretty good at skiing while we were still kids.

'At school I was never the one in the class to make things go – in the first place I was about a foot taller than the rest of the kids. There were occasions when I'd have lopped myself off at the knees if that had been possible. Then I had to go through this male thing of handing it out as well as taking it. They weren't tough guys or anything like that: I was just the odd man out – the big, silent guy.' But, as many a young lady and co-star were to find out, still waters really do run deep. And often dark and secretive.

Eastwood's career was taking off in 1970 when he was interviewed in Las Vegas by a lady reporter who had been in town for several days. She was introduced and he leaned forward with a handshake but no hello, just: 'Yeah, I've been watching her legs for two days.' When a blonde woman sitting across from him made a comment he told her: 'Cool it!' This other woman was Maggie Johnson Eastwood, his now former wife. In 1970 they had been married for 17 years. It didn't seem to cramp Eastwood's style. Over the years, not much has.

'I became hooked on girls at an early age. American kids seem to start dating a lot earlier than European kids, even now. I got my first crush when I was at Glenview [at 14 in Oakland, California] grammar school. Her name was Joan and she was a redhead, a little teeny-bopper. What attracted me, I think, was that she was the most popular girl in class.

It was actually very much a one-way situation. She never showed any signs of being intrigued with me. But for a time I stopped staring out the window and began dreaming up to the front where she was sitting. Not once did I have the courage to ask her out with me.'

He overcame his early introspection; the loner became a lone wolf, prowling alone. What helped him was something that, even in all his daydreaming, he had never imagined – acting.

An English teacher who he reckons was a pretty fair amateur psychologist chose him to play a rebel teenager in that year's school play. He didn't want to. Miss Jones told him he would enjoy it. He suffered hell. He wanted to run away from school. Another pupil, his friend Harry Pendleton, was also in the play. The young Clint tried to talk his pal into 'vanishing', saying: 'They'll laugh at us.' Harry agreed: 'They sure will.' They planned to miss the play but next day had second thoughts. It would be easier all round if they tried to work their way through it.

'I realised at some point that all the kids in the audience were laughing with me and not at me. I suppose it was the first time I realised you could act extroverted without really being so and also that being self-confident didn't mean that people took an instant dislike to you or laughed at you. I was 15, but it was the day I grew up.'

And, by then, girls had taken second place in his life. For a little time, anyway.

'I still wasn't 15 when my dad bought me my first car – an old rattletrap he'd picked up for $25. I've never exactly led what you'd call a monastic sheltered life. The car took my mind off girls for a bit. For the next couple of years it was cars first and girls second. I wasn't actually supposed to drive on my learner's permit except in an emergency. But even at that age I was within one inch of my present height and the cops never stopped me. That summer when I was 15 I left home for the first time. It was just an impulse thing.'

It was his gut talking. An instinct. He drove south towards California's ranch country and got a summer job baling hay. 'At night I could scarcely crawl into my bunk – absolutely dead to the world. But it sure toughened me up. It was about the happiest time of my life up till then. I had a couple of buddies at the time and we all set out to raise a little hell. It began with the cars.'

In a different era Clint Eastwood might have been a real cowboy and an adventurer. He was just a teenager when he started making money delivering newspapers and groceries. He might not have been a social whiz, but he was independent. It's the same today. He's more content casually eating cheese quesadillas and a platter of rice and beans in the kitchen at home, or having a drink or dinner with friends in Carmel, than he is at the White House, chatting with presidents or meeting Prince Charles and Princess Diana, as he did at a 1986 dinner where they all danced until 1.30am to an impromptu Neil Diamond 'concert'.

'I've worked ever since I was 13 years old. My parents had a hard life when they were raising us. My father drilled into me that nobody does anything for you but yourself. Today we live in a welfare-orientated society and people expect more from Big Daddy government, more from Big

Daddy charity. In my young days, that kind of society never existed. That philosophy never got you anywhere.

'I worked for every crust of bread I ever ate. Yet I always had a sense of future. I always had the feeling that, discouraged as I was many times, there was a place waiting for me at the top of the heap. I knew I had something to give. I don't think I had a colossal ego. Just the stupidity, perversity, premonition or whatever it is that gives a person a feeling of hope. That feeling of hanging in there.'

Eastwood had to hang in many times. He chanced death, courted disaster and became a real-life hero before ever a camera rolled to the shout of 'Action!' But many times he felt a lost soul, just a man drifting along. His parents had continued to move around a lot and so, after leaving school, in an attempt to find some fixed point, he went to live with his grandmother for a time and raised chickens – 'I talked to chickens a lot' – in Hayward County on the outskirts of Oakland. He never didn't work but he couldn't settle. America was beginning to boom after the Second World War. The American Dream was the goal. What was happening to the schoolboy dreamer after he graduated from Oakland Technical School in 1948, where he had been a more proficient basketball player than a scholar?

He was breaking his back digging ditches and swimming pools. Or working the midnight-to-7am shift in front of a furnace at the Bethlehem Steelworks near Oakland. The sparks flew in the furnace. Afterwards Eastwood and company would go on the town. Roy Sturges, who once worked alongside him at the furnace, recalled: 'He was a man who worked real hard and paid himself by enjoying himself. We all believed we deserved a few beers and a good time after the hours we put in. And Clint wasn't one to hang back. He was a nice kid. Loyal. Always willing to help out if you had to go someplace early or had a problem at home. He'd be the one to stand in for you. Always there.'

*Loyal.* It's a word you hear much about Eastwood. He plays that role in the most extreme circumstances – and he expects loyalty in return. It is part of the camaraderie he learned mucking in at the furnace or digging ditches or waiting for the cry, 'Timber!' in the Oregon logging fields, when he was a tall, strapping lad and, like most teenagers, felt immortal. He soon learned that he wasn't.

Eastwood had always been fascinated by the logging business and managed to get hired in a mill operating on the Willamette River, near Eugene, Oregon. After only a few days on the job he was nearly killed: 'I heard a shout and looked up and saw the crane driver and I hadn't quite got it organised. A nasty load of giant logs hung suspended over my head. I don't think I've reacted faster in my life. Yet even as I started to run, down came the logs. Any one of them could have crushed the life out of me. I just barely jumped clear – as the logs hit the ground they jammed against the crane, which was a lucky break for me.

'The whole thing was: the money was good in the logging business and so was the food. The guys you met there were like wild characters out of a novel. It was pretty hard living but working outdoors in this fabulous country – rugged mountains, tall pine and fir forests – made it worthwhile. I never stayed long enough to work up into one of the really skilled jobs: if a man doesn't know what he's doing he can really pay for it. Some of the Douglas firs grew 250–300 feet tall and a man who goes up to the top of one of those to lop off the high branches has to be experienced. Log-rolling – that's riding the logs in mid-river – is another job where you either know what you're doing or you don't live long enough to have grandchildren. I earned good money felling trees. I'd pick where I wanted a tree to fall, take my axe and cut a "V" so it would fall in that direction. Then another man and myself would work a two-man double saw. It took two of us because some of these trees were six feet in diameter. Some of the time was spent in the sawmill, which was better pay, but I preferred being outdoors.'

Today Eugene hasn't changed much since Eastwood's logging days except that it's a little quieter. He remembers: 'On weekends we all descended on Eugene and more or less turned the place inside out. Our manners weren't quite Ritz Hotel but the people in town were used to such behaviour from loggers. They were usually glad to see us. We were a lively bunch just out to whoop it up a bit. Most of the action was at a little place out of town where you could get a couple of beers and listen to some music. I've always preferred jazz, but I had fun listening to the badly played country-and-western stuff. It was so corny.

'Occasionally I'd talk to a girl. I can't say there was anything serious, though. It was the wrong time for me. It wasn't that I was consciously steering clear of involvement, but I have this attitude towards responsibility – you don't undertake responsibilities until you are ready to handle them.

'I was earning good bachelor money but mentally I was

still drifting. I had an idea I wasn't going to settle for tree-felling or sawmilling as my life's work, but the way wasn't too clear...'

# THREE

## SWIM OR SINK

'I've even learned from my screenwriters.
When I produced *Heartbreak Ridge* and starred
as Marine Gunnery Sergeant Tom Highway, I say:
"You improvise! You adapt! You overcome!"
Helpful words to remember.'

CLINT EASTWOOD, 2003

THE way forward suddenly became very clear.

Clint had just turned 20 when the Korean War began on
25 June 1950. He knew he would be drafted but later said:
'I guess I was interested in living a little first.'

And that meant San Francisco. He teamed up with several
other footloose friends waiting to go into the army and they
hit town. He's proud of the time they had: 'We enjoyed
ourselves so much that by the time we reported for our
physicals we were so exhausted and partied out that we

thought we might fail our examinations. But we all made it.'

His love affair with Carmel was about to begin. And his infatuation with a girl that nearly cost him his life. Fort Ord is just another army camp – duty, discipline and dishwashing. Basic training was six weeks with no time off. But it was on the Monterey Peninsula and for that Eastwood will always be grateful. As he is that his father taught him to swim.

'I had an idea I might learn something while I was in the army and they had what were called Division Faculty Classes. I went to see the captain in charge and told him about the different jobs I had had since I left school. He asked me if I could swim. "Sure," I answered. He told me: "From this moment, Eastwood, you're assigned to the swimming pool. As an instructor."

'There was already a lieutenant and four sergeants running the pool, so I can't say the work was too tough. Suddenly everybody got shipped out to the front line – except me. I suppose my name just didn't come out of the hat. So there I was, a 20-year-old private earning $76 a month in charge of an Olympic-size pool and organising all the classes. It was a great opportunity. I moved out of the barracks and bedded down in one of the small dormitories attached to the pool.

'So long as I kept my nose clean and ran the place efficiently I was on my own. It was a real sweet set-up.

'Come 6pm I'd knock off and go into Carmel and meet some girl. The money wasn't much, so I decided to take a job at nights. Sure, buck privates weren't supposed to take civilian jobs in their spare time – but there wasn't anything in army regulations that said you couldn't. I signed up to work a swing shift with the Spreckles Sugar Company in the Saunas Valley. For four months, when I'd finished my work at the pool I'd shoot across to the Spreckles place and load sugar sacks or do maintenance work or anything they wanted. What I hadn't reckoned on was I'd need a little sleep now and then.

'After four months I was the weariest swimming instructor in the army. I found myself falling asleep in the pool and drinking more water than was good for me. I figured I needed a change, so I found a job in the junior non-commissioned officers' club. There were two other guys working there permanently, one behind the bar and the other on the floor to keep order, a bouncer. I quit the sugar factory and worked the NCO club, which was only a minute's walk from the pool. It could be fairly wild in there. Maybe six or seven girls and 150 guys!

'The men weren't supposed to drink anything but beer, which was free, but a few of the smart guys would smuggle in some hard liquor and mix it in the beer. And that caused trouble. I had to bounce quite a few of them. Being big was a help.'

Eastwood never did get to Korea. But he nearly got killed anyway. For this time his size worked against him. He tells the story as though he were pitching a movie script: 'It wasn't the girl's fault – she was real nice. I'd met her while visiting my folks in Seattle. I felt like seeing her again and mentioned it to a buddy who happened to be from Seattle. The problem was: how to get there and back on a weekend pass. Besides, there was the money involved.

'He said he could fix it. He explained that if you were in the service and in uniform, the naval air station at Monterey would fly you wherever you were going, if they had an extra seat on the aircraft. So I got a pass and headed out to Monterey. Sure enough, I found a little reconnaissance plane – going up to Seattle. Yes, there was room for me. So I flew up in style. I saw my mother and father and Jeanne. Then I went out with this very nice girl. I felt like I'd had a great weekend when I took off for the air base to hitch a ride back.

'There was nothing leaving for the south. I sat there, feeling dismal, trying to figure out what to do. The problem was: I had to fly back to get to camp in time – or I'd be AWOL. Dilemma: no money but a commercial air ticket. So I hung around asking every pilot in sight. Finally, I heard there was a naval torpedo bomber going to San Francisco. They didn't have any seats, of course.

'"Isn't there anywhere I could hang on?" I demanded desperately.

'"You could try the wings," said one of the pilots.

'He sized me up. "There's just one chance," he said. "But you're too big to squeeze into the radar compartment."

'I'd have turned myself into a midget at that moment, if necessary. But my legs alone looked as if they would fill the radar compartment. This was a little cubbyhole in the tail, with a tiny door, a little porthole and a big panel of instruments. Nobody was actually supposed to fly in there; the door was just for maintenance men to service the plane. But with a little shoving and pushing, they got me wedged in.

'Funny? Maybe. But it wasn't funny a little later. Everything that could go wrong with that trip went wrong. First of all, the compartment door sprang open and I nearly fell out – I guess my bulk was putting a little strain on it. So there I was, a mile or so up and no parachute and holding on for dear life.

'There was a little button you pushed to talk to the pilot, but the intercom wasn't working right and although I could hear him, he couldn't hear me. The pilot spotted the sprung door and warned me. He began shouting at me: "The door's open, soldier! Shut the door if you don't want to fall into the drink!" I kept yelling back at him, but he couldn't hear me. I can't say I was enjoying any of this – and even now, the thought is pretty grisly.

'Anyhow, I yanked out a cable, and got it looped round the handle of the sprung door; that kept it mostly shut. It still left a gap, however – and if you want to feel really miserable, I suggest you spend a couple of hours contemplating a nice long drop the way I did.

'Things got worse – fast! Before taking off, the pilot had warned me that he'd have to fly pretty high and I'd have to use the oxygen mask. As we climbed steadily, I put the mask to my face, only to discover it wasn't working. I fiddled desperately with it and tried to tell the pilot – but he still couldn't hear me. Last thing I remember before blacking out was him sending a message saying that although he could transmit, he couldn't pick up anything, but giving his position, estimated height and flying speed and adding that he had about two and a half hours' fuel left – plenty to reach California.

'I remember nothing after that, except a kind of woozy, twilight feeling. Fortunately for me, the pilot's oxygen supply started going out, too, so he had to lose altitude. It must have been an hour later when I became aware of what was going on again and I realised that we'd hit California. It was easy to recognise, because the whole place was socked in by fog. I could hear the pilot talking again. He was telling the base he couldn't see anything, so he was going to hang out to sea a bit and see if he could get in under the clouds.

'Our danger now was that if we stayed over land, we might crash into a mountain; the pilot had to stay low because of his oxygen. I wasn't really worried yet; I had this feeling that if I'd got this far, I was going to survive. Then as we began circling round I remembered the fuel. I checked my watch and found it was about two and a half hours since the pilot had radioed that he had that much supply.

'I think I felt a little panic right then. I had no way of communicating with the pilot. I didn't know what kind of guy he was. Would he eject and save himself by parachute and leave me and the plane to go down together? I knew he had the canopy above his head open, because the cable controlling it ran back through my compartment. But I couldn't figure I had much alternative except to hold on for dear life.

'The pilot must have spotted a hole in the clouds, because we dipped suddenly and went down fast. Next moment, through the porthole, I saw we were over the sea. I could see the whole coast of California now – beaches, cliffs and mountains, the tops of the latter invisible because of the fog.

What I couldn't understand was why the pilot was flying over the water; why didn't he make straight for the city airport? Only later – much later – did I learn that the guy knew he was out of fuel and might crash on the city before making the airport. It was our lives against those of several hundred citizens. So there we wallowed, a few hundred feet above the sea, about a mile off the coast.

'And then the engine went – and it was a very deadening feeling indeed. You could hear the air whistling – and I was watching the water and the beaches and cliffs and particularly the cables leading to the pilot's canopy; I sure wanted to know when he was going to leave the ship. I noticed he had the flaps down and realised he was going to come down in the water. I started wondering if the plane would float and began preparing for the moment we hit water, wedging myself in so that I would ride the shock.

'I saw the water was rough – it was going to be no easy landing. And then we were bouncing and bouncing – like a pebble skimming over water, and the ocean was just shooting in all over the place. You had the feeling that one moment you were in the air and next in a submarine. And then we stopped. We stopped with our nose down and our tail in the air. I found myself standing on the instrument board. I whipped off the cable holding the door and stepped out on to the back of the wings. The pilot was climbing out of his canopy and he leaped and landed beside me. He looked at me.

'Well, I hit the water and started to get out of there fast; I had an idea that if the plane started to sink, it would suck me down with it. So I just didn't hang around. It was sunset when we'd come down – and now the twilight was settling and it was getting dark. There was a big swell and very soon we were separated. We shouted a couple of times – but we were a long way from the beach and we needed every ounce of breath we had; so it became every man for himself.

'At certain times of the year, the Pacific gets full of phosphorus and you could tell where the beaches were because of the glow as the waves crashed on them. And then – almost the worst ordeal of all – I found myself in the middle of jellyfish! It was a creepy feeling. They were so close you could almost touch them, even see them in the phosphorous water. After all I'd been through, I didn't feel like being stung to death by jellyfish. I just clawed my way through.

'I don't know how long it took me to hit the beach, finally. But it was an ordeal I never want to go through again. When I was close to shore, I had to struggle desperately, because of the fierce undertow. Even when I was no more than 20 feet from the beach, I wasn't safe. I'd swim forward two feet and be carried back six. But, inch by inch, I made it, until finally I felt bottom under my feet.

'I don't know how long I lay unconscious on the beach, but when I came to I was probably a little delirious. I vaguely remember running up and down the beach looking for the lieutenant, shouting his name until I was hoarse. I started imagining that every rock uncovered by the sea seemed to be his body – and I kept dashing back and forth into the surf like a madman. For a time I consoled myself with the thought that he'd probably come in a little distance away. Then, as I went several hundred yards in each direction, looking for him, I felt certain he had drowned, poor guy.

'I remember it was a peculiar contradictory feeling. I felt terribly depressed at this idea; yet strangely elated because it wasn't me. Anyhow, in the end, a little crazy by now, I guess, I began wandering off. I was barefoot – so I stayed at the water's edge rather than go inland. I went round some cliffs and there, about eight miles in the distance, I saw the lights of the radio communications relay station.

'I don't remember anything, except that I looked at that light and kept walking towards it. Later the guys at the RC station told me: "When you came through that door, buddy, you looked like a survivor of the *Titanic.*"'

# FOUR

# SHOOTING STAR

'Nobody pushes Clint.'
EASTWOOD CO-PRODUCER
BRUCE RICKER, 2003

CLINT was never again concerned about mortality; it was fate that dealt the cards. It was typical of him that he should survive on his own strength and merits. His image, his success, is all about the self-sufficient loner who can take care of himself and, if necessary, any trouble that happens.

The code, the driving force of his life, is individuality and getting on with the job. Watch him on a film set and he'll be as likely as some casual worker to help move equipment or pour the coffee, a man in control of himself and the world around him.

That control is all-important to him. And that includes the women around him. He talks of the 'strong' women of film that he admires: 'I love strong-women pictures. I don't like the girl-next-door, namby-pamby stuff – I guess, because I was raised in an era of the strong woman on film, the Barbara Stanwycks, Bette Davises. They were wild; Bette's presence was powerful.'

This admiration had never carried over into his relationships until he married for the second time. Until then he'd always been the Boss. He says his father told him: 'Nothing comes from nothing and don't plan on anything because no one gives you anything in life.'

It's a cynical creed. But it is his appeal. People, audiences, want someone strong. They want to feel safe. They want assurance.

'Part of his sex appeal is the constant mystery – how deeply does he feel? How deeply is he involved in life?' says actress Susan Clark, who co-starred with him in 1968's *Coogan's Bluff*, the second movie in Don Siegel's rogue-cop cycle about a country-boy cop taking on the big city, New York, as well as the bad guys.

His loose-limbed frame, the deep-set eyes and drawn cheeks on his parchment face – he can look ghostly in bad light – add to his enigmatic image. And *nobody* knows quite what he's thinking. For his long-time lover Sondra Locke: 'There's a certain distance, a certain mystery. He's always unapproachable to some degree.'

But not if you're the right lady at the right moment. Fritz Manes is a stuntman and producer who knew Eastwood in the early days. 'Even in Junior High School,' he says, 'Clint was a solid loner – he didn't care for hanging out with the gang. He was always right on centre with himself, very sure of himself, so he didn't need the support of a circle of friends. Not that Clint ever lacked for companionship.

'In high school he had a kind of natural charisma that was really maddening. You could sit in class and do all the little tricks of flirtation, flex your muscles, shuffle your $10 bills, and nothing would work if Clint was in the room. He'd be sitting there doing nothing, just looking at the floor and all the girls would be looking at him as if they were in a trance, locked in on some secret magnetism he had. It was very demoralising for the rest of us guys.'

During his spell in the army Eastwood met young actors David Janssen (who would star in television's *The Fugitive* and *Harry O*) and Martin Milner (television's *Route 66*) and they kept saying Hollywood was also the place for him. He knew better. On the GI Bill he enrolled in a business course at Los Angeles City College.

The move was again motivated by a woman. Eastwood's friend Don Horner had a date with a girl from the University of California at Berkeley. Eastwood had what he recalls as 'tentative plans' with another girl. But Horner wanted to arrange a double date and Eastwood went along. His blind date was Maggie Johnson, a five-foot-seven blonde – a true Californian girl in look and attitude. Clint liked her. A lot: 'Maggie and I hit it off right away. I can't say there was anything special about that night. I liked Maggie's sense of humour. I had no idea about marrying her.'

What happened was like the plot of one of those absurd B-movie romances they were churning out in the early 1950s. He wasn't thinking of marriage or commitment but this tall, suntanned and athletic girl graduated and was off south, home to Los Angeles. He decided to go too.

While at college there, he helped pay his rent by earning $30 a week for managing an apartment building in Beverly Hills. He worked at a garage in the evenings. At weekends he and Maggie went to the beach for barbecues, jazz and dancing, where they mixed with a young aspiring film crowd. His future wife said: 'Clint was only 23 and so good-looking I couldn't resist him. I was plain Maggie Johnson, a college student. We fell in love right away. We were married six months after we met.'

That was on 19 December 1953 – Eastwood was on Christmas holiday from college – and they went on honeymoon to – where else? – Carmel. They were married and living in a tiny, one-room apartment in downtown Los Angeles. He was studying. She was working in the office of a Los Angeles export business and doing some modelling.

It all changed suddenly, as Maggie recalled: 'I remember him coming home one night all excited. He had met someone who wanted to give him a screen test.'

Director Arthur Lubin had also offered tests to David Janssen and another aspiring actor hanging around the studios, called Rock Hudson. Eastwood knows the story frame by frame.

'I'd met the director, who was under contract to Universal Studios, and he asked me: "Did they ever run a film test on you?" It had never occurred to me but I was definitely interested. I had nothing to lose but time. I went out to Universal the next week and it was fascinating. I'd never been in a film studio before. The director and the cameraman asked me if I'd ever done any acting. I told them about the school play. They decided to run a silent test on me to see how I photographed. I didn't feel I'd ever make it – it seemed like a little fun. There was no harm in it. They said they'd call me and I thought: Don't call us, we'll call you. But I was riding high and Maggie and I celebrated with dinner and a bottle of wine.'

It was 17 days after his test that Universal Studios signed him to a contract. When he told his father he was going to be an actor he received the advice: 'Don't do that. You'll never have a chance. It's the stuff dreams are made of – don't do that.'

He paid no attention.

His film career – at $75 a week – began with small parts in even smaller films, like 1955's *Revenge of the Creature* and the talking-horse saga *Francis in the Navy* the same year. He lasted 18 months at Universal.

Clint and Burt Reynolds were fired on the same day by the same studio executive. Reynolds loves the story: 'First he told Clint he had a chip on his tooth and said: "You should get that fixed." Clint never did. He also said: "You speak too slowly – your Adam's apple sticks out too far." When he turned to me I thought he was going to say my ears were too small or something wonderful. You know, I could make them bigger or something. Or put gum behind them and make them stick out. And he said: "You have no talent."

'So we got out. We were walking up the street and I turned to Clint and said: "You know, I can learn to act. But you're going to have a hell of a time getting that Adam's apple out of your throat."'

But for Eastwood acting wasn't as much fun as the story. He did walk-on parts on television shows, some live TV work in New York and dug a lot of swimming pools back in Los Angeles. He was offered 1957's *Ambush at Cimarron Pass*, a cheapie film made in eight days. He calls it 'a Z movie, the lousiest Western ever made', but back then it was work. 'It was unbelievably bad and I said to myself: "If you have to do more of this junk then quit."'

Westerns were the genre of the moment then on US television: *Wagon Train* was an enormous success and the CBS television network wanted their own Western series. With this in mind, they commissioned *Rawhide* and Eastwood's agent, James Arthur, tried and tried to get him a shot on the series. He failed and failed. His wife encouraged him to keep going. And it was a friend of hers who accidentally got him his break. Maggie Eastwood's best friend, Sonia Chernus, was a story consultant at CBS. Eastwood went to visit her and out of the door came Robert Sparks, a producer at the network. He stopped short and looked Eastwood up and down before hustling him into the office to meet Charles Marquis Warren, the producer of *Rawhide*.

The late Eric Fleming had won the role of trail boss Gil Favor, but the network wanted another leading man on the show and had written Rowdy Yates, the ramrod or second-in-command of the trail herd. Eastwood – with Frankie Laine booming: 'Movin', movin', movin', keep these cattle movin'. Rawhide!' – was boosted high up in the saddle for seven and a half profitable years, coddling cattle in 217 episodes of the show.

His work and play on the basketball court, in the swimming pool and the Oregon forests paid off. He did his own stunts, and he looked like he was part of the horse.

The series was a hit around the world. Clint Eastwood became a television star – but not immediately. 'I made the pilot film and the first ten episodes and then nothing for six months. We had to wait until it was aired by CBS in order to see how the audience liked it and if we would continue. But the airing was postponed indefinitely. It didn't happen in September and by the terms of my contract, I couldn't see about other parts. Then, in December, as we were about to take the train to San Francisco to spend Christmas with my folks, a telegram arrived. It said *Rawhide* had been scheduled as a mid-season replacement.'

It began in January 1959.

Eastwood was cautious with his success and remembers his thoughts at the time: 'After a few years I would have liked to have done something else, but *Rawhide* was security. I remembered all those months without work and thought I'd ride it. Another disquieting thought was that few big television personalities ever transferred successfully to theatrical films. What hope did I have?'

He wasn't so cautious about romance. Incredibly, he has pursued a career in one of the most public of arenas but his secret life has only now become public. The way Maggie Eastwood talks, it is as if they had an open marriage for many years. Certainly, people who have worked with Eastwood on his films have talked about how brazenly he has pursued the ladies. And not just to flirt but in a serious way. There was a lot of talk about his extramarital love life – talk that didn't get into the Hollywood gossip columns.

A crew member who worked on one of his films said: 'Clint goes where he wants, does what he wants – goes to dinner with a girl if he wants. Maggie doesn't say a word. Clint is the undisputed boss.'

Eastwood was asked about this and responded at the time: 'Maggie doesn't chain me down. The worst thing is owning people. I don't want to be owned by anybody – maybe shared, but not owned, lock, stock and barrel. Like: "Where were you?" or: "Who's that?"

'That's like two attorneys battling – the beginning of the end. It kills more relationships than anything – clutch, grab, lust. Squelches the spirit. To me love for a person is respect for individual feelings. Love is respecting privacy, accepting faults.

'But don't believe it's a one-way street. The sophisticated woman accepts the chances are a guy's not being 100 per cent faithful. If she talks about it, it only makes it worse; best way to get a guy to be unfaithful is to talk about it.

'The beginning is infatuation – after that it becomes other things. Love isn't across a room: it is a long time. Sex is a small part of life – 99.9 per cent of your life is spent doing other things. And if you accept a guy, you have to make that guy feel important so he gets satisfaction. It's selfish – you give love to get love. Women have the toughest roles – it's easier to be on the offensive than the defensive.'

Eastwood and Maggie, who was also his career mentor, pushing him forward for roles and advising him on scripts, waited 15 years after their marriage in December 1953 before their son, Kyle, was born. When Clint is asked about it he shoots off: 'Planned parenthood', but people close to the couple in those days believe that Maggie had to fight to have her first child. She herself says: 'Clint and I were both "moving" people and we didn't think we could manage in a one-room apartment. We decided we wouldn't have kids until we could afford help.' Kyle Eastwood was born in 1968.

Clint's illegitimate daughter was born four years earlier, on 17 June 1964, at Cedars of Lebanon Hospital in Los Angeles. It was a secret for more than a quarter of a century. *Rawhide* was a success in 1959 when Clint first met Roxanne Tunis, who was then 28 and a tall, stunningly attractive brunette. He was the star. She was a sometime screen extra, stuntwoman and occasional actress. According to those who worked on the series, Roxanne Tunis was no starry-eyed fan. Like so many, she was overwhelmed by the Eastwood charm. They acted like a couple on the set of the series while his wife Maggie was back at home in Carmel.

With Eastwood's help, Roxanne found more success as an actress and became pregnant. He has not talked about it, so we can only imagine the dilemma. He was a star and he was married, and in 1964 the term 'love child' had not even been used.

There was potential for scandal and he was still working at establishing his career, but he was pragmatic – and so was Roxanne. She would have the child but in secret and he would support them for the rest of their lives. There would be no gossip. They have both kept to their bargain and in 2005 Kimber is married for the second time.

Kimber Tunis has her father's face and there is also a family resemblance in her son – Eastwood's grandson – Clinton Eastwood Gaddie, who was born on 21 February 1984, in Oxnard, California. Clinton is from her 1983 marriage to gardener and tree specialist Anthony Gaddie, from whom she is now divorced. In 1974 Kimber had moved from Los Angeles to Denver, Colorado, with her mother. Eastwood provided funds for schooling and holidays and treats for Kimber as well as buying their home in Denver. They were all sworn to a secrecy pact but when Kimber grew up and had a child of her own she said of her father: 'I don't make any decisions without him. He takes the decisions about every part of our lives. He loves his grandson and sees him when he can.'

Maggie Eastwood knew about the other family and even met Roxanne on the set of the film *Breezy*, which her husband was directing in 1972. Eastwood went white – he was totally shaken – when Maggie arrived with their son Kyle and confronted Roxanne. But the two women had a 'civilised' meeting and Roxanne played with Kyle while Eastwood shied away, supposedly concerned about a camera set-up with his star, William Holden.

It was an intriguing time in Eastwood's love life. That year he had also met Sondra Locke, who had auditioned for a role in *Breezy*, a role which Eastwood would decide was not for her. But he remembered her later.

The former Mrs Eastwood will not be drawn into discussions about meeting Roxanne, just as she says, 'No comment' when asked about her feelings towards Sondra Locke. But she does tell us enough to see what was going on in Eastwood's life – a busy one socially as well as professionally – at the time he first became involved with Roxanne.

'With *Rawhide* everything changed,' she says. 'Before

we knew it we had some money, a house with a pool and were forever posing for pictures as Hollywood's latest young and exciting couple. It was new to us, so we didn't mind all the publicity and the pictures. We didn't live the Hollywood life, but we went to some parties. The glamour and the glitter weren't our whole life. In Hollywood people said we had a perfect marriage. Well, it wasn't always perfect. No marriage ever is. In a way, the end of our marriage was inevitable.

'Other women? I was never realistic about some things. I used to always hope for the best. I wanted to protect myself. I wondered about it but I didn't dwell on it because it would probably have driven me insane. I just preferred to hang in there and not to worry too much about it.'

While Maggie Eastwood was keeping her private feelings somewhat concealed, professionally it was Eastwood who was feeling frustrated. He had been hunky Rowdy Yates for seven years – and how long can you take Frankie Laine booming in your ears? When *Rawhide* had begun on American television, there were 40 other Western series in competition on screen. As the years went on, Eastwood learned about film editing, how each show was pieced together, and he asked if he could film scenes himself from horseback. Then he asked to direct an episode. He had watched James Garner move from *Maverick* on television to the big screen and seen Steve McQueen vault from *Wanted Dead or Alive* to become one of the world's top movie stars. But the producers had enough evidence of stars messing up to say no.

Eastwood was fed up enough reluctantly to accept – after

James Coburn had rejected the offer – the lead in a film which had the prophetic title *A Fistful of Dollars*. Much has been written about the minimalism of the film. It has been the subject of scholarly thought: what it meant; who Eastwood's character the Man with No Name was.

In reality, it was a low-budget Western being made for $200,000 in Spain by a non-English-speaking Italian director named Sergio Leone. In 1964 no one was offering Eastwood anything else in the movies. And all involved got lucky.

What was to change Eastwood's life and some aspects of movie-making was his own style and gut instincts. Leone, who died in 1991, had made sword-and-sandals movies like *Sodom and Gomorrah* and this was a similar exercise.

At first Eastwood reckoned that the less his character talked, the more mystique. But he doesn't take the credit: 'It was all there in the script. Even *Yojimbo*, the Samurai picture it was taken from, was the same. Yeah, a little broadness, but I'd been doing 200 *Rawhides* and I was ready for anything different in doing a Western. The Western in America had reached a real dead period as far as imagination was concerned.'

But Eastwood almost didn't become 'Il Cigaro' to the Italians, 'El Cigarillo' to the Spanish or 'Herr Wunderbar' to the Germans and box-office magic worldwide to audiences who hung on his every silence. He recalled his first days in Spain: 'I scuffed around in the dirt all morning waiting for the director and the crew to quit arguing. The talk was all in Spanish and Italian and I didn't understand a word but I could tell there was a violent discussion going on about something. I hoped they'd get it straightened out before we blew the whole morning without getting one shot. Finally, Sergio called me over.

'"OK, Clint, you can start making up," he said through his interpreter. What the heck, I decided – they were always at it. Trouble was, this outfit didn't have much money, so there was always arguments about paying the crew. But then I wouldn't have been in Spain if they had a lot of money – they'd have gone for James Stewart or Bob Mitchum if they'd been loaded. So I figured I'd put up with some disorganisation.

'Making-up was a nice, slow job if you didn't mind the sticky heat and the flies and the dust. The scene called for a lot of make-up because my face was to be badly swollen from being beaten up by a whole gang.

'I came out from under the job feeling hot and uncomfortable and headed for the set. I was literally the most alone man in Spain. The set was deserted. No producer, no director, no crew. Only the big arc lamps standing there like Spanish vultures.

'It seems the crew hadn't been paid for two weeks and they had left the set until someone came through with their money. This wasn't the first time this had happened. It was just one foul-up after another. But this time, with one eye sealed shut by make up and all the other junk on my face, I'd had it.

'Maybe I hurt too easily inside. I used to flare up at the drop of a hat until I learned better.

'I made a decision – I told them they could find me at the airport. Fortunately, Sergio caught me before I left the hotel. He apologised and promised it wouldn't happen again.

Things ran a little smoother after that, but they were far from perfect, but we got through the film.'

Maggie Eastwood remembers: 'He was paid $15,000 for that. Suddenly we heard the critics in Europe loved the film. That's when I knew Clint was going to be a big star.

'Well, for years I was the Woman with No Name. I was this big Hollywood star's wife, yet I never had an identity of my own. He had this thing about being a loner, like I didn't exist at times. He's a very complex person.'

Buoyant and burly Sergio Leone would not have used the word 'complex' about his American star. He found him 'strange' and not at all what he expected when their partnership began. Eastwood was changing the rules: 'I always was a different kind of person even when I started acting,' said Clint, before making the wonderful admission: 'I guess I finally got to a point where I had enough nerve to do nothing.

'My first film with Leone had a script with tons of dialogue, tremendously expository, and I just cut it all down. Leone thought I was crazy. Italians are used to much more vocalising and I was playing this guy who didn't say much of anything. I cut it all down. Leone didn't speak any English, so he didn't know what the hell I was doing, but he got so he liked it after a while...

'The original screenplay had endless pages of dialogue all explaining the character's background, but I wanted to play it with an economy of words and create this whole feeling through attitude and movement. It was just the kind of character I had envisioned for a long time – keep to the mystery and allude to what happened in the past. It came about after the frustration of doing *Rawhide* for so long.

'I felt the less he said the stronger he became and the more he grew in the imagination of the audience. You never knew who he was, where he came from and what he was going to do next.

'I had spent many years playing the sort of Mr Good Guy. There was something I liked about going against every Western tradition. Usually, no one played the protagonist where he enters town and sees a woman and child crying for help and essentially rides on. But that gives him somewhere to go during the movie. He can become interested in the parties against his will. The producers thought something was really awry. "Hey, this guy isn't doing anything – he doesn't even have a name." But when they saw it assembled and how it went over with the public, they realised what it was. The "No Name" guy soon became a very imitated character.'

'Eastwood *was* the character,' said Leone recalling the early days of their partnership in the American magazine *Film Comment* in 1978. A decade later he admitted in a conversation in Beverly Hills that he had felt intimidated by Eastwood – but it didn't stop him cashing in on the cult he had created with his star.

After *A Fistful of Dollars* (originally *The Magnificent Stranger*) in 1964 came *For a Few Dollars More* in 1965 and *The Good, the Bad and the Ugly* in 1966. For whatever reason, and it would seem to be more happenstance and the circumstances of the 1960s than some cleverly thought-out promotion, Eastwood rode off on a mule at the end of *A Fistful of Dollars* and into the sunset and cult status.

The poncho.

The badly chewed cigars: 'If I had to be in an unpleasant frame of mind, I took a couple of draws and, boy, I was right there.'

And the squint and fast draw compromised the picture of the grizzled gunslinger, the anti-hero, the Man with No Dialogue as well as no name.

It was a role of the times.

In the upheaval of mid-1960s Britain, Michael Caine had just created Len Deighton's working-class hero from *The Ipcress File* on screen in 1965, and that womanising bounder *Alfie* the following year.

In America, which was entering equally turbulent times, Eastwood was the icy-eyed icon of the age of Vietnam. 'Clint is the quintessential Western man. He has a certain code and he adheres to it religiously,' said Susan Clark.

After working with him, the late Richard Burton said his co-star in *Where Eagles Dare* had 'dynamic lethargy'. Nearly 40 years on, Eastwood laughed about that description: 'Well, AA [Alcoholics Anonymous] might have been where he was at the time.

'I loved Richard – he was a terrific guy and I enjoyed working with him. And he was great at coming up with things like this. I'm not sure what he meant, though.'

You could also get away with Burton's words for Lee Van Cleef, another American actor imported by Sergio Leone for his Westerns. Van Cleef believed *For a Few Dollars More* to be the best movie by the Eastwood-Leone partnership. In an interview before his death he told me: 'It had more depth to it. There was more subtlety about the film and about the performance. And Clint had the confidence then. He had the character down. He's playing it minimal and it worked.'

Van Cleef, who went along with Eastwood and Eli Wallach in search of hidden gold in *The Good, the Bad and the Ugly*, said: 'We had a good time. Clint was really easy to work with. He was professional. And while it was clear he had that star quality, it didn't make him anything other than one of the guys.'

The actor, who played bad guys for most of his career, knew a lot about his fellow stars. He rode the spaghetti-and-paella train in Italy and Spain for several years after Eastwood returned to mainstream American movies. 'I think Clint's timing was good,' he said. 'He was fresh then, a new face for the movies and he had the experience from all those years on *Rawhide* and working with Leone. I knew when I worked with him that it was just a matter of time. He always had control of the situation. There were all those guys babbling away – at times we couldn't understand them and at times they didn't have a clue what we were saying. But, somehow, it all worked. And then when the movies were seen outside Europe there was no stopping.'

A Japanese film critic put the stamp on the legend when he called the trio of Eastwood films 'macaroni Westerns'. One man's pasta became another man's spaghetti, but it wasn't suddenly all a champagne life – or a very public one.

In the 1960s he had been happy to pose with Maggie by their swimming pool, learning his lines, having her trim his hair and finding other excuses for different sorts of publicity pictures to promote *Rawhide*. But, after filming *The Good, the Bad and the Ugly*, he returned to California with a completely different attitude. He wanted control. Total control of his career and of his marriage. Hollywood thought he had got lucky in Europe. 'Just fluke hits,' they said. He says his thoughts then were: 'I was appalled not only at the way money was misused but also the lack of control that an actor had over characters.'

The Italian producers of the spaghetti Westerns had not envisioned how much of a box-office superman their nihilistic hero was to become and had not arranged all world copyrights. When they were legally able to release the Leone films in the United States, Eastwood hit American cinemas with a one-two-three punch and scored a knockout every time as the three movies were shown in the one year – 1967.

And he kept up the pressure by starring that year in Ted Post's *Hang 'Em High*, which might have been made in the USA but for its strong flavour of Leone. The movie did wonderful business, returning costs in ten weeks, the fastest turnaround in the history of United Artists' studios.

Still more fun and better received was *Coogan's Bluff*, which gave us Eastwood as a hayseed Old West lawman going against the odds in the big city. The film, the basis of the television series *McCloud*, which starred Dennis Weaver, was made the same year as *Hang 'Em High* and was to begin Eastwood's high-energy work pattern.

The critics liked *Coogan's Bluff*. But still they were not convinced about the star. Clint was. He completed *Coogan's Bluff* for Universal Studios on New Year's Eve 1967. That same day he flew to London and reported for work on *Where Eagles Dare* on 2 January 1968. He was being paid $750,000 and getting the same billing as Burton, who was then an acting and marital legend. It didn't bother Eastwood – the man with all that 'dynamic lethargy' – one bit. 'People recognise me wherever I go and like it. But that's just part of success.'

The other part was control and clout. And the luxury of having his views about violence and sex listened to. Of the first he said: 'I am not an advocate of violence, but on the other hand, if it is one of the narrative elements in the story, I am not as upset by it as other people are. The world is a violent place – no one can escape that. In films, when it is justified, violence acts as a sort of release.

'Sex? It's used to stimulate and probably some people wish they were involved in the same situation they are looking at, but sex in the movies is not the type of animal release violence is, although sometimes it is intended that way. When I'm working, I like to use my imagination.'

He needed it after agreeing to star in his first musical, the $20-million-budgeted *Paint Your Wagon*. The director, Josh Logan, was delighted to get Eastwood in 1969, saying: 'Fortunately, this is the year of Clint Eastwood. We were looking for a man who could be a leading man and a romantic threat to Lee Marvin's love for Jean Seberg – he's strong physically and as a personality.'

Yet, when Logan's prized star turned up, driving his pick-up truck, for the first day of filming *Paint Your Wagon*, the studio guard refused to let him in.

'What did I do? I turned around and went back to my office and got on with some work. Then the calls began coming in. I may say I took my time about getting back.'

Considering the film's poor critical and box-office

reception, it might have been better if he'd been kept out – along with the rest of the cast, including affable but vodka-prone Marvin and the fragile and beautiful actress Jean Seberg, both now dead.

Seberg always wanted real men. Eastwood personified her desires. And he was willing to go along with them. Those who were on location in Oregon support long-standing rumours that Eastwood and Seberg had a passionate affair during the making of the film. Eastwood himself has never acknowledged the affair. Or denied it.

He was quizzed about his marriage between the time of filming *Paint Your Wagon* and *Two Mules for Sister Sara*, which found him down in the Mexican jungle. The actress Susan St James was with him, but not exclusively. There was another, never-identified date.

'Maggie doesn't chain me,' was Eastwood's repeated reaction back then to the tales of the many ladies in his life, while his wife was back in Carmel, swimming or playing tennis, entertaining herself. And he expanded in 1969: 'When I finish a film I drift back to my own little area where I can be with people I want to and ten minutes later with no one. I'm really all about Carmel, off-in-the-backwoods stuff. If I get really uptight, I go up alone or my wife will go ahead of me. Most of the time I'm off with a flick – I bounce back and forth. She usually comes to every location after I'm situated, visits awhile, and then leaves. She's travelled all over the world, has demands at home. Selfishly, I like things organised.'

As another fast-gun drifter in *Two Mules for Sister Sara* he rescues co-star Shirley MacLaine's Sara, a prostitute disguised as a nun, from three rapists. Sara, still in nun's robes, then goes on a trek with her protector across Mexico until they take on a French garrison. Years later, Eastwood still gets enthusiastic about the film, which was directed by his friend and mentor Don Siegel, who died in 1991: 'Westerns are designed as men's shows. I haven't worked with many actresses who have been turkeys. Once in a while you'd get a stiff who'd be baking in at the make-up table all the time.'

On location back then, he was asked point-blank: 'Are you happy?'

The question was centred not on his career but his private life.

'Either happy or extremely loyal,' he answered.

'Complex', said Maggie Eastwood. 'Strange', said Sergio Leone. Also troubled? Certainly confident. And easily bored.

'*Paint Your Wagon* took six months to make – it should have been three. It sent me crazy all that hanging around. *Where Eagles Dare* took five months. A monumental bore. I hated seeing money flung away like that. So I decided it was time to make my own pictures. If studios want to chuck their money away that's up to them. I want no part of it.'

Eastwood was about to make the move which would turn him into one of the wealthiest movie stars in the world.

# FIVE

# TOP GUN

'My dad was Scots-English, my mother Dutch-Irish,
strange combinations. All the pirates and people
who were kicked out of everywhere else.'
CLINT EASTWOOD, 1983

CLINT'S answer to his frustration with the film world was
to go into business for himself. 'My theory was that I could
foul up my own career just as well as anybody else, so why
not try it?'

It was 1968 and he was still angry and upset over a
business adviser who had told him going to Spain to make
*A Fistful of Dollars* was a 'bad step'.

He formed the Malpaso Company, named after a creek
that runs through the Monterey Peninsula. It is also,
Eastwood tells you with a smile, Spanish for 'bad step'. He
explained: '"Malpaso" came from a pass through the

mountains, which meant a difficult pass, a bad pass or bad step, as they use in Spain a lot. I've never been superstitious about it. I thought at one time when I picked that name that it might not be very good for Latin-American countries, then I was working in Mexico and they had a resort called the Malpaso Resort. If they're not superstitious, why should I be? I just liked the name. It's like purposely coaxing a black cat in front of your car...'

Malpaso began life in a small bungalow at the Burbank Studios in Hollywood. In 2005 it is still there as the centre of Eastwood's company, known as the Taco Bell because it so resembles a chain of rough-and-ready Mexican fast-food restaurants of that name. In the 1960s Eastwood was happy working there with a few cans of beer, a couple of pencils, a few pieces of paper and was equally frugal about personnel. Already a major star, he had a staff of four. The *Doris Day* television series, in production at the same time, had a staff of 26.

'All you need to get into the Directors' Guild of America is for someone to give you a job. So I gave myself a job. I said: "Kid, you got a job."'

Maggie Eastwood was up in Carmel with Kyle, and her husband commuted up the Pacific Coast Highway. Or maybe stayed at the office. He was preparing for the first film for Malpaso, entitled *The Beguiled* and to be directed by Don Siegel. Released in 1970, it was to be audiences' first glimpse into Clint's personal fascination with sex and violence, of lust conquering innocence.

He plays a soldier during the American Civil War who hides out in a girls' school like a boy in a sweetshop.

Immediately he starts flirting with the students, but in return for his attention they start to poison him, then cut off his leg.

Yet he always had bigger ambitions; in 1970 he had walked into the office of the then President of Universal, Lew Wasserman, one of Hollywood's best connected and most powerful men, and asked if he could direct *Play Misty for Me*.

In those days there was a set procedure for actors who had directing ambitions: they were told to get lost. But Wasserman didn't laugh or throw him out. He said yes; with conditions: 'He said we don't want to pay you, though. You work for whatever your guild minimum is and if the picture does well, maybe we'll give you a few bucks. But he said yes very briskly.'

*Play Misty for Me* in 1971 was Eastwood's debut as a director and arguably the most significant turning point of his whole film-making career. He revealed, but not until a couple of decades later, that the film was based on a real story of sexual harassment. And it was Eastwood who was harassed. He was 19 and the girl was around 23, he said, and quietly explained: 'There was a little misinterpretation about how serious the whole thing was.'

He used his own experience and that of a disc jockey in California's Mendocino County to create his character in *Play Misty for Me*, which remains a highly regarded cult film. Jessica Walter had the best part as the demented fan stalking disc jockey Eastwood and his screen girlfriend, a role which gave Donna Mills her breakthrough.

Mills, who went on to become immensely popular as

Abby in the long-running soap *Knots Landing*, was then very much a newcomer to Hollywood. 'I had done some guest shots on television, including Burt Reynolds's show *Dan August*.' Apparently, Burt and Clint were talking and Clint had tested 300 girls for the role of the girlfriend, which is a lot of auditions. 'Burt told him to watch my part on *Dan August*. Clint went in and saw a rough cut of the show and said: "That's the girl."'

'He hired me right from it. I was on a soap in New York and I never met him until I came out to Hollywood – it all happened that fast. It was the first time he had directed and it was wonderful. He really was wonderful. He knew exactly what he wanted. We shot the film in six weeks, which is not a long time for a major feature.

'I liked him a lot, but he was married and we were very proper. I have always made it a rule of my life that I never go out with married men – no matter how attracted I am to them or how appealing they are. I think it's a real heartache for everybody involved.'

She did have one refreshing love scene with her co-star – under a freezing-cold waterfall. 'Clint brought out a bottle of cognac to warm us up – by the time we both got through the scene we were bombed. Clint and I became very good friends after the movie and stayed in touch a long while.'

And he had made another point to the Hollywood executives who questioned his decision to give Jessica Walter the grand-standing psycho role. 'The studio people said why do you want to do a movie where the woman has the best part? My reaction was: Why not? I figured, why should men have all the fun playing disturbed characters? If you think about it, the best characters – the roles with a little conflict and zip to them – are the villains.'

Unless they're *Dirty Harry.* Inspector Harry Callahan was the Man with No Name but with a clean shave and in a neatly cut suit, shirt and conservative tie. And he had the big .44 Magnum, which liberals dubbed 'an angry erection'. Of course, in 1971 *Dirty Harry* was an instant box-office success as a fast-moving film directed by Siegel, by now Eastwood's unofficial partner. Harry was the great cop who was stopped from catching his man – a sex killer played by Andy Robinson – by bureaucracy, by the system.

The blue-collar appeal was instant – here was another anti-hero but this time trying to do everything possible to clean up the streets. D.H. Lawrence had observed years earlier: 'The essential American soul is hard, stoic, isolate and a killer.' And *Dirty Harry* translated that thought of the literary man for the man in the street worldwide. But in the Vietnam era the controversy was fierce. When the Philippines announced they were using *Dirty Harry* as a police training film, there were howls of derision.

The advertisement for the movie ran: 'You Didn't Assign Dirty Harry – You Turned Him Loose'. Eastwood would never be drawn into the political debate that went on around the film. But he did have answers about the violence it shows: 'Violence is a fact of life. It's what people are most curious about – like slowing down to see car crashes on the highway. It's unusual. It goes on the front pages of newspapers, not the back page. That's what people want to know about. What about people who don't accept that? I tell them to fuck off.'

He's adamant: 'A lot of people thought it was a political film and it wasn't at all. He's just an individual who has a certain philosophy about victims of crime. But that story was a bit ahead of its time.

'Nowadays, there's organisations for victims of violent crimes and for the families but in those days there wasn't any of that. I don't necessarily agree with Dirty Harry's philosophy all the way down the line. I don't disagree with the importance of rights for the accused either. But we were telling a story.'

He says Dirty Harry was a rebel who makes mischief. 'But was he a leftist rebel or a rightist rebel? He was just a guy who hated bureaucracy and wanted to get a job done; now is that "far right"? I don't think he thought of himself as a political man. He thought of himself as a passionate man trying to solve a case. Dirty Harry was just a person who had questions about the law – I don't think there is a person in America, anywhere, who isn't frustrated by a lot of our court decisions.'

Eastwood's instincts proved accurate when the worst urban violence ever in the United States forced President George Bush to send in the National Guard and the army to take back control of the looted and burning streets of Los Angeles in the late spring of 1992.

It wasn't only Los Angeles which turned into an inferno following the acquittal of four LA Police Department officers in the beating of black motorist Rodney King. There were demonstrations and riots across America, including Eastwood's home town of San Francisco.

In 1971 the *Dirty Harry* scenes the fans adored and most

imitated were those most loathed by the civil rights groups. Especially the scene where Harry is pointing his big gun at the wounded bank robber he is standing over:

'I know what you're thinking.

'"Did he fire six bullets or only five?"

'Well, to tell the truth, I kinda lost track myself.

'But seein' how the .44 Magnum is the most powerful handgun in the world and that it would blow your head clear off, you got to ask yourself – "Do I feel lucky today?"

'Well, do ya, punk?'

At that moment Harry pulls the trigger and it clicks on an empty chamber. The punk is messing himself. Harry flashes his roguish grin.

Americans called him a fascist. French film buffs already were rating him an auteur. Audiences were turning out for everything he did.

With *Play Misty for Me* and *Dirty Harry* in the same year, 1971, he was on his way as the biggest box-office star of the 1970s. And about to meet Sondra Locke, who would end his marriage at a cost to him of more than $20 million. And who would later shatter his faith in 'the loyalty of friends' and sue him twice. And who would become one of the very few women throughout his life that he did not part on amiable terms with.

During their long relationship, Locke, who married sculptor Gordon Anderson in 1969, remained married. As Maggie Eastwood has said, the end of her marriage was inevitable. What was extraordinary was how long it stayed together, at least officially, given the private pressures and extramarital relationships involved.

But hard-working Eastwood was still pursuing his other passion, film-making, seemingly oblivious to the complications of his private life. In 1972 he made the Western *Joe Kidd* on location in Arizona. It was familiar territory. Just a bigger star role. Eastwood was the gunfighter protecting Mexican workers against moneyed interests. He also had to protect himself against the ladies, one of whom, ever forward, approached him in the film's location hotel and asked: 'What does it take to stay the night with you?'

'A lot of things crossed my mind, but I just laughed and scratched my way out of the problem,' he said later.

The movie-making continued as in 1973 Eastwood directed the love story *Breezy*, which starred William Holden. He was casting the film and interviewed Sondra Locke, who had won an Oscar nomination for her first film, *The Heart Is a Lonely Hunter*, in 1968. At that time she was 21 and played a 14-year-old in the much-admired screen adaptation of Carson McCullers's novel. She desperately wanted the role, especially with Holden leading the cast. She didn't get it. But the producer and director of the film would recall her later.

Inspector Harry Callahan returned in 1973 in *Magnum Force* to more outcry and in 1974 Eastwood co-starred in the buddy picture *Thunderbolt and Lightfoot*, directed by Michael Cimino, alongside the young Jeff Bridges.

Eastwood was on the list of the Top Ten box-office stars with John Wayne and Paul Newman from 1969 and by 1975 he was top of the heap – literally.

*The Eiger Sanction* was a slight international espionage story but the thrills were in the mountaineering stunts. Eastwood did his own. And nearly got himself killed while only rehearsing for Swiss location scenes. He took on rock faces at California's Yosemite National Park. With him was cinematographer-mountaineer Mike Hoover, who watched as Eastwood 'flamed out' from the rock face and was dangling in space, unable to get to safety. Hoover remembers how:

'He looked at me and said: "Gee, I don't think I can make it."

'I said: "Well, Clint, you really don't have much choice, do you?"

'Then he reacted characteristically – he got pissed off.

'He pulled in his chin, he gritted his teeth and with absolutely no technique at all, just blood and guts, he moosed his way up.

'No skill, no brains, just pure muscle. It was gruesome to watch.'

Much more gruesome was the filming on the Eiger when a British climber and stuntman was killed and Hoover himself narrowly escaped death. David Knowles, who was 27 when the film was being made in 1975, was from Preston, Lancashire. Eastwood was hanging from a rock face a few yards from Knowles, who was hit by a falling boulder and killed, while Hoover, who was struck by the rock, had his pelvis fractured.

Filming went on and all the climber-stuntmen accepted the accident for what it was. 'They are a breed apart – they strike up a great camaraderie between themselves,' recalled

Eastwood. Hoover remembered it differently: 'He always comes off as very callous and pragmatic but inside he's mush. He was shaken by the accident – he even started to cry. And he was ready to shut down production of the film. He's the first guy to do the dirtiest job – and not in a show-off way. Clint seemed so simple I thought he was phoney, but after a while I realised how sharp he was. He isn't verbal, but he's one smart mother.'

Which is why, after making *The Eiger Sanction*, Eastwood said: 'I will never do anything like that again – just too damn dangerous. Even though I had practised for weeks, it was still terrifying. I don't see how you can ever get used to dangling on the end of a rope, thousands of feet above nothing, held up by a man you hardly know. And when a glacier moves with that terrible groan, that's terrifying. One of the British guys said I'd get used to it. I never did.'

Professionally, Eastwood has always been surefooted – none of the Malpaso stuff, those bad steps; sometimes a difficult hurdle but nothing dramatically wrong.

But he was struggling to reach firmer ground with his family – now including a daughter, Alison, born in 1972 – when, smack in the middle of the 1970s, he began pre-production thinking about 1976's *The Outlaw Josey Wales*, one of his classic films.

The plot has emotional links with his own life at that time: 'I loved the story. I don't know why but I'm always attracted to characters who are always in search of family. I have an affinity for people who are close together...'

Josey Wales loses his family to a band of guerrillas during

the Civil War. He goes after the bad guys. Then a crazy
Yankee captain slaughters surrendering rebel troops. Josey
survives and picks up an oddball team of pilgrims on his
travels as he seeks revenge: a dying frontier boy played by
Sam Bottoms, an old Indian with some of the film's best
lines, portrayed by Chief Dan George, and a lost young
woman – Sondra Locke.

Locke is a wisp of a thing. Blonde and fragile. Born in
America's Deep South. Which in *The Outlaw Josey Wales*
was fine – on the surface. She had attended a 'cattle call' –
an audition of more than 2,000 actresses – to win her part
in *The Heart Is a Lonely Hunter* but was concerned at her
success in it: 'I was afraid it had put me into some kind of
sexual oblivion. I played a practically pre-puberty tomboy
and some producers thought I was a boy.'

Eastwood changed her image in *The Gauntlet*, which
followed *Josey Wales* in 1977 and mirrors its humour.
Here she is in skin-tight jeans and an open top, taunting a
bunch of bad-boy bikers: 'Let's see what you've got
between your legs.'

In that film she's a very tough good-time girl helping
Eastwood's hard-drinking Arizona cop. But it was *Josey
Wales* that made them into something of a contemporary
Spencer Tracy and Katharine Hepburn. They made love
together. They made films together. Polite people only
discussed the films.

It was a long relationship – a major commitment by so
high-profile a star as Eastwood. Maggie Eastwood did what
was required and that was to support her husband in all his
endeavours. It could not have been easy.

Eastwood and Locke sparkled on screen. Off screen they did too. During filming of *The Gauntlet* the battle-of-the-sexes sparring sometimes overflowed off screen. Locke appeared with Eastwood in six films, including the Dirty Harry excursion *Sudden Impact* in 1983.

She says they had lived together as man and wife from 1977. In a rare, exclusive interview at the Hotel Bel-Air in Los Angeles, she talked about their lives together in great detail. She would become less forthcoming about their lives apart when it all became a legal matter, but in that interview she gave an insight into Clint's intense private life.

She always felt lucky in their relationship, she said. People talked. It was part of the territory. She accepted the strange set-up. She was married. He was married. They were a couple. When you listen to her talk about her life before and then with Eastwood you get an understanding of the man and woman who were Hollywood's Odd Couple for so long: 'The only way to get a rest is just to leave Los Angeles – to get out of town. To get away from business is the only way to relax. I've always done that. We did that.

'Some friends of mine have some places up in Oregon and in northern California and Idaho and it's such beautiful country I take off there and collapse. I read and walk. And you know, it's amazing. I find everybody asks me what do you do, don't you get bored? I find that when I get in the country I don't know what it is but I find there's never enough time in the day, the day goes by so fast and I'll think: Oh, I wanted to write such and such a letter today or something else. Well, there's no time. I suppose the smallest task seems a monumental thing at the end of the day.

I go with friends but away from business and away from Hollywood, and the telephone.

'Quite frankly, any career I've had is because it just came to me because I am the worst at producing a career. It just is totally against my grain. I don't like going to places where I don't know people, I don't like new people. It's a terrible thing to say and it has to do with Hollywood. That sounds a cliché in a way but it's basically true. I'm just no good at pushing my own career. Period. So it's amazing that I've had one at all.

'I've worked in a lot of Clint's pictures but I've never got into the celebrity circuit. I think that he's the same way too in that respect. He keeps himself outside of the Hollywood scheme of things. But basically I'm so bad at that. I love to work. I really love acting. I love the film process. I love the set. I'm interested in all aspects of film-making.

'I really love movies, ever since I was a child, but I am so bad at business. Agents or managers don't really do anything that much for you. They're very good at negotiating if someone wants you and once in a while an agent probably has done a lot for a client, got them started or pushed them hard, but in the general sense, I think it comes down to the person. You have to get out there and you have to make the contacts and you have to be seen, you have to know this person, that person, you have to make yourself available. Out of sight, out of mind.

'I've never done that and it's not that I don't care about my career and that I don't want to work, because I've been disappointed that there aren't enough roles that I was sad that I didn't get. There isn't a lot to get you excited most of the time, but there have been a few things, you know. I think working once a year would be ideal really! An actor can make one really good film a year, that's accomplishment because there isn't that much great material.

'I really don't mind leisure time. Even if I were getting offers right and left, I'm not the person who wants to work all the time. I'm compulsive in accomplishing projects, but I don't always have to be focused on something, it doesn't have to be movies or working... I always think: Oh, I'll never work again. I think actors, no matter how successful they are, always think: Oh, this is the last one, I'll never work again. I can remember when I did *The Heart Is a Lonely Hunter* with Alan Arkin and he said that. And at that time Alan was very hot, everyone was interested in him. I remember thinking to myself: Oh, this is incredible, all this.

'But I got that part just as part of the process of a talent search because I was right out of high school. I had never done anything except local theatre and I was very interested in it and I auditioned. That's the only time I've ever pursued acting in my life. I remember Alan Arkin said to me – I wondered what I should do after this, should I go to Hollywood, it was filmed in Alabama – "Well, Sondra, I always think every time I finish a job, I always think I'll never have another job." And I remember being stunned and thinking how it's just part of the territory. So it's not that I'm so secure in it, that's not true at all. I'm probably very insecure, but I enjoy being off enough.

'If you get to the black side of it, I feel that in many ways I did myself an injustice because this is such a place, this town – especially where actresses are concerned – it reminds me of when I was in school and everybody was always interested in the new girl in town, the new family moves in and everybody is always saying: "Oooh, wow, have you seen this…?" and they've got the daughter and the son and that's kind of the way this town is.

'Once you get through that crack you have to move fast and furious because once you've been around for a while it doesn't matter, your reputation or anything, they're always looking for the new girl in town. So you have to make the most of it at the time it erupts. I didn't realise that. In fact, I was so naive, that when I auditioned for *Heart*, I thought: Gee, this is easy. I went in, I auditioned, I thought I was the best person for the part, so naturally I would get the part and then I was nominated for the Oscar and I thought: This is too easy. What is everybody talking about? I thought: That's the way it always works: you go in, you audition for the part and the person who gives the best audition gets the part. That's how dumb I was. Then after a while it began slowly to sink in that that's not the way it works at all.

'Rarely it works that way. It worked in my case because they were looking for an unknown and naturally they were going to take the person they thought was the best, with no political reasons for doing anything else, but I learned quickly that was definitely not the case. After *Heart* – this is terrible – there was a picture with Noel Black directing. I thought he was such a good director. He did a film called *Pretty Poison* with Tuesday Weld and Tony Perkins and it was a marvellous little picture and he had a film at Fox called *Run, Shadow, Run* and he wanted me to do it.

'At that point in my life, I was determined that in this acting game you have to act. Because the only downfall with my first film was that I realised that everybody thought I was that girl in *The Heart Is a Lonely Hunter*. And I got no offers other than the exact same character and I was still high and mighty and determined to prove that I am not this character. I'm something totally different, I can be anything! And so I took this film because it gave me the opportunity to do something totally different from the first role I had done. Robert Forster was in it and in 1968 he was very hot and it seemed like a real good combination. That's when Fox released *Star*.

'They lost so much money on that Julie Andrews film they didn't do a lot of advertising on the other films they had. They just pushed the picture out there and it got lost in the shuffle and a year went by with my life and career and that film did nothing. Then I did a picture with Robert Shaw, called *Reflection of Fear*. It was a wonderful part and once again there was a lot of in-house fighting – not that I'm saying these were the greatest pictures ever made, but they were certainly good pictures worth release – but the film once again got lost out there and didn't really catch on. Every film has to have its own kind of release. So that's the way it goes; who's the next girl in town?

'I didn't feel bitter about that. I felt angry at times. I still feel angry at times. I don't like to name names, but I think a lot of people get a lot of attention they don't deserve. But that's the ballgame. That's just part of it. Not everything is always fair. It's a very unfair business. It's so subjective that there are no … nothing makes any sense.

'So, I have felt angry and really annoyed at certain things and people at times. But I realise that I feel very lucky for what I have, based upon how little I put myself out. When I really sit down and talk to myself, I realise I have no complaints because I didn't go out there. If I'm going to complain at least I should exert myself. It's not that I'm lazy, it's that I don't know how to do it. It's just not a talent of mine. I remember doing a film with an actress and she was amazing. She was on the phone all day and they weren't social calls. Everything was related to business, do you know so and so, could I meet them, it was obsessive. She was perfectly happy with it. I'm not saying that's wrong. It's just that it's totally foreign to me. If I tried to do it I don't think it would work because I just don't have the talent for it. I'm not goal-directed at all.

'I always wanted to act, to be involved with film and I like the production end as well. I like all aspects of it. I always wanted to be involved. I don't know if I still am because I may be too far gone to change my ways but in school and always in my life I was one of those people who could learn anything. If somebody told me they were going to put me in law school, I would have been an attorney. If somebody said they were going to put me in medical school, I would have been a doctor. I'm not even saying this to compliment myself because what happens on the other side is that I don't have the goal orientation to make myself do any of those things, but I just had that knack to do anything.

'I was born in Tennessee and Marion Dougherty, the casting lady, who's very well known in the business, conducted a talent search for *The Heart Is a Lonely Hunter* and went from city to city, primarily in the south, but also New York and Los Angeles looking for someone for the part. I heard about it, read about it in the papers and I auditioned. I drove to southern Alabama. It would make a wonderful film and Clint thought it was one of the greatest stories. I auditioned locally and then they took me to New York and I spent a few weeks there auditioning and reading with various other candidates for the other roles.

'After we did the picture, I came here to Los Angeles and I've sort of been stuck here ever since. I did have a compulsion then, I wasn't alone because Gordon Anderson – my husband, we grew up together, we were like playmates when we were children – really pushed me to do it. He made me do it. I don't know if I would have done it... I would have done it, I think, but it seemed like one of those things that couldn't happen and it's hard to convince yourself that you could really get the part, nationwide talent hunt and all that.

'He was very interested himself, he's an artist but he was also an actor and was doing very well in New York. He actually went to New York and was studying there. I somehow felt responsible for his giving up acting because I think he saw how absurd it was and he saw things that I had to go through – idiotic things most of the time – and he has so many other talents, so he just sort of fell back on those. He does miniature sculptures, mostly by commission. Many collectors sort of get on to him and they want favourite characters in a novel or film and he would sculpt these characters. Collectors are maniacs. Once they get on to you... He's well known among people who collect miniatures or those sorts of things. He works in porcelain. He's done a few things of me. I became Alice in Wonderland once.

'Clint was totally responsible for *Sudden Impact*. It started out as a small project that he was thinking of producing and didn't even have ... he wasn't even in it ... it was just a small story that caught his eye and he thought it was interesting and would make a good film. He thought he'd produce it. Then the final writer who did the actual screenplay just got the idea off the wall, out of the blue, of making it into a *Dirty Harry*, a murder/suspense film, and suddenly it became a *Dirty Harry*. It was just a small story that probably no one would have been interested in, no one would have seen the potential. In the end, Clint did and turned it into a *Dirty Harry*.

'He does that, he moves before anyone knows it. A fast draw. The films that I've been in, my two favourites are *The Outlaw Josey Wales* and *Bronco Billy*. I loved *Bronco Billy*, I thought it was very brave of Clint to make it because obviously it's not what his fans would like to see and yet people who love that kind of film, a more sophisticated audience, loved it.

'But *Josey Wales* was the first film I did with Clint and I think it's a classic film. Orson Welles once said on the *Merv Griffin Show* [on American television] that *Josey Wales* was one of the best directed films as far as he was concerned and that if Clint hadn't directed it, everyone would have called it a classic. But because Clint had a certain stigma that goes with being the kind of star that he is, he doesn't get the credit often that he deserves in the area of performing or

film-making. He is simply associated with the macho
superstar. But Welles said that and I was very impressed
because I agreed. I think it's wonderfully directed. It's a
beautiful film.

'The attitude still makes me angry like it makes me angry
when I don't get certain things or certain roles or certain
opportunities that I think I could do a good job at. It's also
part of that game that you accept certain constants in the
business and I always go back to Steven Spielberg's
comment when he first did *Jaws* and it was such a big hit
and the picture was nominated for a Best Picture Oscar and
he wasn't nominated for Best Director. I was very impressed
with his comment. They were interviewing him on television
and he said: "Well, everybody loves a winner but nobody
loves a winner.' And I thought: That's true.

'I feel frankly that applies to Clint. He's one of the few
people in the business who personally believes films are big
efforts and you're only as good as the people surrounding
you. Clint does, in effect, do everything in his films from
start to finish. He picks the properties, produces, directs,
stars and edits, picks the cast. I think people take him for
granted and he's been such a big star for so many years it's
just, "Well, that's that." That's all there is and it's not
really true. For many years to come people will look at the
films and say: "Hey, that was wonderfully directed." *Play
Misty for Me* was wonderful suspense. For me one of the
hardest things to accomplish – and I see films all the time
– is suspense.

'We met originally when I was auditioning for a role in
*Breezy*, which he didn't cast me in. I've always played

younger. I was 17 when I did *Heart* and played 14. He just wanted a maturity. We've talked about it and I say: "How dare you not cast me in that film?" He says: "Well, I just sensed there's a certain maturity about you that comes across in spite of yourself. There's no question you could have acted the part, but there was just a certain immaturity in this other actress that I thought was better for the film." So that was the end of that.

'At that time, I had been out here [Los Angeles] a few years and I had gotten rather blasé about a few things: an audition is an audition. I remember I wanted that part very much. It was one of the few scripts I had read since I had come to Hollywood that I really wanted and then when I heard that William Holden was playing in it, I thought: Oh, I've got to do this, I've got to do it. I was very disappointed. Jo Heims, the lady writer, wanted me to do it. She called me up and we talked and I said: "I'm really doing my best." It didn't work out. Clint told me later that he thought I had an interesting quality, whatever that is, and I stuck in the back of his mind and I guess the next thing that came along that he thought I might be right for was *The Outlaw Josey Wales*.

'My agent got a call asking me to come in and meet him. That was it. I think basically it wasn't that large a role – it was just that it had a special quality about it – but it was the chance to work with Clint because I did admire him and what he had accomplished in the business and also I thought it might help... I had done all these interesting little films that hadn't gotten released and I thought this was perfect to be in a Clint Eastwood picture. Everybody will see me! It will be a commercial success! It's about time! I loved the story, the script.

'And I lost my eyebrows. We were sitting around a campfire and in order to get the light we had to make the fire so enormous that when I had to stand by it during the scene, I singed my eyebrows. That was one of my best acting moments not to scream out! He's notorious for not letting actresses wear make-up. I can't get used to my face except one way. If I go to a big party I look very strange to myself with a lot of make-up, yet I'm wearing this beautiful dress, I should have on more make-up. The face doesn't go with the dress. One of my fantasies was always to do period film.

'People get preconceived little niches for you and although I had a lot of work behind me when I started working with Clint several of the films weren't seen. And then you become ... well, a lot of people think she only works with Clint and he is such a dynamic figure that it's easy for him to overwhelm, everyone wants to know what he's thinking, what he's doing, and then you become a part of that.

'That did happen to me there's no denying it. I think it would be wise for me to find something uniquely my own to do. The thing about getting caught up in Clint's image is inevitable. But it hasn't happened only to me. It's happened to other performers in his pictures.

'There's something I suppose that's so powerful about him and the fact that he runs his own show, that sets him apart from the rest of the business. We've talked about this. He talks about it too with the actor Andy Robinson, who in the original *Dirty Harry* played the villain. Andy is a wonderful actor, but things never came round to him the way they should have but I think … it was a double whammy in that one because he was playing a villain and once you play the crazy villain then everybody sees you as the crazy villain.

'Clint's private but it's not deliberate in any way. If it were, we didn't accomplish anything. At least not the sort of publicity I wanted. He's sort of secret, as I said. Like doing the first *Dirty Harry* without anyone knowing about it until the last minute. He just doesn't like to tell anybody what he's doing. It extends to all parts of his life.

'I basically am the same way. It's a bit going back to the thing of not being able to promote my own career. In a way it's the same personality quality. I don't go to cocktail parties and flow well with the traffic. I've never been very good at talking about myself, which is one reason I never give interviews. I find I can talk easily with you. I don't like talking about myself. But I've always been that way. I always want to know more about the people I'm with and I start withdrawing when I'm asked questions about myself and it's not that I have big secrets, it's just the way I am.

'In the beginning, when I first came to this town, I did make attempts to follow suit. I had a press agent, I had one of the best and, in my opinion, nothing worthwhile was accomplished. I would give these interviews, force myself and I'd read them and most of the time – and I'm not blaming the journalist because something in living 3-D is very difficult to translate into black and white, one-dimensional things – humour was lacking, inflections weren't there. Even when I would be quoted verbatim, I would say that's not me. So I just withdrew more.

'Just after my first picture I came to this town and met a few people and right away I was always the vulnerable girl abused in some way or held back with a fragile character or emotionally disturbed or something like that. Then Clint used me in *The Gauntlet* in which I played a very tough girl. I like dichotomies anyway, it intrigued me. I always liked the bad seed.

'It gives another dimension to the character to look one way and act another, so I loved playing the part in *The Gauntlet*. She was tough. Well, pretty soon everybody suddenly said: "Oh, she's tough and she's hard." I found this really impossible. I was browsing through a bookstore one day and picked up an encyclopaedia of actors and flipped to my name to see what they're saying about me – in fact, it was an English publication – and it says: "American actress of the type hard-boiled." I laughed and laughed. You can't win for losing!

'How do I see myself? Very confused! I don't know. Sometimes I see myself as not specific enough. Because I'd always prided myself all my life on being able to be so versatile, being able to learn anything, being able to adapt to anything. I was always able to do that to the degree that I'm ... even don't have enough of a handle on myself. Actually I'm very down to earth, grounded, a directed person even though that sounds contradictory. But at the same time it's easy to be so many different things. I always thought that was what acting was all about and probably one of the things that attracted me to it. Then I thought: No that's not right. You have to project a certain image and be a certain way to get a certain career going. I've never done that.

'Except I've got this image as sort of an extension of Clint, if you will, which is not me, so it's...'

# SIX

# MAGNETIC MAN

'Every woman feels she has a chance with him.'
SIERRA PECHEUR, 1980

HE looks you straight in the eye when you ask about his relationship with Sondra Locke, but it is clear that after all the years his heart is not in denials. Or explanations. It happened. Girls happen.

In more reflective years he did explain why he had settled his disputes with Locke out of court: 'That's the vulnerability of being a motion-picture actor – somebody trying to gain financially off of you. All you can do is sit back, and if somebody sues you, that unfortunately automatically allows them in our legal system to say anything. It doesn't have to be true.

'Sometimes you have to let people hang themselves a

little bit. I'm not sure how many people believed Sondra Locke. In the long run people hurt themselves. There is something to karma. If you spew enough negativity, it has to come back to you in some form, I do believe that philosophically.'

More secular were the British pubs he visited with Richard Burton while filming *Where Eagles Dare* in the late 1960s and when he got into partnership to open his own bar-restaurant in Carmel he gave it what he believed was a pub name: the Hog's Breath Inn. He could have called it anything he wanted, for his association with it made the place an instant success. There were tourists. And there were girls. Girls who looked as though they had walked out of the pages of *Vogue* or *Elle* or the Polo Lounge at the Beverly Hills Hotel. Meet a star. Be a star?

The female staff there were always gracious and always loyal and usually stunning. Eastwood is a good boss, no matter what the endeavour. Paul Lippman was at one time a part-owner with Eastwood of the Hog's Breath. He maintains Eastwood was a romantic Casanova at the pub. He chatted up all the girls. Especially the blondes. 'Clint liked small or slight women – he called them "squirts" or "shrimps" and "spinners".'

According to Lippman, it was lust at first sight. He said that when he and Eastwood double-dated they would talk about their girls the morning after. But he said that Eastwood said of his morning-after bedside manner: 'We don't talk – we watch cartoons.'

Lippman says Eastwood liked unknown women whom he would not later accidentally meet. He maintains Eastwood had swift encounters, including one with a brunette 'who taught him transcendental meditation'.

Eastwood denies the 'Dirty Clint' charge, saying: 'Other than having a couple of beers together a few times, we didn't see each other or socialise. He and his wife once owned part of the Hog's Breath but we were never close. I won't apologise for any of my behaviour because I haven't done anything wrong.'

During his relationship with Locke, the actor's reputation as a ladies' man – albeit a low-key one – never lost momentum. But in public, at Hollywood functions or at the White House, it was Locke who was on his arm.

But she was not his partner on film when he returned for the third time as Inspector Callahan, the Mean Machine of San Francisco, in 1976. This time Dirty Harry got a woman partner, Tyne Daly, who would later become famous worldwide as tough but tender Mary Beth Lacey in the television series *Cagney and Lacey*.

In *The Enforcer* – then a topical mix of politics and terrorism following the kidnapping and subsequent trial for bank robbery of heiress Patty Hearst – Daly got a taste of the action awaiting her on television. In the film the Mayor of San Francisco is kidnapped and Harry and Daly's Detective Kate Moore are on alert. Moore dies – another partner gone for Dirty Harry. Victim or not, it was a good scene-stealing role and Daly recalled: 'I was really proud of my work on *The Enforcer* because I had to act even more than usual. I just can't stand the sight of guns but I didn't want to turn down the chance to play opposite Clint. I just had to swallow my feelings, look into his eyes and get on with the show. Clint taught me to handle guns like an expert. Everything I did on *Cagney and Lacey* I learned from him. He's a good teacher.'

And frugal. He's not known as 'SkinClint' for nothing.

During *The Enforcer* a blue Cutlass car had ploughed through a store window. In 1977 the same car – engine removed – is finally to go out of service. Eastwood was star and director of *The Gauntlet* and, on location in the Nevada desert near Las Vegas, here was one more special effect. On cue the car blows, the roof spinning through the smoke with other debris as flames play around the dummy-victim in the driving seat. Eastwood is still to survive a police ambush, a car bombing, a state-line shoot-out, a helicopter attack, a showdown with a motorcycle gang, a fright on a freight train – and that's before he hijacks a Greyhound bus and drives through town with 300 policemen blasting at him with machine guns. Just another Clint Eastwood love story.

In *The Gauntlet* he plays Arizona cop Ben Shockey, who is nowhere near as smart as Dirty Harry and likes the bottle too much. He is trying to get prostitute Gus Mally, played by Sondra Locke, back from Vegas to Phoenix to be the key witness in a mob trial. Speaking on location then, Locke said: 'You can't say there are no good roles for women when you see this. She's very feisty – she's got a different nature from mine.'

So, of course, has Eastwood. These were the early days of their romance. Locke talked about him sometimes in strange contradictions. 'He's one of the most sensitive, gentlest men in the world – with the most horrifying temper. Yet he wouldn't kill spiders – he helped me get over my fear of

them. I have the greatest amount of respect, admiration and fondness for him and I think it's mutual. I love working with him but there's nothing specific in the works... Nobody is going to complain about playing opposite Clint as a romantic lover on screen.'

Eastwood was quizzed about her at the time and smiled a reply: 'Good spontaneity.'

He also defended his women in films: 'When feminism came in I was one of the early targets. What they didn't notice was how many of my films have good roles for strong women. Sondra in *The Gauntlet* had more to say than I did. And despite the fact that the character is a hooker we didn't cast for some busty, gum-chewing, dumb blonde. We made her an intelligent, strong woman.

'I'd never cast myself opposite a woman who was there merely for sex appeal. I cast it a little off. Good casting would be to make her a princess – she is a princess. But to cast as a hooker – that's the twist.'

It was not an argument feminists readily accepted. Eastwood's attitude to that was much the same as to the gossip about him and his leading lady. Also, there was the question of Maggie Eastwood and Locke's husband, Gordon Anderson. Locke maintained in 1977: 'Gordon and I don't sit down and talk about it. He figures if there's any truth to it, I'll be the first to tell him. If there's anything to know, he'll know it.'

Nevertheless, it was Eastwood she visited in Carmel. Or went skiing with in Vail, Colorado, or the Sun Valley Resort near Ketchum, Idaho. We might suggest the situation suited Eastwood. It took pressure off him to get divorced. It gave him time to play pub playboy at the Hog's Breath. Man, wife, mistress – recall the late Sir James Goldsmith's famous warning: 'When a man marries his mistress, it creates a vacancy.'

Others said the situation was fine by Locke because it took the pressure off her – she was frightened of embarrassing her strict Baptist parents in Wartrace, Tennessee. Even after all the publicity, her mother, Pauline, said at her home: 'Sondra tells me these rumours about her and Clint are not true and for us not to pay any attention to them. Sondra and Gordon are still in love and are still married and living together – no matter what people say about her and Clint. And there's no talk of divorce.'

A curious set-up. Especially when we were later to learn that during her relationship with Eastwood the actress would at times sleep over with her husband. It was reported in America and never denied that the trio would go out on dates together, along with lots of other Odd Couple gossip.

In 1978 Eastwood and Locke were an established movie team when they made *Every Which Way But Loose*. It was a change of pace for the actor. He played a laid-back truck driver, Philo Beddoe, who is chasing Locke's country-and-western singer, Lynn Halsey-Taylor, across America. To finance the trip he has the help of friends Clyde, an orang-utan, and Orville, played by Eastwood repertory company member Geoffrey Lewis. They start bar-room brawls – Eastwood's the fighter – and bet their travel money on the results.

Eastwood admits Clyde was not always easy to work with. A little temperamental? 'Orang-utans are shy and stand-offish – they're not like chimpanzees, who are total extroverts. With Clyde what we'd do was simple: I'd give him half a can of beer, he'd relax, and we'd do the scene. We had to get it right on the first scene, though, because Clyde didn't have much patience.'

What about Eastwood's kissing scenes with Clyde? Full on-the-lips stuff? 'You've got to understand that people get sort of attached to Clyde. Besides, Clyde is a very warm-lipped primate. They say you should never play a scene with a child actor or an animal – they'll steal the scene every time. But at that stage in my career I thought: What the hell – I'll take a chance with an orang-utan.'

In 1979 Clint Eastwood had a new love in his life – a $100,000 red Ferrari, a competition car that you push to the limit, a speed machine. He took a high-performance driving course at an exclusive California school. He was still involved with Sondra Locke, and he and Maggie Eastwood separated in January 1979, after 26 years of marriage.

Then Eastwood and Clyde, the orang-utan, defied the critics and turned *Every Which Way But Loose* into the third-biggest box-office success for Warner Brothers (following *The Exorcist* and the original *Superman*), earning more than $60 million – then magical numbers – in America alone. The film went on to be equally successful in Europe. Eastwood also planned to team up again with Don Siegel, who would direct him in *Escape from Alcatraz*, a fact-based tale of convicts doing what was regarded as the impossible: getting free from the prison known as 'the Rock', which sits so bleakly and ominously out in San Francisco Bay.

Eastwood was almost 50 in 1979. It was all classic male menopause – younger girl, separation from wife. Proving that age is no limit to achievement, even the films were good, action-packed manhood movies. It was like Jack Palance, at the 1992 Oscars, doing one-arm push-ups before a television audience of one billion viewers to show that, even at 72, he didn't need a health certificate to work. But Hollywood is very much that way – they think insurance, they concern themselves about the bottom line, the profit and the loss of such should a star die or be unable to complete a film.

No worries about Clint.

By the spring of 1979 he had raced with another star driver, Paul Newman, at Riverside Raceway in California and had arranged to take a course at Bob Bondurant's School of High Performance Driving in northern California. It is a place often used to train drivers of international businessmen and politicians to avoid kidnap in high-speed chases. It also gives exclusive courses to laymen. Eastwood took a five-day course along with acting friends Gene Hackman and James Brolin, who is now married to Barbra Streisand.

At the Bondurant School they said Eastwood was very dedicated. 'He was a good, clever driver – careful but not afraid to take risks,' said an instructor who had to be persuaded to admit that Eastwood even attended the school. 'We don't really like to comment on clients for security reasons, but it's some time ago. It's a real hazardous course.'

And so, of course, is marriage. Maggie Eastwood made the decision to separate after all the loyal years. She didn't ask for a divorce then. Maybe it was just a way to tell her husband that she had needs too. Eastwood was totally taken aback by her request for a separation. He thought things were fine. 'Like everyone else, we had our good times and our bad times,' Maggie reflected later.

Eastwood moved out of their marital home, a giant spread of a place near Carmel with priceless views over the Pacific. He rented a house in Hollywood to get on with making *Escape from Alcatraz*, both on the sound stages and on location at the prison, which no longer functions as a jail but as a tourist attraction.

By now Eastwood himself was a major attraction on the big and the small screen. After he and Maggie separated he was asked in a major American television interview with Barbara Walters about it. There was much preamble about what was or wasn't the case. Eastwood replied: 'I'm legally separated, if that's what you mean. People have problems within marriages. Everybody has them and some people manage to resolve them or work them out and others don't. Whether she helped me or I helped her – I mean, we have a very good relationship. She and I are probably better friends and having much more amiable conversations, more sensible conversations about philosophical differences or agreements now than we ever have.'

Walters asked: 'Is Sondra Locke the number-one relationship in your life?'

Eastwood replied: 'She's a very extraordinary girl, a very intelligent girl, very smart. I enjoy her very much as an actress and personally and I ... she's one of my number-one friends. She's just a very special person.'

Although not yet divorced, he was asked: 'Can you imagine remarrying?'

'I'm not a person who preplans life,' he answered. 'I pre-plan as far as films and the education of the kids and what not, but I think one has to be relaxed about life.'

Walters asked him about sex appeal, about why women throw themselves at him and went on: 'Yet, you don't think you're sexy?'

'Do you fool around on the first date?' asked Eastwood.

A flustered and reddening Walters tried to bluff. 'I could do this interview all day,' she replied, stumbling. Eastwood offered his enigmatic smile.

But on location at the Rock he was grim in the inhuman world that had been recreated for Don Siegel's cameras. Everything about the movie was tough and it was clear Eastwood was out to prove himself. In the film he played Frank Morris, who, on 18 January 1960, arrived at America's equivalent of Devil's Island. Morris had escaped from several prisons. In the first scenes we see the Warden, played by Patrick McGoohan, telling him he won't escape from Alcatraz.

When a pair of brothers Morris knows arrive at the maximum-security prison, they begin to plan just that. The scheme is elaborate. Using makeshift tools, they manage to get through the ventilation grilles leading from their cells to a shaft which goes to the roof. They make dummy heads for their bunks – heads with human hair from the prison barber shop. Raincoats strengthened with contact cement work as a base for their gateway shaft. On 11 June 1962 the trio went for it. Frank Morris and Clarence and John Anglin were never heard of again. The authorities believed they would find their bodies in the icy waters of San Francisco Bay. They didn't. Their escape – or death? – remains the only unsolved case in the prison's history. Within a year the prison had been closed.

The story fascinated Richard Tuggle. Al Capone had been held at the Rock and Richard Stroud – the Birdman of Alcatraz – was another infamous inmate. But when Tuggle heard the tale of the escape Frank Morris masterminded, he asked: Has anyone made a movie about this? His question was to team him with Eastwood – a chance but pivotal combination.

Tuggle only decided to write a screenplay of the story after he lost his job as an editor at a San Francisco health magazine. He then approached publishers McGraw-Hill, who had the rights to a story based on the incident. Amazingly, the novice Tuggle managed to persuade them to give up all film rights to the story. The first-time film writer heard that Don Siegel had once been interested in the project and the chain to Eastwood – the actor whose 28 films to that time had earned more than half a billion dollars – began. Within five years Tuggle would be directing his own screenplay, *Tightrope*, which showed Eastwood delving into the dark side of one man's sexuality.

But in 1980 there were memories of the actor's past. American television viewers voted *Rawhide* the golden-oldie series they would most like to see again. By then Eastwood, at 50, was playing a different kind of cowboy, called Bronco Billy. He never thought he would make a film like *Escape from Alcatraz*, explaining: 'I surprised myself. I never was too big on prison movies even as a kid, too much confinement, not enough sprawl to them. But there was a real suspense story in *Alcatraz* – a guy with no education but smart enough to scheme himself off the Rock. I liked it.

'The same way I liked *Bronco Billy* right away – it's the sort of film Frank Capra might have made about a romantic, dreamy bunch of losers getting their act together. So, I look at the whole picture, not just my role in it. I look for an entertaining story. When I go to the movies, I go for the action, the laughs, then I have a few beers. I don't go to intellectualise. If you analyse too much of anything in this life, you'll analyse your way right out of it.'

Eastwood made *Bronco Billy* on location in Boise, Idaho. Bronco Billy is a poor man's Buffalo Bill with a rather dog-eared Western show. As the title character, Eastwood sported pearl-handled six-shooters and a white rodeo shirt. Sondra Locke played runaway heiress Antoinette Lily, who joins this particular circus. Her relatives are trying to cheat her out of her inheritance. Bronco Billy is trying to show her the ropes. Although it did not have major box-office impact – comparable to an Eastwood shoot-'em-up – it was a memorable, breakaway film for him. And for it he again rounded up some of the usual suspects, Geoffrey Lewis among them. Lewis, the father of Juliette Lewis, who was nominated as 1992 Best Supporting Actress for her role in Martin Scorsese's remake of *Cape Fear*, played a scheming fortune hunter in *Bronco Billy*. He also appeared in *High Plains Drifter*, *Every Which Way But Loose* and *Any Which Way You Can* – in the latter two movies as Eastwood's good ol' boy buddy Orville.

'Working with Clint is always a pleasure,' says the actor, who lives in California's San Fernando Valley. 'There is no giant star ego thing about him – you just go in there and sweep up the work and then relax. He doesn't make a song and dance out of it.'

'Clint's kind of a guru director,' says Sam Bottoms, who is another Eastwood company regular. Bottoms – brother Timothy and Joseph are also actors – goes on: 'He gets this laid-back Zen feeling to come over the set. And, of course, as an actor, he can do just about any role he picks for himself. I'll make a prediction though – I don't think Clint will ever hang up his guns. He'll go out blazing.'

'Clint likes to shoot films fast and clean,' says Bob Daley, who has long been Eastwood's producer. 'He expects a lot from himself and. he expects others to measure up and keep pace with him.' Back when they were making *Bronco Billy* – the character is really a New Jersey show salesman who promotes himself as the Fastest Gun in the West – they all realised they were witnessing a new phase in Eastwood's life, reflected in the new style and attitude of the film. One of its songs – a duet by country-and-western star Merle Haggard and Eastwood entitled 'Bar Room Buddies' – made America's Top 40 country-and-western charts in 1980.

He seemed to have moved on, escaped the chains of middle age. He was asked a question then and replied: 'Happy? I *am* happy. Many people with everything are too complicated to be happy. I'm not.'

As part of his Western show, Bronco Billy would shoot blindfolded at a busty blonde being spun furiously around on a Wheel of Fortune. The kinky implications of the skimpily clothed girl strapped down on the wheel were clear to Eastwood the man – and the director.

'Oh, sure,' he said on the film set when a film technician teased him about it, and then he added smiling: 'We've been hustlin' gals for this wheel all week.'

Tessa Richarde, who has a Monroe bosom and breathy voice, was 'the gal on the wheel'. It didn't take a lot of persuading to get her up there. Just listen to her. Breathlessly, she said: 'Clint has a certain star quality. He's got that mystery in his eyes, a distant twinkle. And he wasn't at all like the tough guy I imagined. There's a gentleness about him that makes him very sexy. He's got a rugged boy look, but he's very sensitive. He can look fierce one moment and loving the next. He's very soft-spoken but at the same time he's so overwhelming that you can actually be afraid of him. Yet you immediately feel you can trust him. He makes you feel part of the family.'

Sierra Pecheur played an Indian squaw in *Bronco Billy*: 'When I first encountered Clint the big surprise was his humour. I had no idea how rascally he is. He has this little air of devilry right between his eyes. He's very playful, a real charmer. Macho doesn't really apply to Clint. He's strong, yes, but not macho. There's a finesse to him. I don't mean effete – I mean, there's a nice delicate feeling of sensitivity to him even when he's being ferocious. And he's definitely sexy – though maybe magnetic is a better word. Not a cold kind of magnetism but a playful, pleasure-filled delicious kind of energy of life. To women, he's got romantic presence, an essence.

'There's an old saying about Clint Eastwood – every

woman feels she has a chance with him. It's not blatant sexuality. It's more in the possibilities than in anything overt.'

Also, there's an old story about Eastwood being approached by a man who offers him his girlfriend for the night saying: 'Only for you, Clint. You're the only other guy in the world I'd want her to make it with.' Eastwood makes an excuse and leaves the conversation.

Jack Green was the camera operator on a string of Eastwood films going back to *The Gauntlet* and including *Bronco Billy*, *White Hunter, Black Heart* and *The Rookie*. Green was promoted to director of cinematography, as well as Oscar glory, when Eastwood's returned to the period Western with *Unforgiven*, which was filmed in Canada and went into cinemas in America and Europe in late 1992.

An amiable man, Green talked on location in Savannah, Georgia, while he was director of cinematography for Lizzie Borden's film *Love Crimes*. Eastwood was not involved in that movie but would have liked the atmosphere, with its Southern ladies, one moment coy and the next sexually aggressive. Green said: 'Clint likes to have close people close to him. There's a certain security in that. I think there's about 15 of us who have worked on most of the movies. He's not a show-off or anything like that. If he's having beers with the guys that's exactly what he's doing. He's not out to impress people. Of course, he doesn't have to. The ladies? He doesn't have to impress them either.'

But Eastwood the Casanova was having problems with Sondra Locke in late 1980. He had taken off skiing in Vail, where he openly dated several girls. One local businessman was an eyewitness: 'At the busiest bar in town, Shadows, he invited women to sit at his table while other girls were hanging over the back of his chair. He loved all the attention he was getting. Girls were slipping him phone numbers and he was smiling and laughing and loving it all. No matter where he went in town, he had a beautiful woman on each arm.'

This led to a short separation between the couple. Later it would be revealed there was more involved than Eastwood playing the pub playboy.

At the same time Maggie Eastwood was trying to get on with her life and the man she chose to share it was former used-car dealer Henry Wynberg, the man who squired Elizabeth Taylor between her two marriages to the late Richard Burton.

Famous names. Taylor. Eastwood. Wynberg?

The man whose association with Taylor had made him the most famous second-hand car salesman of all time became 'an international millionaire', a 'millionaire playboy', and was dubbed a string of other meaningless titles.

At the time he was immodestly dignified about it: 'I'm just a nice-looking ex-used-car salesman who happened to meet a charming lady.'

When he was fined $1,000 after pleading no contest to charges that he turned back odometers on four cars he sold between July 1972 and May 1973, Wynberg then was describing himself as active in 'various stages of entertainment'.

After his relationship with Taylor ended in 1975, when he was in his early 40s, he was accused of having sex with four girls aged 15 to 17 on several occasions at his Beverly Hills

A dashing young Eastwood in *Rawhide*, 1960.

*Top*: With Maggie Eastwood, née Johnson, his wife: 'Clint was only 23 and so good looking I couldn't resist.' They married on 19 December 1953 and stayed so for 31 years. She has called herself the Woman With No Name.

*Above*: Happy families? With Maggie and Kyle, Eastwood's son, born in 1968, fifteen years into their marriage. Their daughter Alison was born five years later.

As the Stranger in Sergio Leone's *A Fistful of Dollars*. Eastwood, who had had enough of his role as hunky Rowdy Yates, reluctantly accepted the lead in the movie with the prophetic title.

Eastwood admires actress Jo Ann Harris, who appeared with him in *The Beguiled*, at the film's screening in 1970. Directed by Don Siegel, this was the first Malpaso production where audiences glimpsed Eastwood's personal fascination with sex and violence, with lust over innocence.

*Top*: With his date Jocelyn Reeves, a Carmel resident, Eastwood arrives at a gathering in Los Angeles to draw attention to the Campaign for Californian Environmental Initiative of 1990.

*Above*: At Swifty Lazar's Oscar party with Dani Janssen, the blonde widow of Eastwood's army-days acting friend, David Janssen. There was talk that Eastwood would be husband number five.

*Top*: His directorial début, *Play Misty For Me* was a significant movie for Eastwood. In 1991 he revealed that it was based on a real story of sexual harassment and it was Eastwood who was harassed.

*Above*: With Sondra Locke in *The Gauntlet*, in which Eastwood starred and directed. 'Many of my films have good roles for strong women. Sondra in *The Gauntlet* had more to say I did.'

ooking mean in *High Plains Drifter*.

'Dirty' Harry Callahan.

home. He was also charged with providing the underage girls with drugs and alcohol. Then an aspiring photographer – years later, in 1990, he sold private pictures of Elizabeth Taylor to European magazines – he faced another charge of taking pictures of 'a sexual nature' of the girls.

Wynberg pleaded guilty in 1977 to statutory rape of a 16-year-old girl and admitted giving drugs to four high-school girls in return for sex. He was convicted on all counts and sentenced to 90 days in jail.

In October 1980 he was saying in California that he had been with Maggie Eastwood for 18 months: 'I'm happy with Maggie but we've been trying to keep it secret. We first met at a dinner party in Beverly Hills. It was at the home of a mutual friend and we've been together ever since.' Wynberg would seem a strange choice to step into Clint Eastwood's shoes. But, he was attentive. They played tennis together. They skied together. They went swimming together.

He met Maggie Eastwood at a dinner party after the collapse of her marriage. He had met Taylor at the home of President John Kennedy's one-time brother-in-law, the late, tragic British actor Peter Lawford, after her first failed matrimonial merriment with Burton. It may not have been merry widows but the Dutch-born Wynberg, who had moved to America when he was 17, seemed to have a grasp of being in the right seat at the right table at the right time.

He said in 1980: 'Elizabeth Taylor is a very moral and loyal lady and I have found Maggie to be the same. I find Maggie extremely mellow and relaxed in her attitude to life – she is a nice, stable influence on me. I think we all need a stable influence if we can find one. There are too many people partying around and I have been through all that nonsense. There is nothing quite as nice as a quiet little dinner at home ... and going to bed early is wonderful.'

At the time Wynberg said this, there was much speculation about Clint and Maggie divorcing. The arithmetic of such a divorce argued that Maggie Eastwood would receive something more than $25 million for an end to her long marriage to the world's richest star. The divorce wasn't about to happen – yet.

Clint Eastwood was bemused by all of it. But, even if it was begrudgingly, he had to admit that his wife seemed happy and there were no objections to his children travelling abroad on holiday with their mother and Wynberg. Except that he was about to ground his son Kyle as he wanted him to co-star in a new movie with him. He had completed *Any Which Way You Can* as well as *Bronco Billy* in 1980. Even for Eastwood there had to be a time to breathe before starting *Honkytonk Man* in 1982.

In this picture he played Red Stovall, a hard-drinking Depression-era country-and-western singer trying to get success before the late surges of tuberculosis finish his chances. Sounds corny? It certainly would not be the sort of material you would have gamely walked into a Hollywood conference with, offering a grin and: 'Hey, have I got something for Clint.'

But, remember, this is a changed man. Eastwood was directing. Sondra Locke, who does not appear in the film, was coach for Kyle Eastwood when he was cast as his father's nephew in the film. It's another familiar story: the youngster trying to keep the elder on the straight and narrow path. Eastwood recalled of his son: 'He listened well and thought out the part. When he didn't, I was there to remind him.'

Nepotism, you ask? Dangerous? Rejection? Ego problems later in life? Clint Eastwood sees none of that: 'He's a very natural kid and he's been totally immersed in film. He was always obsessed with it. When other kids would be watching cartoons, he'd be watching *Of Mice and Men* – the original 1939 version. That's why I thought he'd be able to handle that size of a part.

'Kyle kept asking me to let him have a part in a film and I realised that the boy in *Honkytonk Man* was just his age at the time, so I let him have a go.'

Kyle Eastwood was 14 when he co-starred (literally in the billing) with his father and he recalls his early teenager's reaction: 'I liked stealing the chickens. I liked driving the car.'

Legendary country-and-western singer Marty Robbins recorded the title song but suffered a fatal heart attack before the film was released in cinemas. But the music was part of the new Eastwood following his 'Bar Room Buddies' duet with Merle Haggard and Eddie Rabbitt's song 'Every Which Way But Loose'. Eastwood was happy with the film. The critics were not. And, more hurtful, neither were audiences. The film went into cinemas a few months after *Firefox*, also made in 1982. In *Firefox* director Eastwood starred himself as a superhero American-agent pilot who goes into Russia to steal a supersonic, super-duper Soviet plane. (Eastwood had last played a pilot in 1955's *Tarantula*, when he was called upon heroically to bomb the giant spider.)

*Firefox* had spectacular special effects but not much effect on audiences. Eastwood was not ruffled by two misses in a row. 'It's a little ironic,' he said then, 'that some of the critics who didn't like what I was doing in the 1960s say they don't like what I'm doing now because it's not as good as the stuff I was doing in the 1960s.

'They said Harry was on the edge of being a fascist. Now they ask why I'm not going to do Dirty Harry again. But where would you take him now? Without the very good combination and the very good writing the Harry films had, there's no point in doing it again now except for monetary reasons.'

And Clint Eastwood is a most practical man. Dirty Harry returned in 1983 in *Sudden Impact*. Eastwood had found another reason than money to make it – a feminist reason. The killer is a woman. And played by – guess who?

Forget good ol' boy Clint. On a random count Dirty Harry blows away 14 problem people – aka 'scum' – during the film and falls in love with Sondra Locke's character, who kills three men and a woman in revenge for a gang rape a decade earlier. There is no country-and-western soundtrack with this film, in which Top 40 hits have an altogether different meaning.

This is Dirty Harry gone astray. Inspector Harry seems to be flaying out at everything. It was 1983 and it seems Eastwood was lashing at his own devils. Sondra Locke is an anguished painter, Jennifer Spencer, seeking the men who raped her and her sister. When she finds them, she shoots them in the groin. And then in the head. Boom, boom! Is this an eye for an eye and an ear for an ear?

What it was was a vigilante film – the fourth and most exploitative of the Dirty Harry series. Eastwood and Locke are teamed as soul mates, Dirty Harry and Dirty Harriet, in the most violent lurid film. It was also an instant hit, the most successful of the Dirty Harry films, earning more than $100 million within weeks.

Critical redemption for Eastwood was only a short time away. In *Tightrope* in 1984 he played Detective Wes Block, who wanders New Orleans's nocturnal sexual playground. 'Go on, make my night,' Block might have said to the many ladies of the evening he encounters.

Eastwood protege Richard Tuggle's film is set in the city's French quarter, where someone is murdering prostitutes – prostitutes with a liking for sadomasochistic sex. In the tradition of film noir, the thrust of the tale is that the criminal is a distorted image of the cop.

When Eastwood's Wes Block visits the brothels and finds the hookers he meets seductive, he holds back, agonises and then gives in to his compulsions. But the girls he has sex with start getting murdered and he must confront his own demons, his double nature, his dark side.

Block is shown as a single parent – 'My wife didn't want tenderness' – bringing up two blonde daughters, one of whom is played by eleven-year-old Alison Eastwood. ('I thought it was only fair to let her have a turn at being in a film, too.') He's a man trying his best to do the decent thing. Then he has to investigate the killings at night, and it's a tour of erotic specialities, with the girls dangling delights like handcuffs and producing whips and vibrators and lots of symbolism with a red lollipop.

The critics loved the bondage and kinks, Block rubbing himself all over with baby oil and handcuffing a young lady to a bedpost. Finally, with Dirty Wes, Eastwood was a true auteur.

Genevieve Bujold plays Beryl, who runs a help centre for rape victims. Beryl understands Block – and the killer. When she and Block become lovers, she even offers to put the handcuffs on for him, but he unlocks them. He no longer wants total control.

Eastwood was in control, at least professionally. In 1984 he was named the world's top box-office star for the second year in a row. He had knocked his old friend Burt Reynolds off the top spot in 1983 making cinema history – it was his sixteenth appearance on the Top Ten list, which was more than any living star. There were no hard feelings from Reynolds. He and Eastwood were going to make a film together in a dazzling display of superstar power. But that top spot made a difference financially. Eastwood was paid $5 million and Reynolds $4 million to make *City Heat*. The film was to change both their lives. Reynolds would lose his star power and find his whole life irrevocably changed. And Eastwood would officially lose his wife. He and Maggie Eastwood finally agreed to divorce in 1984 after 31 years of marriage.

# SEVEN

# RIDING HIGH

'There are two American art forms, the
Western and jazz. It's funny how Americans
don't support either of them any more.'
CLINT EASTWOOD, 1985

EASTWOOD felt *Tightrope* had been tough going and
decided his next film should be fun.

*City Heat* sounded just that and for the first time in his
career he agreed to be packaged with another star. You can
see the potential of Eastwood and Reynolds, the two biggest
box-office stars in the world – a modern-day Clark Gable and
Spencer Tracy or James Cagney and Pat O'Brien partnership,
the charisma of a friendly-enemy relationship.

The plot had them caught between rival mobs during the
1930s – a comic romp with bullets flying all over the place

along with the laughs. It was to be directed by Blake (*Pink Panther*) Edwards, who also wrote the script but before a camera was even loaded he walked away from the project and actor-director Richard Benjamin took over.

Eastwood says he had asked Edwards to make some character changes but nothing was done: 'I think it ended amicably. At least, it did on my part. I said: "I'll step back." The studio said: "No, no, we don't want you and Burt to step back."'

Later they probably wished they had. This potential firecracker of a movie went off like a damp squib. It was more than just a box-office disaster for Reynolds.

During the filming of *City Heat* he was accidentally hit on the face. He thought he had broken his jaw, but it was much worse. The bash he received during the fight scene developed into temporomandibular joint disorder (TMJ), affecting his balance and sensory perceptions. He lived on soup and got thinner and thinner. Reynolds says: 'People were willing to believe I had AIDS because it was just too good a rumour to let go. I'm sure it started with two gay hairdressers as a joke: "Charlie Bronson, Clint Eastwood and Burt Reynolds have AIDS..." and when I wasn't showing up and got thin.'

While Reynolds struggled to restart his career, his long-time friend's wife Maggie Eastwood was considering marriage to Henry Wynberg, from whom she had been inseparable since they first met. But she still wasn't a 'free' woman. In the summer of 1984 she filed for divorce.

The settlement – she and Eastwood had agreed to a property settlement four years earlier – was not to be discussed but sources say that given the property market of the early 1980s, the divorce package provided Maggie with around $28 million.

'She realised that she and Clint weren't getting any younger and she wanted them both to be free to remarry,' a friend in Carmel said. There was another less generous theory from a man who has known both Eastwood and his former wife for many years: 'She lost hope that Clint would get tired of Sondra and go back to her. She realised they would no longer live as husband and wife again, so why stay married? But she likes having a man around the house and that's why she married Wynberg.'

Eastwood, of course, didn't marry Sondra Locke. Instead, in September 1984, he was on location in Sun Valley, Idaho, starring in and directing *Pale Rider*, his first pure Western since *The Outlaw Josey Wales* in 1976. The film is set in the California gold rush of 1850. Eastwood is the anonymous stranger wearing a preacher's outfit and a couple of weeks of beard. He goes to the aid of a bunch of independent miners who are being muscled out of their claims by a conglomerate mining concern. Some saw the film as the other side of *High Plains Drifter*, in which Eastwood's character represented the devil, whereas this time the allegory cast him as one of God's avengers. Simpler folk thought it simply a homage to director George Stevens's 1953 landmark Western *Shane*, which starred Alan Ladd, Jean Arthur, Van Heflin and Jack Palance.

The stars in *Pale Rider* included Sean Penn's brother, Chris, as one of the bad guys. 'It was,' he recalled, 'a dream come true. I'd seen every Clint Eastwood film there is and had wanted to do a Western since I was a kid. I even got to tell Clint to get out of town.'

Also in the cast were Michael Moriarty and Carrie Snodgress – on the side of good – and giant Richard Kiel, who was memorable as the villain Jaws in the James Bond adventure *Moonraker*.

Eastwood made quite an impression on Sun Valley (population 12,000), especially during the slack business period between the end of summer and the beginning of the ski season. And time on location gave an insight into Eastwood at work and the demands and pressures he puts on his team. On *Pale Rider* the cast and crew numbered more than a hundred: he took his own village with him.

It was about the end of August 1984, recalled Kathy Wygle, director of the Laughing Stock Theatre Company, when she was first contacted by a casting director from Warner Brothers Studios in Los Angeles: 'They asked if I would like to assist them in casting some minor roles in a Clint Eastwood movie that would be shooting up here,' she recalled. 'I had about five days to get four people for [each of] 14 roles.' Wygle strolled around town until she found people with the right look: 'We were able to cast three speaking roles and lots of featured extras.'

Loren Adkins, a Wygle discovery, called the mining set 'real authentic'. The 80-year-old retired Forest Service employee had reason to know: he'd been there. 'I was six years old in 1916 and my dad ran a butcher shop in Placerville [California]. I remember the screens they used to wash gold-laden dirt down the hills.' Up on the hillside, smoke puffed out from tin chimneys on a cluster of weathered wooden shacks. At that point in the filming schedule the mining camp had been completely pillaged by the bad guys. Smoke still rose from abandoned campfires.

Paul Calabria, who with partner Karen Dew handled the set's smaller livestock, was 'chicken wrangling', alternately unleashing a dozen chickens from their pen when a scene was shot, then gathering them up again when it stopped. 'These aren't trained to come when they're called, like the chickens we keep in Los Angeles,' Calabria explained good-humouredly. 'These are "non-pros"' (Hollywood talk for 'not in the business'). He threw his feathered charges a baleful look, adding: 'When we first let this batch go, they went *everywhere* – we were picking them out of trees!' Then he grinned, saying: 'Now they're much better, though. They're becoming Hollywood chickens … they want more money.'

Eastwood, in full costume – boots, spurs, black vest, grey shirt – moved quietly about, setting up the last shots of what had been a long week of ten-hour days. Accompanying him was his son Kyle, visiting for the weekend. Eastwood moved from actor to actor, giving directions for the next scene. On set, as the cameras rolled, Eastwood and Michael Moriarty began methodically to smash a huge boulder with heavy sledgehammers, soon to be joined by other miners. After about ten strokes, the director stopped and, wiping his brow, said calmly: 'Well, that's enough of that.'

The atmosphere surrounding the actual filming may have been calm and steady, but several miles away, on the set where the cast and crew would move to in a week, the pace was breakneck. The construction crew had been at work for a month, building a small Western town from scratch. This was not to be just a one-dimensional, false-facade town either; the buildings would be used inside and out. One crew member paused just long enough to explain: 'Hey, we gotta move fast – Clint's right on our butts.'

The 12 buildings stood in various stages of readiness. Some were finished outside but needed furnishing; others were still in the bare-frame stage. Workers scrambled around to the cacophony of hammering, drilling and sawing that obliterated anything but the loudest of conversations. Three commercial truck-and-trailer rigs stood nearby, overflowing with set dressings, and lumber was strewn everywhere. Production designer Edward Carfagno, moving quickly in and out of the various locations, was an elusive target. Finally he was located in the set's dry goods store inspecting the picks, sledgehammers, mining pans and everything else that an 1850 mining town would carry. He appeared unruffled by the impending deadline. 'We'll get it done in time,' he said calmly, 'but we actually needed more like five or six weeks.'

Although a sign posted 100 yards down the road advised sightseers to keep out, no fewer than three groups of locals circled the site in an hour. One contingent, a tiny troop of cub scouts, hiked up behind one of the buildings, accompanied by den mothers Teri Boderstab and Pat Peebles. 'One of their classmates is in the movie, so we thought it would be fun to bring them up here for their first meeting of the year,' Peebles explained. 'This movie is the talk of the town!' Cub business at that moment concerned the signs proclaiming the town LeHood, California. 'Now why do you think Mr Eastwood came to Idaho to make a movie about California?' Boderstab asked her charges, who had no trouble with the answer.

'Idaho looks more Western!' 'It's more natural.'

'Because there's too much smog in California!'

In the meantime the cubs speculated among themselves about Clint. 'It's been "Clint" this and "Clint" that all the way up here,' Peebles said, laughing. 'You'd think they were personal friends of his.' Their speculation concerned Eastwood's mode of transportation: whether his limousine would be able to make the eight-mile trip up the rutted dirt road.

'No, Clint'll fly in by helicopter,' said one scout. After all, they reasoned, he was a star. The star chuckled when told of the scouts' various speculations during a lunch break the next day. 'I'm the guy who asks not to use limos!'

Eastwood seemed to have no problem doing a Western after nine years out of the saddle. 'Isn't it beautiful here! Ninety per cent of my last pictures have been shot at night. Here we'll only have two night shots.'

Why a Western? Why now?

'Two fellows I'd used before came to me several years ago with this idea, and I liked it and gave them some ideas. I didn't know exactly when we'd shoot, but I do like fall – the sun's low and the light's good.'

Eastwood was matter-of-fact about his much-discussed rapid directorial style, which Richard Kiel figured came from his work with Sergio Leone. 'Actually, Leone is slower than I am,' said Eastwood. 'I give a lot of the credit to Don Siegel [who directed him in *Two Mules for Sister Sara*, *The Beguiled*, *Dirty Harry* and *Escape from*

*Alcatraz*]. He was always organised for speed.' He pondered for a second, then added: 'But you learn from everyone you work with. I'm surrounded by the best crew around, and we all like to move at the same tempo. I think if the director is slow and ponderous, it can hurt the final product. The movie might not be as satisfying and, besides,' he shrugged, 'I'd get bored.'

In Hollywood, Eastwood's long-time producer Fritz Manes – taking time away from the location to help with the trailer for *City Heat*, the videocassette of *Tightrope* and the television version of *Sudden Impact* – offered his thoughts on *Pale Rider* and Westerns: 'We've been sitting on *Pale Rider* since '78 or '79. There were other things we thought required more urgency as far as filming went, since they were fairly timely, such as *Firefox*.

'Clint's always been fairly obsessed with the project. His whole bent was Westerns from the start, and I can't tell you how many fans have asked him or written to ask when he would do a Western again. You can't feel as secure with *Pale Rider* as you would with, say, a sequel to *Dirty Harry*. However, my feeling is that there's going to be no problem.

'I guess themes just run in cycles … detective movies, then cars, drugs, outer space and whatever. But everybody loves cowboys. They know the hero always comes out on top – it gives people a good fantasy to live with.'

Eleven years before *Pale Rider* was made Eastwood galloped across the world's cinema screens in a film that many regard not just as a fantasy but as the ultimate one and *the* last great Western ever made. *The Outlaw Josey*

*Wales* was more than the white-hat-black-hat-tall-in-the-saddle-good-versus-evil Western.

Arguably, no one but Eastwood could have pulled off *Pale Rider* in the middle of the 1980s or maybe even in the couple of decades gone before. *Shane* had been more than 30 years earlier and the 1985 update would seem all too elliptical for the MTV generation.

In 1976 Eastwood also went up against the odds with *Josey Wales* – Westerns in the 1970s were financial leprosy as far as Hollywood was concerned and equally contagious – but he gambled on his edge, his instinct. And he won.

Eastwood had learned to have patience; to explore film properties, buy the rights and then wait for the best time to produce them. First of all he had to relate to the story.

You only have to look again at *Josey Wales* to know that. It opens with him tilling honest soil on his Missouri farm as the American Civil War is ending. Then guerrilla raiders burst this particular bubble of tranquillity, torching his home and killing his wife and child, and he becomes the outlaw Josey Wales. At a glance it seems the story of so many films all across the genres.

But this tale had a remarkable genesis. It was written by half-Cherokee Forrest Carter, a self-taught Indian poet and storyteller. He was persuaded to sit down and write one of his stories and Whippoorwill Publishing in Arkansas printed the book. They published exactly 75 copies of *The Rebel Outlaw: Josey Wales*.

The book was sent to Eastwood's producer, Bob Daley, who found it moving and a page-turner. Unusually, he sent it from the office to Eastwood, who was in Carmel. The company decision-maker also felt it had 'soul' and wanted to turn it into a film, in which Josey Wales loses one family but gains another, albeit a family of camp followers.

Although the action is conventional the detail is realistic and there is much wry humour, usually provided by Chief Dan George acting as the ageing, folklore-overloaded, tough-as-old-boots Indian chief Lone Watie.

Much of Eastwood's attitude to life – and death – is reflected in this film. The Civil War is shown as a wanton waste of life. But the message is not sledgehammered at the audience like some Oliver Stone film. Instead, you get Josey Wales muttering: 'Dyin' ain't much of a livin'.' And when Josey blows away a couple of bounty hunters his badly wounded saddle partner (Sam Bottoms) says: 'Wish we had time to bury them fellers.' Josey spits tobacco juice on the face of one corpse and says: 'To Hell with them fellers. Buzzards got to eat, same as worms.'

Ah, the Wild West philosophy. Eastwood shoots a great line.

And it is very useful punctuation in the trek across Texas around the army, the bounty hunters and the bad men who sell whiskey and women to the Indians. Sondra Locke is in the frame as lost Laura Lee, who, with her grandma Sarah (Paula Trueman), completes Josey Wales's Mild Bunch.

But although all around him might be nervy and frightened, Eastwood's hero is never rattled. He is the invincible man of fiction. The gunplay is conventional and so is much of the a-man's-gotta-do-what-a-man's-gotta do psychology.

The twists are provided by Eastwood as director. Here we see the actor-director so frustrated by the lack of challenge during the *Rawhide* years ('I called it *Rawmeat*') trying to stretch the genre into the post-Vietnam and Richard Nixon 1970s in America.

Of course, one must not dwell too much on the auteur aspects. One reviewer of a literary tome on Eastwood's motivations suggested that reading too much between the celluloid frames invited the reaction of the crowd to a blowhard in Mel Brooks's *Blazing Saddles* when they chanted: 'Blow it up your ass, Harold.'

But, nearly a decade after *The Outlaw Josey Wales*, few critics were echoing that sort of sentiment towards Eastwood. He and Sondra Locke had enjoyed a very established and stable relationship. Curiously, as Eastwood the film-maker's career blossomed, Eastwood the lover-partner-companion's long-term relationship with her wilted.

Professionally, Eastwood was on top in 1985. He had finally won respect as a serious artist. Privately, he and Sondra Locke were not the blissful couple they had once been and they would never work together again.

And Maggie Eastwood was getting married again. Her former husband made it clear that if there ever was a wedding, he wouldn't be attending. He never got a chance – his ex-wife didn't tell him about it.

Eastwood was 55 and very set in his ways, a man who needed things done his way. He was shaken by Maggie's decision to marry again. It was something he never thought would happen. Whether it was strictly subliminal or premeditated, he was encouraging Sondra to get involved in projects he was not associated with to make herself independent of him.

'Of course, she gets Clint's pictures – she's his girlfriend.' Sondra Locke says it was comments like that that made her go it alone with *Ratboy*. Well, not exactly alone.

When she decided to direct and star in the film – Rob Thompson's story about a woman who discovers a freaky, rat-like being she then tries to exploit – she needed a crew. Eastwood wasn't making a film at the time, so she hired his: 'I could have hired people I didn't know, but the Malpaso crew I'd worked with for years and knew well. They're one of the best crews in the business, talented and fast,' she said before filming began.

She also said something which showed the heady aspirations one can get by being with such a major star as Eastwood: 'I was looking for a good, challenging role for myself and I saw nothing there. Then I picked it up and reread it. There was something unique about the story. I just couldn't stop thinking about it. It haunted me – so much so that I decided: it may not be the role I'm looking for but why don't I direct it?

She approached Warner Brothers, who distribute Eastwood's films, and surprise, surprise, without much hesitation they agreed she could make the film. Eastwood stayed away from the project apart from watching some daily footage of what Locke called 'a little fairy tale'.

Maggie Eastwood, meanwhile, was living out a Hawaiian fantasy. On 6 April 1985 she went through a sunset wedding ceremony on the lawns of the Mauna Kea Beach Hotel in Hawaii with Henry Wynberg, who after the ceremony tempted fate: 'For Maggie and me there's no one else now. We're sure this is it for the rest of our lives.'

His bride said: 'There's only one man in my life now and that's Henry. I just want to cry with happiness.'

Kyle and Alison Eastwood were among the 15 guests who wore flower leis for the ceremony – the newlyweds wore white-orchid leis. Two of singer Paul Anka's daughters also attended the ceremony, conducted by the Reverend Walter Frutiger, a local minister. Wynberg, who lived with Elizabeth Taylor for 14 months in 1974 and 1975, said he had not told her he was getting married. And Clint Eastwood was kept in the dark too. 'They'll have to read about it in the newspapers,' Wynberg had announced with disdain. When he did, Eastwood told friends the marriage wouldn't last. It didn't.

By then Eastwood was riding high on *Pale Rider* and his outing as the sexually twisted Wes Block in *Tightrope* had won critical raves. Early in 1985 there was talk of an Oscar nomination for the role. He was more pragmatic than those touting his performance: 'I'm popular with the public but that doesn't make me popular at the country club.'

He called it right. No Oscar nomination.

But his work was celebrated at the British Film Institute and he was the superstar of choice at the 1985 Cannes Film Festival, where the ultimate status symbol remains the yacht. Eastwood was aboard the *Broke* that year, a yacht rented for him by Warner Brothers Studios. It was under 24-hour paparazzi watch.

And starlet patrol. There were girls everywhere who would have been happy for Eastwood to make them stars, if only for the night. Or day. Or afternoon.

His presence at Cannes resulted in one of the biggest press

conferences in the history of the festival. Some questions were rather bizarre. Was he, when he killed a bad guy in *Pale Rider*, in fact killing his father, Sergio Leone? Eastwood thought not but said everyone could have their opinion. There was reverence and indignation at the conference, which was held in a hall five times larger than the normal press salon.

'Aren't there any good screenwriters left in Hollywood?' asked one French journalist, putting down what he called 'trite' dialogue in *Pale Rider*. Eastwood kept cool. Even if the Frenchman didn't like the film, he couldn't complain about the price – the press gets in free.

Would he like to dedicate the film to anyone? 'Yes, I'll dedicate it to every person who's been missing a Western in recent years.'

Eastwood has God-like status in Europe, especially in France, where he has become as revered as the late Steve McQueen. Other honours that year were a retrospective at the New York Museum of Modern Art, the Deauville Film Festival and the Montreal Film Festival, precursors of his Screen Actors' Guild Life Achievement Award presented in March 2003.

Asked at Cannes about this sudden serious acceptance, he replied: 'I think a lot of people who are critics now came of age with my movies. Maybe they had a good experience with a girl at one of my movies and feel they owe me something.'

But Eastwood also had detractors – especially now that he was being taken seriously. He also has a tremendous memory and has never forgotten slights against him from even his earliest days in Hollywood. Which is why those who talk against him shoot him in the back, as it were. He would make better films if he worked with better writers, actors and directors, say some.

'He doesn't like to share the screen with a powerful, name actress; or submit himself to be directed by a big-name director,' said one producer.

'He's cheap. He's won't normally pay more than $50,000 for a script, which is a tenth of the going rate,' said a successful Hollywood writer.

Eastwood sat on a couch in his office at Burbank Studios and listened to the remarks by his detractors, who naturally wanted to remain anonymous. On the issue of scripts he said: 'That's not true. If it's a good screenplay, I'll pay for it. But I'm not going to hire somebody just because he's got a great name. Even the most expensive guys turn out crap.'

On big name co-stars: 'This is one thing that does bother me about the business here and in New York. Everybody's after the same actors of the moment. Nobody comes up with Carrie Snodgress [*Pale Rider*] or Jessica Walter [*Play Misty for Me*] and Sondra wasn't exactly running with activity when I used her in *The Outlaw Josey Wales*.

'The point is there are dozens of fine actresses out there who are as talented – and some more talented – than Jessica Lange or Sally Field or Sissy Spacek. But these other actresses are not the gals of the moment – the fad of the moment – so nobody hires them. This is what really drags me about the business. I hate the way they discard people, particularly the women. One minute they're given all the praise and the next minute they're dustmops. It's a real shame.

'So, I've tried to use good people who maybe don't have the big names... None of these so-called hot actresses is a heavy-leaguer like Vivien Leigh but they're gals of the moment and two years from now they'll be others. I just don't see the reason to work with them. It's not just money that's stopped me.

'I've paid some big money to actresses – Genevieve Bujold in *Tightrope*, for example. My flashpoint is just the iniquities of the business. You've got the Golden Globe crowd who don't know a thing about acting and who don't even try to learn. And then you've got the Academy Awards group, which is more political and so often gives Oscars to actors who don't have popular appeal and therefore aren't threatening – people like Ben Kingsley.

'I'm not putting these people down. I'm just saying that a popular movie star like a Paul Newman doesn't have a chance against them.

'So, I'm inclined towards the underdog. I guess I've always been rebellious in that way. I think it had to do with how I was raised. My father used to say to me: "Show 'em what you can do and don't worry about what you're gonna get. Say you'll work for free and make yourself invaluable." That approach builds your confidence. If I hadn't been brought up that way I might have reacted differently to the criticism received early on in my career in terms of the contents of my films – Dirty Harry being called a fascist is one of many examples. I might have said to myself: "Well, I've had some success, I'll do something a little more middle-of-the-road and not offend anybody." But by not offending anybody, you do offend somebody – yourself.'

# EIGHT

# HIZZONER

'Some people think that when you're older
you're supposed to sit down and watch TV reruns
and squeeze beer cans. That isn't for me.
I like to be involved.'

CLINT EASTWOOD, 1985

PATT Morrison was working as a reporter for the *Los Angeles Times* in August 1985 when she flew up to Carmel from Los Angeles to write a story about one of California's most popular tourist resorts. The story was perfect for her because it involved an absurd situation – and she's excellent at deriding pomposity and deflating egos.

The essence of her story that summer in the *Times* was that the City Fathers of Carmel were going all out to stop the selling of ice-cream cones. Some people thought that snacking in the street, even in hot weather, was undignified.

Ms Morrison thought that stupid, and said so. The headline on the story shouted 'SCROOGE CITY' and told how the city council denied a businessman a permit to sell ice-cream cones using an ordinance forbidding take-out food. But there were also the laws banning children from the parks, frisbees and drivers stopping to watch the sunsets.

Eastwood was not amused about what he regarded as a negative image being broadcast across America – the newspaper wire services picked up the story – about the town he loves. He did not regard the incumbents at City Hall with the same sentiment. In fact, he'd just about had it up to here with them.

And so Patt Morrison became responsible for Clint Eastwood going into politics and becoming a candidate for Mayor of Carmel, 'Hizzoner', the boss of the five-member council and 18-strong police force.

After his separation from Maggie Eastwood he had built his own home two miles from Carmel, with a six-foot-high fence with nails on top to discourage racoons around the property. By 1985 he had lived in the area for nearly 14 years.

Both his children went to American public (that is, not private) schools in the area. He had made financial contributions to town charities, specifically the Sunset Cultural Center, and continues to do so. When you walk through Carmel with him he is so low-key that there is hardly a glance.

If a group of tourists spots him, it is a different matter – stares and cameras clicking. But in his sports jackets and jeans, maybe a windcheater on a chilly evening, he does not advertise his fame. He'll most likely drive into town in his pick-up truck. Giuliano's is one of his favoured restaurants and Susan Negri, who runs it, said: 'When he comes in for dinner, the women all seem to want more coffee. But he never pushes. When he arrives without a reservation, he'll wait for a table just like anyone else – often he'll come back later rather than cause a stir.'

But, in 1985, he stirred things up. Quaint, style-conscious Carmel, with no street numbers and no cemetery, appropriately got the Man with No Name to deal with.

Eastwood – 'I'm no property developer' – had planned to build a two-storey office building next to the Hog's Breath Inn. George Brook-Kothlow, the architect who designed the building, and Eastwood's former home, said the city 'never offered any clear-cut direction to what they were having a problem with'. Eastwood's next-door neighbour is Russ Harris, who remembered: 'It's one thing to maintain the charm of the community but what really riled up Clint was that their decision seemed totally arbitrary. What really irked him is, if that was happening to him, what was happening to the little guy in town?'

This is what happened then: regulations designed to keep business in the background obstruct all development despite the fact that the city's budget ($6 million in 1985–6) operates from such revenue. Property taxes are small. The 1929 city charter is clear that Carmel belongs to the people who live there and business is 'subordinate to its residential character'.

All shop signs needed approval, as did any outside design changes. If you wanted to put in a skylight or paint the front door, you had to make an appointment with the Planning Commission.

The city said Eastwood's proposed building would be too close to the sidewalk. They said the exterior contained too much glass and not enough wood. Eastwood and his partner, Maggie Eastwood, with whom he continued a business relationship, sued the city, saying the regulations were 'vague, subjective, ambiguous, unintelligible and obscure'.

In November 1985 the two sides settled out of court. Eastwood could build but to modified plans. He was not happy. There was a new glint in his eye.

Dirty Harry and some of his other screen characters have tended to lose patience with bureaucracy and take the law into their own hands. Eastwood considered becoming the law.

'We all knew he was frustrated,' said George Brook-Kothlow, 'but there was no indication he'd personally get involved other than to support a new candidate with a more viable point of view with respect to commercial versus residential interests.'

As the new election year approached, Eastwood, not rushing in like a fool, commissioned a telephone poll to see if the residents of Carmel wanted a new mayor and if they wanted him in the $200-a-month job – a position of little money and lots of aggravation.

What the poll showed was there was no great support for the current administration of Mayor Charlotte Townsend, who was then 61, an earnest, friendly and sincere 'local neighbourhood lady'. But a lady who liked the neighbourhood the way it was.

In the summer of 1985 Eastwood was asked point-blank by *Rolling Stone* magazine if he would ever run for political office. 'That's something nobody has to worry about,' he replied.

That all changed at 4.20pm on 30 January 1986. Before the 5pm deadline that day Eastwood arrived fresh from the opening round of the Pebble Beach National Pro-Am golf tournament and dropped off his nominating petition for mayor. It was endorsed by 30 – 10 more than needed – registered voters.

Ronald Reagan, former actor, was in the White House. Clint Eastwood, actor, producer, director and one of the world's most popular cinema attractions, wanted to be in Carmel City Hall.

'I don't need to bring attention to myself,' he told Carmel's weekly newspaper, the *Pine Cone*, in his first interview as a candidate – also the paper's first world exclusive – adamantly going on: 'I'm doing this as a resident. This is where I live; this is where I intend to live the rest of my life. I have a great affinity with this community. There used to be a great deal of camaraderie, a great spirit in this community. Now there is such negativity. I'd like to see the old spirit come back here, that kind of *esprit de corps*.'

Every morning Eastwood runs several miles as part of his daily workout. Now he was running for something altogether different. But still, he argued, for his own well-being.

Eastwood was stumping for less government intervention. He wanted to do something about the problem of tourist parking. He decried restrictive zoning laws. And he was particularly hot on the ice-cream issue. 'I can recall a time when you could walk down the street in Carmel and pick up an ice-cream cone at a shop – now you'd be fined.'

To those who wondered about his being mayor and a movie star, Eastwood, who had taken off most of 1985 – he cited 'personal reasons' when asked about this during the campaign – to spend more time and try to have more influence over his two teenaged children, promised: 'The city will be my absolute priority. I'll be a lot less active in films than I have in the past.'

He went on the campaign trail. Usually his politician's outfit was a tweed sports jacket, grey slacks and shirt and tie. He went on the tea-and-biscuits circuit. He attended the Monterey Bay Republican Ladies' Club. He went anywhere he could to get a vote. He kissed babies. He shook hands. He refused autographs, but with a polite: 'Thanks for asking.'

Eastwood said more in one day on the campaign trail than he had in 30 movies. He was as gushing as Zsa Zsa Gabor the day I went with him to the Kiwanis Club, a Rotary Club-type organisation. Of course, the campaign didn't just interest the residents of Carmel. There were media from all over the world. At the Kiwanis Club a pushy and apparently not requested aide wondered what a Japanese film crew wanted to know about Carmel. 'Nothing ... but in my country, Mr Eastwood is biggest star,' came the reply. Eastwood overheard this. He arranged his rangy six-foot-four frame to find the film crew's level and did the interview.

Today Carmel, tomorrow Washington? It was a question time and time again. He was diplomatic: 'I've been there four times. One time Nancy Reagan called up and said Prince Charles and Princess Diana are coming and they want to meet you. There will be 80 people. I said: "That's very nice, count me as one."' Political ambitions? 'Ronald Reagan can get on with running the country. The fact we have construction-site toilets behind the Pine Inn is really disgraceful.'

It was only outsiders who considered Eastwood a sure thing at the 8 April 1986 election. But his celebrity was no assurance of that. Carmel is used to famous faces, and residents include Doris Day, Paul Anka and Joan Fontaine; what Eastwood had to do was convince the town that his politics were not some whim and he was not a fluke. The message he gave to town meetings was straightforward: 'I hope the voters of Carmel base their decision on election day not on my career as an actor and producer but on my involvement in this community and my experience and desire to be a good mayor. This is between my neighbours and me.'

The ballot on 8 April was probably the most intensely scrutinised small-town election in American history. Eastwood received 2,166 votes – 72 per cent of the total – easily defeating incumbent and former librarian Charlotte Townsend. 'I would like to think we can now take the community out of the hands of the few and put it in the hands of the many, the people of Carmel,' he said in his victory speech. Later he was asked if he wanted to be known as Mr Mayor and replied: 'Nah, just Clint.'

Eastwood had cast his own vote at All Saints Episcopal

Church, having arrived in his old pale-yellow Volkswagen convertible. The event was treated like something from a presidential election – the candidates were outnumbered 50–1 by the media – and there was a curious ballet as photographers jostled for the best camera angles. It was like Cannes without the starlets.

A day after his victory Mayor Eastwood was meeting with friends to discuss the election and future moves. A telephone call interrupted the meeting. The caller asked Eastwood: 'What's an actor who once appeared with a monkey in a movie doing in politics?' President Ronald Reagan, who was an actor in 1951 and made *Bedtime for Bonzo* with a chimpanzee co-star, was on the line from Washington. Eastwood, who co-starred with Clyde the orang-utan in two films, assured the president that his political ambitions ended at the Carmel city limit.

'He used my line, "Make my day", so I borrowed his "Get government off my back,"' said the mayor. The late James Stewart, who appeared in Eastwood's favourite film *Mr Smith Goes to Washington*, also telephoned congratulations.

Eastwood decided not to retire from film-making for all of his two-year term as mayor. He had found the ten-week campaign tiring. Clearly he would rather have been making movies than drinking weak tea and attending 55 coffee mornings. But he was happy to have won. A week later, dressed in a grey suit and red tie, he was sworn in as mayor. His mother was there. And so was his sister Jeanne, and Charlotte Townsend handed over the gavel to him. As he again said his priority would now be Carmel and not the movies, you could almost hear the groans in the corporate offices of Hollywood.

On 6 May, at his first council meeting, Eastwood dealt with an agenda of 50 items, keeping his promise to get on with the job. He also sacked four planning commissioners who had made decisions he did not agree with including turning down his plans to build the office next to the Hog's Breath Inn.

Within two months of his being in office, there were more changes in Carmel than in the previous ten years. Ice-cream cones were on sale, a new car park had been built, steps to the beaches were under repair, more public toilets had been installed, ramps for the handicapped constructed and a new pedestrian bridge erected. The next move was to lift the ordinance banning high-heeled shoes.

But any frivolity was suddenly lost when Eastwood election campaign worker David Archer, then 42, was arrested for rape and murder. Archer was caught after being chased by police down the Pacific Coast Highway. Eastwood said 200 volunteers had helped him in the campaign and Archer was simply one of them. Archer, charged in Carmel with killing a repair man during a robbery and raping a woman at a party to celebrate Eastwood's election, maintained he was very close to the mayor. He said he would call Eastwood to testify at his trial. He never did.

And Eastwood returned to more mundane matters of local government. He could be found in someone else's garage trying to decide whether it could be moved three inches north. A typical day started with meetings at City Hall at 9am, a tour of the town – on foot – and then budget or planning-commission conferences. Evening council meetings often lasted six hours and sometimes continued after midnight. On the long-standing Eastwood movie principle of the less talk the more action, he limited speeches to three minutes.

As promised, he did make being mayor of Carmel his priority. However, he still managed to make two films during his two-year term. One was *Bird*, the story of jazz great Charlie Parker, which he produced and directed. The other was *Heartbreak Ridge*, which he produced, directed and starred in. And which got Hizzoner in hot water with the US Marine Corps.

While Mayor Eastwood was taking control in Carmel, first-time director Sondra Locke had completed filming *Ratboy*. It opened in American cinemas in the summer of 1986 but turned off the critics and didn't turn on any audiences. Locke was philosophical about it. She was also impressed by Eastwood's election, which she called an 'idealistic gesture'.

For the movies, Eastwood himself was preparing a crowd-pleaser with *Heartbreak Ridge*. It was fun if formula stuff. He would star as Gunnery Sergeant Tom Highway, who had to knock an inexperienced grab-bag of sloppy Marines into shape during the invasion of Grenada in 1983. Of course, he could drink, fight and curse better than anyone else in the Marines: Eastwood meets *The Dirty Dozen*. Except he was too dirty.

The US Defence Department gave their full co-operation before filming began, but after screening of the film on 14 November 1986, they objected to 'an excessive amount of profanity'. They then withdrew support for the film, which led to the cancellations of benefit screenings for the Marines and tributes to them being scrapped from the film's credits – an enormous publicity boost for *Heartbreak Ridge*.

In the film Eastwood plays quintessential Eastwood. A man of straightforward principles, he likes nothing better than a fight or a drink or vice versa. A special unofficial screening was set up for members of the Marine Corps, who liked the film and Eastwood's old-fashioned stereotype character and thought the language was realistic. But officially, the Corps completely distanced themselves from the film.

Eastwood was in Carmel chairing a city council meeting when the flap started. Typically, he found the bureaucratic reaction silly. 'It's a shame that a charity has to lose money because of somebody who's got a bee under his rear end somewhere. It's not something of national security. In the words of Alfred Hitchcock, "It's just a movie."'

Marine Corps official Lieutenant Colonel John Shotwell said the whole tone of the film was objectionable. Especially one scene where Eastwood as Sergeant Highway pumps an extra round of ammunition into the back of a Cuban soldier he has already shot. Eastwood said that in combat, Marines occasionally do make sure the enemy is dead. He got quite irritated by the fuss, although admitted the script took some liberties and that he ignored the other services involved in the Grenada invasion: 'There were a lot of people there. We were showing 12 guys, a small reconnaissance platoon. What am I supposed to do, spend another $5 million showing the army's invasion? It's insane.'

Eastwood, again typically, counterattacked. In the original script, Sergeant Highway's squad is rerouted to Grenada while on their way to Beirut to replace Marines killed during the terrorist bombing in 1983. That is, in fact, how some Marines got to Grenada. The Defence Department wanted no mention of that and Eastwood eventually agreed to take it out of his film. 'They didn't want to acknowledge that incident and that's sort of altering history. I'm sure relatives of people killed in Beirut wouldn't like having that history denied.'

Securing government co-operation is a balancing act for film-makers. The film people get access to military bases and equipment and the armed services get Technicolor recruitment advertisements. The navy was turning away recruits after Richard Gere's role in *An Officer and a Gentleman*, which was made without its co-operation, and Tom Cruise's *Top Gun*, which was made with it. Even when John Wayne's 1949 *Sands of Iwo Jima* is shown on television, Marine recruitment gets a boost. Ironically, there is a scene in that film which might appear more harmful to the Marines' reputation than *Heartbreak Ridge*. Wayne's Sergeant Stryker, angry with a recruit who falls over himself during a bayonet training, intentionally slams him in the jaw with a rifle butt. That was, and is now, a court-martial offence, but the Marine command in Washington approved all of this film.

'It was the only scene I objected to,' said retired Brigadier General Leonard Freibourg, who was a major representing the Marines on the filming of *Iwo Jima*. 'I went to DC with it and the answer came back the next day. DC said: "Tone down the severity of the blow, but let it go. It's a good story point."' The butting incident seems to be there to set up a comic-relief scene a few minutes later, where Sergeant Stryker shows the clumsy recruit how to get into the bayonet rhythm by doing the Mexican hat dance with him. The closest that *Heartbreak Ridge* comes to that brutality happens when Eastwood rips an earring off one of his troops, and it, too, is played for laughs.

Retired Colonel George Gilliland, who talked Darryl F. Zanuck into making *The Halls of Montezuma* at 20th Century-Fox in 1950 and served as the Marine liaison officer during the filming, said that the entire Marine Corps command wanted to help write the script. Gilliland himself objected to the casting of Richard Widmark in the starring role, because he had pushed an old lady in a wheelchair down a flight of stairs in 1947's *Kiss of Death*. Widmark got the part anyway, and Gilliland said once the film was under way there was no conflict between the government and director Lewis Milestone. But occasionally he had to fight for moments of authenticity. He said: 'They had one scene where a grenade goes off and ten guys jump into the hole it left. I said: "Grenades don't leave holes." They said: "Well, they did in *For Whom the Bell Tolls*. I said: "Well, now there are ten million men who know better."'

Mario Van Peebles, who co-starred as a wise-guy recruit in *Heartbreak Ridge*, said that no one expected any problems with the Marine Corps. But he had one when he reported for filming on location at Camp Pendleton, about 50 miles north of San Diego, California. The drill instructor thought he was a new recruit: 'The first one yelled:

"Motherfucker, get down now and give me 50 push-ups. Now!" Then another instructor looked at me and said: "Don't go eyeballing the sergeant, boy! Git down!" I did the push-ups. I felt it was in my best interest.'

Peebles, who appeared regularly on the *LA Law* television series, was hand-picked by Eastwood for *Heartbreak Ridge*. The male model turned actor was born in Mexico City and taken around the world by his composer-writer father, Melvin Van Peebles. Eastwood, again, had recognised talent others seemed to have overlooked: 'Clint instilled a gung-ho attitude in me. He told me to be all I could be. We got to be pals. He even let me write three songs for the movie.'

It's another example of Eastwood going that little bit further for people. He genuinely seems to want to help, maybe to pay a little back for his own good fortune. And, of course, there is his memory.

Actress Marsha Mason had been set to co-star with Eastwood and Burt Reynolds in *City Heat* in 1984 but after rewrites she felt the role wasn't her: 'I really hated to leave the project. I felt badly about it but my character was so different – actually it became a completely different movie and I couldn't connect with it any more. Clint was wonderful about it. He's extremely down-to-earth, very unspoiled, very modest. He's certainly not Dirty Harry – there's none of that character's intensity, wariness or sense of menace.'

And when Sergeant Tom Highway needed an ex-wife in *Heartbreak Ridge* it was Marsha Mason who got the call. As Aggie, now a waitress who has waited through the Korean and Vietnam wars for her man, she was the one who got to play with softy Eastwood. Mason said: 'He married this young thing and then went off carousing with all the other ladies. Now he's trying to figure out how to get Aggie back, so he's reading the women's magazines. "Did we have a meaningful relationship?" he asks me. He's in kind of a crisis.'

Eastwood agreed with that. And says that's what drew him to the character. The actor himself was being drawn in many directions at the time. He was concerned about fulfilling his job as mayor, about his children, about Sondra Locke – he was trying to juggle all the balls in the air, which makes it even more interesting when he talks about his Sergeant Highway.

'It's about love, really. Not only between Tom Highway and his ex-wife, but among friends, people, fellow mankind. That sort of thing, that's the subtext of it. Highway is a man at a crossroads, in life and in his career. He's approaching mandatory retirement, and he's trying to come to terms with the world he'll be facing after the service. He's been a problem soldier, too. He's a brawler. He drinks too much. By this time, he probably should have been promoted to the maximum rank. Especially being a Congressional Medal of Honor winner. But he's a little bit of a screw-up.

'Highway sort of represents the old military, as opposed to the new military – the "Be all you can be" recruiting slogan, or "It's not just a job, it's an adventure," or "The Marines are looking for a few good men." All that kind of stuff where guys work on computers and seem to be having a good time. But he's from the old infantry school. He's scarred up. He's a fighter, and none of that new stuff makes sense to him.

'He's never really understood women at all. He's been with

a lot of women, but now he's trying to get a handle on it through his relationship with his ex-wife, which he would like to get sorted out. But she just throws it back at him in a very honest way: "The only reason you want to get together now is because it's all coming to an end." So he's sort of a lost soul, an empty soul. Sort of a guy who's very hard-boiled, but at the same time searching for the sensitivities of his own soul.

'I think, he's like a lot of men. There's a lot of very macho guys who are that way, because they don't realise there's something else there. They've matured in some ways but not in others. But there often comes a point where you look back and realise that you don't know a lot. Highway's that kind of guy, and that's what appealed to me. That and the fact that it wasn't an action film. I've done a lot of those, and they're fine, but here we're looking for characters with other elements to them. If you've been around as long as I have, they'll let you do that.'

There were those who said the voters and residents of Carmel were indulging Eastwood in his role as mayor. That may or may not have been the case. But it is a fact that Hollywood studios were willing – and would have been betraying their stockholders if they hadn't – to indulge a star with such a box-office record.

Eastwood persuaded Warner Brothers to get the script of *Bird* for him from Columbia Pictures in a behind-the-scenes deal whereby Warner gave Columbia a film called *Revenge* which was perceived as a strong commercial property by the late, renowned producer Ray Stark. (Ironically, it would be an unusual thing, a Kevin Costner flop, some years later.)

At first Stark, one of the most canny of Hollywood moguls and one of the few major deal-makers left from the Golden Age, was suspicious. He thought Warner wanted the *Bird* script for Prince, who had had a huge success with *Purple Rain*. When he was told it was for Eastwood he laughed. 'What, Clint Eastwood playing Charlie Parker?'

Nevertheless, Eastwood was displaying clout, as Sondra Locke would say, to the nth degree, and the script switch went ahead. When the negotiations were over, Eastwood was like a little boy. Clearly it was never a commercial project. But for every *Bird* in the hand were there not two *Dirty Harries* in the bush?

A long film, at 163 minutes, *Bird* is also dark. Whatever demons drove Charlie 'Bird' Parker, a saxophonist of genius and a pioneer of modern jazz, to such creative heights and to the depths of dissolution and destruction in 1955? A film about a man drinking and drugging himself to death at 34? Ah, but it's a jazzman killing himself. And Eastwood is a jazz fanatic. Nevertheless, Parker's story was not uplifting. When he died watching television, the examining doctor estimated his age at 60. *Bird* is a harrowing story – a film made in purgatorial darkness.

Parker – he was called Bird after the nickname Yardbird, given to him in Kansas City, where he ate a lot of chicken while hanging around the Reno Club, a meeting place for jazz musicians – had fascinated Eastwood for years. He had been following the resurgence in traditional jazz – Lu Watters, Bob Scobey and Kid Ory – but then first heard Parker play when he was living in Oakland. He didn't understand him initially, but it got him very interested.

His mother was a Fats Waller fan. At 15 Eastwood could play the piano well enough to perform at the Omar Club on Broadway in Oakland. The regulations were slack – the teenager played for free meals. He was still at school and the only instrument available was the flugelhorn. It wasn't considered very hip. Eastwood played it anyway. But he concentrated on ragtime and blues piano and he can be heard, years later, at the piano along with Mike Lang and Pete Jolly as part of a three-keyboard boogie-woogie number on the soundtrack album of *City Heat*.

Eastwood was a fan of Dave Brubeck, Coleman Hawkins, Howard McGhee and Hank Jones. When he was in the army at Fort Ord, he heard Gerry Mulligan and Chet Baker, and in the army he also met Lennie Niehaus, a former saxophone player with Stan Kenton. Eastwood's memory again... Niehaus had written the music for *Tightrope*, *City Heat*, *Pale Rider* and *Heartbreak Ridge*, and when *Bird* flew into the picture, he had to bring out his saxophone again. It was his job to teach Forest Whitaker, who had the title role, how to play. Niehaus says Eastwood's personality has not changed over the years: 'He was sweet-tempered when I knew him in the army and he's the same gentle man now. You never hear him yell.'

He could however be very tough when necessary. During the filming of *Bird* he would regularly be back and forth to Carmel to take care of council business. British producer David (now Lord) Puttnam, who was then head of Columbia Studios, had complained that executives had to work at weekends – a complaint which had seemed risible to most of Hollywood. And to Eastwood: 'If David Puttnam really wants to give up his Sundays, let him try being mayor of a small town.'

Of course, it was Eastwood's choice to juggle politics and film-making.

Yet why another film about a druggie jazz musician? 'Charlie Parker was a guy who was ahead of his time,' says Eastwood. 'He was one of those people influential in forming the last major harmonic change in music. He was a drug user, but he put down people like himself who used them.' Eastwood says he did not want to shove any anti-drug message down audiences' throats. He wanted to present the story and have people make their own decisions. He has never smoked except on film and has never experimented with drugs. He says of his growing-up days: 'We sort of lived by the saying: "If there's anything better than a woman and a cold beer you better not tell me about it. It might kill me."'

*Bird* was only the second film Eastwood directed in which he did not appear – and where he 'could dress like a bum, my usual fashion'; the other was *Breezy* in 1973. In that film the late William Holden is the older businessman involved with Kay Lenz's California blonde Breezy, who is years younger. The rumour at the time was that Eastwood was attracted to the script because he was involved in a similar situation. Sondra Locke, of course, had auditioned for the role of Breezy.

Holden didn't care about that. During filming he was still marvelling over Eastwood's powers of persuasion. Holden, who died after a fall at his apartment in Santa Monica in 1980, had enjoyed a remarkable career – in films like *Stalag*

17 and *The Bridge on the River Kwai* – for more than three decades when he agreed to star in *Breezy*. He thought he knew all about Hollywood and deal-making, yet he worked for Eastwood for no salary and instead received a percentage of the profits. Sadly for Holden, the film was not a great hit. In fact, the American actors' union, the Screen Actors' Guild (SAG), contacted Eastwood six months after the film was released and told him that just to keep things proper he had to pay Holden $4,000 – minimum SAG wages – to keep within union rules.

Eastwood makes his own rules while filming. Tom Stern, who has been the chief lighting technician on five Eastwood movies, explains: 'He's so fast because he has all of us pulling for him. I have the lowest seniority of the core group. His wardrobe man has been with him since 1959. Clint's not particularly verbal. He talks with his hands, so you flounder for a while and it took me a picture and a half to understand him. He's completely committed to his intuition.'

And he keeps things cool, according to long-time executive producer David Valdes: 'Tempers never flare, you're never walking on eggshells. On a lot of sets there is always panic, but not with him.'

While Eastwood was filming *Bird* there was a move to get him into national politics. The presidency of Ronald Reagan was in its final reel in 1987–8 and after the Gipper why not Dirty Harry?

In Carmel they were selling 'Clint Eastwood for President' T-shirts for $12.95. Eastwood's fans claimed he was more macho than George Bush, more conservative than Robert

Dole, another presidential candidate. 'Based on name identification alone, he would be a viable national or state-wide candidate,' said Senator John Seymour, chairman of the Californian Republic caucus, trying to enlist Eastwood. 'He looks good, he sounds good and he can do what none of the other famous hot dogs can do – say he started at the grass roots.'

And that's what they were in Carmel. During one city council debate, an interminable series of speeches about whether a Stop or Slow sign should be erected at a busy intersection, the mayor observed: 'With a Stop sign at least they'll slow down after they've gone through it.'

Eastwood enjoyed the council meetings. There were some offbeat moments. Twice a 30-something blonde stood up at meetings and pledged her undying love to him and asked him to marry her. The second time he quietly told her: 'I tried marriage once, ma'am, and it didn't work.'

Politicians are always being accused of throwing money at problems they can't cope with. They use taxpayers' money. Eastwood used his own to stop a development project to build town houses on the 22-acre Mission Ranch on the southern edge of Carmel. He paid more than $5 million for the property, which remains home to migrating birds, sheep, cows, residents and tourists who visit the Mission's restaurant and Old West saloon.

Yet despite his cool and potent public face, there is much internal churning for Eastwood. He keeps things to himself. On the surface there is no problem, but... He tells one story of the night before he was about to make his debut as a director with *Play Misty for Me*. He was in bed thinking through the movie, scene by scene, and how he would film each one. He says he felt uneasy because he was convinced he had forgotten something. What had slipped his mind was that he was also starring in the film. He switched on the light, picked up the script and started memorising his lines.

Internal and external man. There are also two Eastwoods in Hollywood. There is the producer-director of films like *Bird*, the influence-maker who urged Warner Brothers to make the Oscar-nominated *Round Midnight*, director Bertrand Tavernier's homage to American jazz in Paris. And there is the cool cowboy or cop who attracts giant audiences – he's the one the accountants love. But over his career, for every outing as Dirty Harry or commercial venture like *Heartbreak Ridge*, there has been something for himself. Which was why he ran for mayor of Carmel and not President of the United States.

# NINE

# White Hat, Grey Heart

'Hollywood has always been a cage …
a cage to catch our dreams.'

John Huston

CLINT Eastwood had no plans to go into national politics and despite massive support he decided early in 1988 not to run again for mayor. Instead he spent his last few hours in office bracing a wet chill swirling off San Francisco Bay as helicopters chattered overhead. Dirty Harry Callahan was back for the fifth time in *The Dead Pool*.

People whose names appeared on gambling lists were turning up dead and Harry was set loose to investigate. This was one for the box office – *Sudden Impact*, made five years earlier, had by then earned more than $150 million.

The accountants were happy. Eastwood was editing *Bird*

– which had very limited time in cinemas in America and earned only $2.2 million at the box office but won ovations at the Cannes Film Festival and worldwide critical plaudits – while filming *The Dead Pool*. He said he wanted to see how Harry was coping 'at this stage of his life'.

Eastwood himself was at a professional crossroads. Other stars of his generation – Paul Newman, Warren Beatty and Robert Redford – had been maintaining a lower profile, producing or directing rather than starring. The austere *Wall Street Journal* had wondered in print if he wasn't getting a little long in the tooth to be still running around in shoot-'em-ups.

Eastwood wondered aloud if the *Journal* wasn't slowing up a little itself, having, he thought, lost a lot of its zip.

Dirty Harry had all the zip needed to turn a gang of thugs who interrupt his meal in a Chinese restaurant into chow mein in *The Dead Pool*. Too old? Getoutahere.

For years Eastwood has followed the advice of Durk Pearson and Sandy Shaw, the husband-and-wife authors of the Life Extension books. Nearly 60, he said he felt better than at 40. The regime was a three-mile jog, two hours in the gym and meditation twice a day – all of that every day. He maintains his diet: low-fat, high-vegetable, no red meat except for the occasional hamburger. He takes choline selenium in yeast to feel more alert, deanol for verbal ability, L-arginine and L-dopa to help him exercise and other vitamin supplements for his skin. He golfs, he skis, he swims and frowns when you raise an eyebrow: 'Sex can be overrated.'

In his early 60s he was fabulously fit and you almost

had to run to keep up with his loping strides when he took off around Carmel or across the Warner Brothers studio lot in Burbank.

He needs reading glasses and wore them for the last Carmel City Council meeting he presided over, on 5 April 1988.

'I think he gave a freshness to the town – I'm a little annoyed he didn't decide to run again,' said restaurant owner Kate Curry that day. But seven others stepped in to try to replace him, including divorcee and mother of three Jean Grace. Eastwood decided to support her in the election.

Sondra Locke was then living mostly in Los Angeles – she would be seen at public functions with Eastwood but rarely in Carmel – and Mrs Grace admitted after lots of romantic gossip: 'I'm very fond of Clint. We go to parties. We go to dinners.' Eastwood has never commented on how political or romantic his relationship was with Mrs Grace, who replaced him as mayor.

He would talk, though, about his two years in charge of the cosy, 50-seat chamber: 'I've enjoyed it. It's been very challenging. The nature of the process isn't as effective as the private sector but you try and move efficiently through the process and include everyone and all their input. My celebrity may have hindered in the sense that a lot of times people would want you for appearances here and there that really had not much bearing on city business.

'Trying to juggle film and being mayor? Sometimes I said to myself: "What sort of merry-go-round is this?"' But it wasn't the workload that stopped him trying to be elected again: 'I have to take care of the personal stuff for awhile,' he said, adding pointedly: 'If you miss time with your family you wonder if it's retrievable time. Sometimes it isn't.' The decision made at the last minute was for himself and his children – Kyle was 19 and Alison aged 15. 'Formative years,' said their father, indicating that if they had been older his decision might have been different. The verdict on his tenure as mayor was largely favourable. He won praise for increasing the number of public toilets in town, improving facilities on the beach, breaking a long impasse over the expansion of the library and getting a greater share of water from a local dam.

And Eastwood was still taking a major share of the movie action. As he filmed *The Dead Pool* he was already planning to star in *Pink Cadillac* and preparing for *White Hunter, Black Heart* to film on location in Africa in 1990. He didn't seem to want to be at home. But he was still enamoured of Dirty Harry and said on location of his fifth outing as the loose cannon San Francisco cop: 'It's like revisiting someone you haven't seen for 18 years. You figure: "I'll go back and see how he feels about things now. How is he existing 18 years later?" All Dirty Harry has ever wanted is to make some sense of the system.

'Originally, the part was written for an older man than I was when I first played it. He was a guy who had been on the force a long time, a mature guy who was fed up with what he saw happening to people. The laws are crazy, he was saying. A lot of people felt that way. That's one reason the films are so popular.'

The role of Inspector Harry Callahan had been turned down by John Wayne and Frank Sinatra before Eastwood pinned on San Francisco Police Department badge number 2211.

*The Dead Pool*, although not as financially successful as *Sudden Impact*, was another money-maker, earning more than $80 million. The reason, according to psychiatrist Stanley Platman, was that these films attract both men and women. 'It's the Clint Eastwood style of manhood that most people admire. He is not only a movie phenomenon but an "ideal man" – the kind of man that men would like to be and the type that most women fantasise having a relationship with. People are always hungry for manly men. His give-'em-hell approach is a refreshing change from what they see around them. It may be "with it" to say that men should be free to express feelings but inwardly many people consider the man who shows his pains and problems as a "softy".

'Both men and women find the hard-hitting, take charge, action-orientated man very appealing and admirably suited to our times. They don't really consider the Clint Eastwood style of punch-'em-out manhood a thing of the past. Men see him as a buddy, a "stand-up" guy who's loyal and unswerving. And women see him as an ideal protector, the man they'd like to have on their side when they cross a dark parking lot.'

Dr Platman, former clinical Professor of Psychiatry at the University of Maryland, went on: 'Almost everyone knows someone they'd like to take a swing at – a neighbour, boss or relative who drives them up the wall. Eastwood handles that sort of frustration the way we'd like to but can't. He serves as our personal "hit man". And he has this extraordinary independence. He does his own thing and bows to no one. Every role he's played – cowboy, pilot, detective – heightens his image as a loner. He is the supreme example of the man who has made his own rules and made them work for him. He represents our most prized fantasy – to be totally independent and self-sufficient. And he doesn't water down his appeal by overexposure. The less we know about someone, the more apt we are to believe he is all we would like him to be.'

Maggie Eastwood was finding out that Henry Wynberg was not at all what she wanted him to be. Her marriage, her children entering their far more aware late teens, were putting pressure on her – and on her former husband.

With Wynberg there had been squabbles over money and drink. What had seemed an idyllic match during that Hawaiian ceremony had now collapsed into bickering. Maggie Eastwood had talked to her former husband about it. They had 'family' conferences about it. One was in London in August 1989.

They giggled about reports that Eastwood was dating Jane Brolin, the former wife of actor James Brolin. They had in fact been family friends for years and legendary Hollywood divorce lawyer Marvin Mitchelson, who died in 2004 after a long battle with cancer, confirmed at the time: 'It was Clint who referred Jane Brolin to me.'

Maggie Eastwood filed for divorce from Wynberg on her return to California from London in August 1989. Part of her petition to the court was that Wynberg be ordered to stay away from her Pebble Beach home because he was 'hotheaded and has been verbally abusive towards me in the past especially when he has been drinking'.

Wynberg was to remain in the spotlight by meeting up

again with his old flame and drinking partner Elizabeth Taylor – in court. Wynberg, who in 1992 was married to 19-year-old Costa Rican Carla Golanz and living in Costa Rica, claimed he inspired Taylor's best-selling Passion perfume. 'I said in 1973: "Darling, your movie-star career is over. You need something for your old age."' He argues that she did create her perfume pension but that he did not receive any cash or credit. In Los Angeles Superior Court in 1990 he sought $5 million in cash and an additional 30 per cent of the $70 million annual profits from sales of the fragrance. Eventually he agreed to settle for $4 million.

Maggie Eastwood's marriage to Wynberg is something Eastwood will not be drawn on and this, of course, is in deference to their children Kyle and Alison. But the family ties, the family matters, had all been troubling him for some time. As always, he wanted control, especially over his children. But he was determined that he would never be involved in anything messy. His divorce from Maggie had been controlled, contractual and quiet.

He could never imagine himself getting into a public situation like Liz Taylor, who, in the Passion case, appeared in court for two days before the proceedings were stopped by an out-of-court deal. But it was his need for control that was to result in his public mess; a situation he had spent his career avoiding. The private man was going to be accused of a series of sins by his long-time lover Sondra Locke.

Eastwood, the world's richest star, was Establishment towards the end of the 1980s. The Man with No Name was joining the great names of the movies like Orson Welles, Frank Capra, Alfred Hitchcock and the Bergmans – Ingrid and Ingmar – and a host of others who had become the subjects of serious film studies.

The Clint Eastwood Cinema Collection was established at the Museum of Modern Art (MoMA) in New York and at the Wesleyan University Cinema Archives. MoMA was to preserve prints of his films from *Play Misty for Me* to *Bird*. Wesleyan University, in Middletown, Connecticut, was to archive scripts and other papers, production material and memorabilia relating to Eastwood's career. He liked the preservation concept although he has always called himself a 'today or tomorrow man' rather than one who lived in the past.

Jeanine Basinger, curator of the Wesleyan Cinema Archives and Professor of Film Studies at the University, says: 'We have been showing Clint Eastwood films in the classroom since 1971. We were honoured to place his papers in our archives along with other film artists – Clint Eastwood belongs in their company.'

And so, he felt, did some of his wardrobe from the spaghetti Westerns: 'There's a poncho that's close to my heart – it sort of started me off – that's there.'

Elevated as a film artist in late 1988, Eastwood was also rolling along making *Pink Cadillac* with the statuesque Bernadette Peters as his co-star. It was *Any Which Way*-type stuff except his co-star sported an eye-catching figure rather than lots of fur. Eastwood was a bounty hunter who gets involved with Peters, playing Lou Ann McGuinn, who is on the run in a 1959 pink convertible De Ville. Peters was initially concerned about Eastwood's reputation for not doing a lot of film takes – his more wham-bang-thank-you-ma'am school of film-making: 'I was worried about that. But then I just fell into the swing of it, which is to capture the moment by what happens. You can't do that with every actor, but Clint is so right there, that he makes it easy, to work off each other. I learned a lot from him in doing the movie. It was a good lesson he taught me. And you do work fast, which Clint has a theory about. It is so you don't hang around all day waiting for the set-ups. You don't get sluggish. You don't get distracted or lose interest. You don't forget where you are. It's a good way to work. It's so relaxed and that's so unusual. There's no pressure at all. I just said to myself: "Oh, boy, this is *great – enjoy it.*"'

Eastwood's work style is much admired, especially in the modern cost-conscious Hollywood. Terry Semel, president of Warner Brothers, the studio which has distributed Eastwood's films since 1975, said: 'People think of Clint Eastwood as a movie star and they know him as a director as well. But behind all that he is in effect the chairman of his Malpaso Company and he oversees every inch of every one of his films. During his tenure here he has been the most reliable and organised maker of films we've dealt with. Clint's a person who knows himself well. He's a very smart business man, always on or under budget in a day and age in which costs have escalated.'

Warner Brothers should have been pleased with him – he accounted for 18 per cent of their revenues from movies. That did not include the $1.5 million that went on the books every week from worldwide distribution of Eastwood movies on television, cable television and video – what's amusingly known as ancillary income.

In what Semel calls an 'extremely unusual' arrangement, Eastwood works without a formal contract through Malpaso Productions. But informality is clearly one film for them, one for me.

'Very talented people have their ups and downs on certain movies but they will always prevail,' said Semel. 'The business we are in is about batting averages.'

There is no public record of what Eastwood's films have earned over the years but the last semi-official reckoning put it at nearly $3 billion in 2003. Considering his wealth, Eastwood has few indulgences or man toys. He has a helicopter to commute between his home in Carmel and Los Angeles and there is what he calls 'a bunch of stuff'. From his teenage days it was always women and cars and cars and women. He owns several cars, including the 1951 GMC pick-up truck he drove in *The Bridges of Madison County*, a 1965 Plymouth police car, assorted trucks, a VW convertible, a 1932 Ford roadster and a 1986 Mercedes 500SL. He has also supported many charities anonymously, many of them to do with the environment, since long before green became fashionable.

It is also claimed that he and actor William Shatner, Captain Kirk of *Star Trek*, helped finance a private raid on Laos to free American prisoners of war. Retired Green Beret Lieutenant Colonel James 'Bo' Gritz told the *Los Angeles Times* that he led mercenaries in the raid, which was code-named 'Lazarus'. They had heard, he said, that about 100 Americans left behind after the Vietnam War were being held in a village 100 miles east of the Mekong River on the border between Thailand and Laos.

Gritz claimed the operation had US government support and his men were equipped with 'nuclear fire-plan boxes' with which they could communicate with mission members in Washington. Three days after going into Laos, the mercenaries came under mortar and assault rifle fire: one was killed and three badly wounded. Gritz, who was decorated for services in Vietnam and Special Forces activities in Latin America, had been involved in two other attempts to locate POWs. Eastwood would never confirm that he helped finance the abortive raid by putting up $20,000 for the film rights. Shatner said he gave $6,500 as part of a payment for the rights to Gritz's life story.

'Clint has an extremely responsible way of working,' says Malpaso producer David Valdes. 'He spends each dime as if it were his own.' And given his wealth, he has every reason to believe it is.

Although low-key and easy-going, a man who does not flaunt his wealth and who plays down his Dirty Harry image, like all celebrities Eastwood has always been aware of the dangers of extortion, kidnapping and crazed fans. Since 1983 he has had a permit from Monterey County officials to carry a concealed weapon, a .38-calibre pistol. In his application to Monterey Sheriff's department he wrote that he was the victim of 'various death threats against my life including that of kidnap in 1978'. FBI officials in San Francisco said they investigated the 1978 case but have never revealed the results. Eastwood has renewed his gun permit annually.

Stronger evidence to justify Eastwood's fears came in 1992 when he was involved in an incident with a real-life twist to *Play Misty for Me*. Brian Keith Nuen had been an Eastwood fan since he was eight years old. By 1992, at the age of 30, he could be classified as an obsessed fan.

He made a series of threatening calls to Eastwood at the Malpaso production offices on the Warner Brothers studio lot at Burbank, threatening Eastwood and the actor's family if he did not pay $5 million. The calls were made between 4 and 29 March 1992 and were recorded on voicemail. On tape a man identified as 'Brian' said God told him that Eastwood owed him money for three films and that if Eastwood did not pay by 11 April 1992, he would die within two weeks.

In one of the calls the message demanded a Jaguar, a pick-up truck, a gun rack, a rifle, a cowboy outfit and money for petrol as well as compensation 'for all the bills that you told me you'd reimburse me for when I came out to California for the first time via your guardian angel wavelength'. In a message of 4 March 1992, the caller said: 'Hey, Clint, we have a compromise – just send me the $5 million cash ... thank you for the responsibility for being my guardian angel in the first place and everything you get that went with it. Just send the cash by 11 April, that's $5 million, US currency, and we'll work the rest out later – thanks a lot, goodbye.'

Nuen – Eastwood told the FBI he had never met him or heard of him – was arrested in Ellicott City, Baltimore. He told special agents that although he had made explicit death threats, he had no intention of killing Eastwood. He said he would not discuss his relationship with Eastwood without the actor present, said agent Bill Hargreaves. Included in

Hargreaves's official report is the following: 'Nuen related that if the deadline was not met, Eastwood would be in a horrible moral and ethical position. Nuen stated that he did not expect Eastwood to live longer than two weeks after 11 April. Nuen related he would not harm Eastwood – he believed that God would handle the situation.'

In May 1989 Eastwood had other obsessions on his mind. On the 28th he was to fly to Africa to make *White Hunter, Black* Heart, a thinly disguised portrait of legendary film director John Huston's quest to shoot an elephant rather than get on with filming 1952's *African Queen* with Humphrey Bogart and Katharine Hepburn. And his private life after more than 13 years with Sondra Locke had hit the fan.

From Los Angeles or San Francisco you fly over to Salt Lake City in Utah and then pick up a twin-engine prop plane which takes you over the mountains to Sun Valley, Idaho. It is rugged Hemingway country and along the main street in the Sun Valley capital of Ketchum the walls of the bars and restaurants are covered with memorabilia of the macho author. This is a real man's Aspen.

'People here like to ski hard and play hard,' says actor Adam West, who played Batman in the 1960s campy television series. West has lived on the outskirts of Ketchum for many years. 'You don't see a lot of posing going on on the slopes here. People come to ski and they're usually people who like a good party. Someone like Clint doesn't get bothered here. He just gets on with having a good time.'

In 1988 Eastwood needed a good time. While he had

filmed *The Dead Pool*, he had edited *Bird* and taken it to Cannes, and he had committed to doing *Pink Cadillac*. He was running hard. And then the former mayor had authorities after him for being 'dirty'.

That summer health inspectors found violations 'too numerous to list' at Eastwood's Hog Breath's Inn. Monterey County's environment health director, Walter Wong, said there was inadequate refrigeration, unsanitary conditions, improper food storage, structural problems that made it difficult to clean the kitchen and an 'extremely dirty kitchen'.

Mr Wong reported: 'The dangerous part was that the refrigeration was not working. Food is supposed to be kept at 40 degrees – this was at 68 degrees.' Health inspectors closed the kitchen and Mr Wong said: 'If it gets to the point where we think food poisoning is possible or there are excessive violations, then we close it immediately. I really couldn't justify letting them remain open when there was a potential for people getting sick. I think they pretty much agreed with us.'

The Hog's Breath bar stayed open. Work began on the kitchen and it opened again two weeks later. Eastwood was not happy with such a negative thing happening. It was just another hassle in what was turning out to be a trying year.

Yes, he did need a good time – and time to himself. His relationship with Sondra Locke was extremely rocky. They had become more and more estranged while he was Mayor of Carmel. He didn't encourage her to visit him in the town and he was enjoying the single life.

'He flirts around but he's very much a gentleman,' says Steve Strnadk, who is the bartender at Bud's Pub Too.

Playboy? Strnadk smiles: 'I've never seen him put the hard hustle on a woman.'

But the town's favourite son also enjoyed the freedom of just hangin' out at Bud's, where he and a group of male cronies are known as 'the barnacles'.

At 58, Eastwood was not so much set in his ways as cemented in them. In Sun Valley he was friendly with Barbara Minty, the former wife of screen idol Steve McQueen, who died in 1980 from a heart attack during a cancer operation. Eastwood and the stunning former model, who was 33 in 1988, were seen out at dinner and dancing at the Ketchum Country Club, a country-and-western bar-restaurant. And Sondra Locke believed there were other ladies.

Nevertheless, at Christmas that year she and Eastwood did what they had been doing for the past seven years and flew to Sun Valley, where they owned a holiday home – and where an almighty row exploded over a series of concerns and frustrations on both sides.

Eastwood wanted his son Kyle to live with him and Locke at his home in the rich Los Angeles suburb of Bel Air, but Locke wasn't sure. She was nagging him about his dates and remoteness. He never wanted to talk about their problems. And the more she complained, the more irritated he became. He retaliated over a long-standing sore point – her husband. Locke maintained her 1969 marriage to West Hollywood sculptor Gordon Anderson was never consummated. They were childhood friends in Shelbyville, Tennessee, and after their marriage moved to Los Angeles – Locke calls their relationship 'tantamount to brother and sister'.

In 1982 Eastwood had bought a house on Crescent Heights Boulevard in the Hollywood Hills for Gordon Anderson to use. The understanding was that this was a gift for Sondra Locke. But, in fact, strangely, both Sondra Locke and Gordon Anderson were named on a lease of the property, with regular rent due to the landlord – Clint Eastwood. And the rent was paid from a joint account in the names of Locke and Anderson.

When Eastwood and Locke began living together in 1977 they moved into the house in the up-market Los Angeles suburb of Sherman Oaks in which he had lived with Maggie Eastwood. Locke felt uncomfortable there, living among the trappings of Eastwood's earlier life, among the family photographs and memorabilia. She talked to Eastwood about it and he told her that if she found a house she liked he would buy it for her. She found one – quickly. The two-storey stucco house with Spanish-tiled roof offered 5,000 square feet of Bel Air living space but was in need of renovation. Eastwood paid $1,125,000 for the property and Locke spent the next three years redecorating it. It sits behind high fences and electric gates.

The house in Sun Valley, Idaho, also has a security system and the surprising thing was the squabble between Eastwood and Locke didn't set it off. The screaming ended when he ordered her to return to Los Angeles. She did. And, after all the years, they would spend only two more nights together. In January 1989 she and Eastwood talked about ending their relationship and some sort of settlement for her. Then she consulted Los Angeles lawyer Norman Oberstein, who assured her that something would be worked out amicably.

No one, it appeared, wanted any fuss. And anyway, thought Locke, the relationship would soon be back on an even keel again. As she and others have said many times, you never know everything that Clint Eastwood is thinking.

In the matter of Locke versus Eastwood the pack of cards that was left of their relationship began collapsing on the morning of 3 April 1989, when Locke took an early morning phone call at the Bel Air house. It was Eastwood on the line. They needed to talk. He would be right over to the sprawling home they had shared on and off for more than nine years.

Eastwood did not hedge around what he wanted to say. He said Locke was sitting on his only real estate in Los Angeles and he wanted her to move out of the house. Dismayed, Locke told Eastwood she could not believe that was all he could say after their 13 years together. Despite all the arguing and tension, this was the moment she first really understood that their relationship was ending.

Locke, who had her forty-second birthday three weeks later, saw her life vanishing before her. She was shaken. And she was tired. She was directing her second film, the thriller *Impulse*, at the time and had had only four hours' sleep the night before. She begged Eastwood to stop any more talk about them breaking up until her film – starring Theresa Russell as a cop working under cover as a hooker – was completed. He appeared to agree. He, if anybody, understood the pressures of film-making. They would talk again after she had finished *Impulse*.

The days rolled on, filming *Impulse* on location on the streets of Los Angeles. On 10 April Locke received a letter on the set of her film. It was addressed to Mrs Gordon Anderson. It was from Eastwood's lawyers and read in part: 'Mr Eastwood has asked you to vacate the premises. You have refused to do so. This is to let you know that in view of your intransigence the locks on all the entrances of the house have been replaced ... your possessions accordingly will be placed in storage.'

Sondra Locke fainted on the set. A guard was placed at the Bel Air property to ensure she did not enter it. She says she still didn't fully understand the emotional explosion but tried: 'Maybe it was all the pressure of having so much power for so long, maybe it was the pressure of life goals, maybe a person reaches a certain age... He came to that point and I think, unfortunately, the sad part is that it couldn't be dealt with in a friendly, humane way.'

It became instead a fierce battle. She was making her film, barred from her home and living with friends and with her husband Gordon Anderson at the Crescent Heights property in the Hollywood Hills. She had to borrow clothes from friends. She had no idea where her 1971 Mercedes was or the whereabouts of her adored parrot, Putty. Distraught, she went back to lawyer Norman Oberstein. He listened to her story and they decided to try to resolve matters by writing a 'strong' letter to Eastwood and his attorney, Bruce Ramer. The four-page letter, dated 24 April 1989, read in part: 'Clint had obviously timed his "blitzkreig" assault to maximise the emotional harm inflicted on Sondra. Clint also knew that Sondra was engaged in the most important professional work of her career and was preparing to shoot a difficult and key scene in the picture. If it gives you and

Clint any personal pleasure or sadistic satisfaction, you did your work well – Sondra collapsed on the set and was left an emotional wreck. It is all she can do to hang on and complete her work – which everyone recognises is the key to her future independence.

'Why you and Clint are bent on a course which could cripple her ability to function and thus jeopardise her future independence escapes me. Why you and Clint desire to inflict on Sondra what you both knew would be intense personal pain is equally puzzling...

'When Sondra consulted me in January, I concluded that Sondra's best course was to have patience and give you and Clint time to work out a settlement proposal... I was obviously mistaken in assuming that Clint would be reasonable, fair and responsible.

'I even went so far as to incorrectly opine that Clint would not take the law into his own hands, harm Sondra, or seek to eject her from the house without benefit of court proceedings and some notice. I based that assessment of Clint on the good reputation he enjoyed among the people who knew him best, upon my own pleasant dealings with him, and upon my belief that a deep-pocket defendant with top-notch lawyers would not risk the exposure generated by lawless self-help. I won't make that mistake twice.'

Oberstein went on to criticise Eastwood's behaviour as a 'well executed, calculated and cruel plan'. And then he was to open the way for headlines around the world with: 'The insensitivity and cruelty which marked the manner in which Sondra was summarily ejected ... without notice or warning is truly unparalleled in my experience. I promise you, however, our objective is neither to garner the last dollar nor obtain a settlement in light of Clint's substantial ability to pay; rather it is to meet Sondra's minimum expectations in light of a 13-year relationship.'

Oberstein outlined his client's claim:

A one-time flat payment of $250,000.

Four years of financial support of $15,000 a month.

One year at $12,500 a month.

One year at $10,000 a month.

One year at $7,500 a month.

Ownership of the Bel Air house.

Ownership of the Crescent Heights house in the Hollywood Hills.

Attached to her claim was an outline of a palimony action she later filed in Los Angeles Superior Court if her claims were not met.

Under Californian law unmarried couples have the right to sue for a 50/50 share of all assets acquired during the time they lived together. The precedent of 'palimony' was established by Marvin Mitchelson when he represented one-time actress Michelle Triola in 1975 in her landmark case against the late Oscar-winning actor Lee Marvin.

Sondra Locke's case was more complex. She was still married to Gordon Anderson, so she would be a woman married to one man suing for palimony from another if Eastwood did not accept her terms.

Eastwood got Bruce Ramer to inform 'Mrs Gordon Anderson' that her terms were not on. Angered by the tone of her lawyer's letter he was not willing to pay her off with $1.3 million and the two houses.

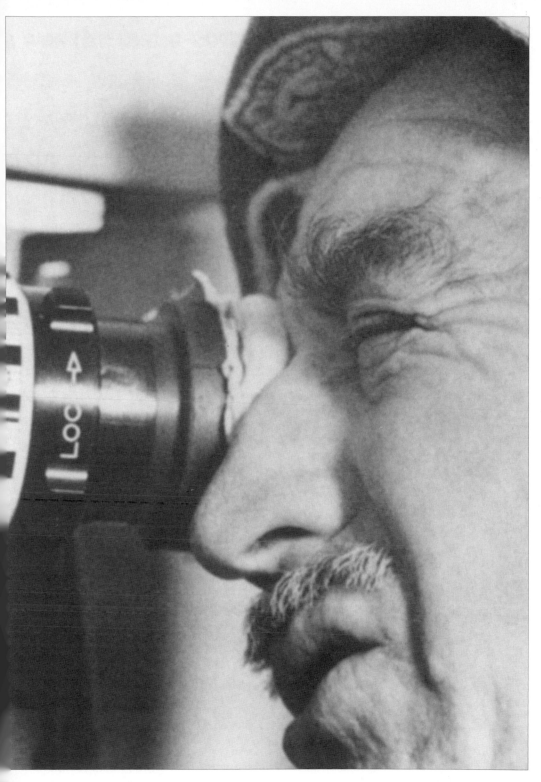

Film director, Don Siegel, Eastwood's friend and mentor. It was Siegel who co-signed Eastwood's application to join the Directors' Guild. For Eastwood's début as a director with *Play Misty For Me* in 1971, he used Siegel's crew and persuaded him to take a small part in the film.

*Top*: Burt Reynolds and Eastwood, two of America's biggest box-office draws at the time, appear with Sondra Locke and Loni Anderson, *far right*, at the world premiere of *City Heat* in Los Angeles, 5 December 1984.

*Above*: In Africa on the set of *White Hunter, Black Heart*, which Eastwood directed in 1990 and in which he also plays the part based on film director John Huston, in the guise of John Wilson.

Keeping it in the family.

*Top*: Kyle Eastwood on film with his father in *Honkytonk Man*. Sondra Locke was coach for young Eastwood when, aged fourteen, he was cast as his father's nephew.

*Left*: With daughter Alison Eastwood, aged twelve, and Jennifer Beck, co-stars in *Tightrope*. In the detective drama, Alison plays Eastwood's daughter Amanda Block.

*Top*: Forest Whitaker as Charlie 'Bird' Parker in *Bird*. There are two 'American art forms, the Western and jazz.' Eastwood's comment was appropriate to his art. With his Westerns under his belt, he fulfilled a longstanding ambition when he directed *Bird* for Warner Brothers.

*Above*: Sonia Braga, the Brazilian actress and sex bombshell, in *The Rookie*, where she makes love to Eastwood in a sadomasochistic scene. Braga was personally chosen by Eastwood for the role.

*Top*: Out and about on mayoral business. When asked if he wanted to be known as Mr Mayor, he replied: 'Nah, just Clint'.

*Above*: As Marine Gunnery Sergeant Tom Highway in *Heartbreak Ridge*.

Eastwood enjoyed a triumphant return to form with *Unforgiven*.

*Top*: Morgan Freeman (Ned Logan) and Eastwood (William 'Bill' Munny).

*Above*: With Gene Hackman who won an Oscar for Best Supporting Actor for his portrayal of Little Bill Daggett. The film won Best Picture and Eastwood won Best Director.

*Top*: Coaching Hilary Swank for *Million Dollar Baby*, she got an Oscar for Best Actress …

*Above*: … while Morgan Freeman got an Oscar for Best Supporting Actor. Clint picked up an Oscar for Best Picture and Best Director.

With second wife Dina Ruiz whom he married in 1995. 'Dina keeps me on my toes, let's put it that way. We both enjoy family a lot, we both enjoy pets and we love to play golf.'

And on 26 April 1989 he was slapped with a $70-million lawsuit.

It didn't make his day.

# TEN

# CELEBRITY JUNGLE

'Love – that's the key to any man. I think in the
last years of his life that has been one of his lesser
productions. He probably has to beat women
away with a club.'

PETER VIERTEL ON EASTWOOD, 1990

ON the third floor of Los Angeles Superior Court on Spring
Street, in the city's downtown, there is a special section
which is guarded at all times. The files are behind a wire
cage and inside a court official warily watches over them.
File C722032 tells the love-hate story of Clint Eastwood
and Sondra Locke.

Judge William Hogoboom, who is retired from the
Superior Court bench, was brought in to referee the couple's
estrangement. On 31 May 1989 he agreed to hold hearings

behind closed doors at a secret location in West Los Angeles to stop any circus atmosphere following on from Locke's palimony lawsuit.

This wasn't settling out of court – it was trying to settle in camera. And it was after the case had been set to be heard in public in the court of Judge Dana Senit Henry on the same date.

But Eastwood's lawyers had pressed for private hearings, for Locke's lawsuit leaked all over the world's front pages. If lawyer Oberstein's letter had been strong, Locke's 22-page lawsuit was heavyweight vitriol. She contested: 'From the start of our relationship Clint told me that he wanted us always to be together and that he would take care of me for ever. Clint repeatedly assured me that regardless of whether we were married, everything he had was ours together.'

In return, she undertook wifely duties, tending to the household, social activities and 'Eastwood's personal needs'.

She asked for unspecified damages, although with Eastwood's wealth estimated at around $140 million she would be able to claim at least half that amount. She also wanted the two houses in the Los Angeles area as well as an equal division of other property.

And she wanted the court to order Eastwood to stay away from the Bel Air estate 'because I know him to have a terrible temper ... and he has frequently been abusive to me'.

Locke described the man she had loved for more than a dozen years as volatile and distant. She said he persuaded her to have two abortions which he himself arranged. And he talked her into having a sterilisation operation, she alleged in her lawsuit: 'At his specific request I underwent a tubal ligation.' She also claimed that by being locked out of the Bel Air home she had 'suffered humiliation, mental anguish and severe emotional and physical distress and suffered mental and physical harm'.

After the lawsuit was filed an American newspaper quoted Locke alluding to Casanova Clint and saying: 'I'm going to make sure the court knows every woman Clint's spent the night with – I'm going to go all the way back to how he started living with me before he got a divorce from Maggie.'

It all made Eastwood shudder. Throughout his career he had been able to separate his public and private lives. But now? He was angry and he didn't want to give in to pressure – but did he want his life paraded through open court?

Officially, at the time, he made only one public comment: 'I am deeply disappointed and saddened that she's taken this kind of action. It will soon come to light that these accusations are unfounded and without merit, however, this matter will be dealt with in an appropriate legal arena.'

Eastwood was shaken by all the attention on his private life. Here was a man who objected to his home town being dubbed Scrooge City. And here he was being described as some evil-tempered fiend. He did everything he could to introduce some kind of damage control and got the co-operation of Judge Hogoboom to take the case into secret arbitration.

The judge sealed all documents in the case and Eastwood's answers to his former lover's charges have never been made public. But in file C722032 he specifically rebuts Locke's charges about the abortions and sterilisation – not that it happened but who made the decision.

In his legal papers he said: 'I adamantly deny and deeply resent the accusation that either one of those abortions or the tubal ligation were done at my demand, request or even suggestion.

'As to the abortions, I told Locke that whether to have children or terminate her pregnancies was a decision entirely hers. Particularly with regard to the tubal ligation I encouraged Locke to make her own decision *after* she had consulted with a physician about the appropriateness of and the necessity for that surgical procedure.'

The 'Locke' must have hurt her.

But was it better or worse than 'Mrs Gordon Anderson'?

Later Eastwood would call her in a conversation 'the person'.

Sondra Locke had made an Oscar-attention debut in film with 1968's *The Heart Is a Lonely Hunter* and it was a promising beginning but her identity rather got lost on celluloid after that.

The ethereal-looking actress made six films with Eastwood but she was always part of the Eastwood ensemble and never really the co-star. She got the biggest part towards the end of their relationship, in *Sudden Impact*. Eastwood was trying to give her more of a platform in the same way he would encourage her to go it alone by directing *Ratboy*. Locke enjoyed her role as a woman out to kill a team of rapists but nevertheless she felt, as she had throughout their relationship, that she walked in the tall man's shadow.

She was never regarded in Hollywood as more than 'Eastwood's girlfriend'. She knew it and she accepted it. She could get people on the telephone because of her connection but that didn't change their perception of her.

After the palimony action happened: 'The total control men like him exert can be terrifying. Women get sucked into it because they want to please but it's dangerous for there is no compromise with absolute power. Clint had been both my lover and the father I was never really close to as a child. I was too dependent. Love, to me, meant absolute trust. I gave Clint my all, holding nothing back and demanding nothing. It's a feminine failing. I thought Clint and I would be together for ever then suddenly it was all over. I was devastated. I thought I'd been annihilated. I'd put so much of my life into this man's hands and suddenly it was gone. I felt as though I'd lost 13 years of my life.

'I never really thought it would happen. When you find yourself in an unfurnished apartment with not one thing that represents what you'd thought you'd worked for you wake up one morning and, like *Twilight Zone*, somebody says: "Hey, too bad, you've gotta start over."

'My objective was to be treated with some kind of respect. To be without my home, my books, my records, my fairytale collection – everything that defined me for 13 years – is not fair.'

But during that 13 years she had stayed married to Gordon Anderson, who was 57 in 2005 and remains a man of some mystery. He has never spoken about the bizarre set-up involving him, his wife and Eastwood.

Sondra Locke kept a wardrobe of clothes and make-up at the $650,000 house which she and Anderson found and which Eastwood bought. She would spend days at the house, cook dinner for her husband and then go back to her lover for the evening. Eastwood paid all the utility bills at the Crescent Heights house.

Judge Hogoboom held a series of private hearings on the palimony case. Everything was kept secret but he did give Locke interim relief, allowing payments to her while the negotiations were going on. And they went on and on.

Finally the judge ruled that there was no palimony case as Locke was married throughout her relationship with Eastwood. This was in the summer of 1989. But the ruling was in arbitration and not legally binding. Locke refused to accept the decision and pursued a full hearing in Los Angeles Superior Court. Eastwood left the negotiations to his lawyers and flew to Africa to confront altogether different beasts in *White Hunter, Black Heart*.

Locke had also carried on working with *Impulse*. Her star, Theresa Russell, believes the movie helped Locke cope: 'I talked to her and said: "Maybe it's a good distancing thing." It seemed to work out because she is basically a strong person.'

But Eastwood was also showing his strength and refusing to give in on the palimony action. There were lots of telephone calls between California and Zimbabwe.

Eastwood was getting fed up with women and lawsuits in 1989. First there was the palimony action. And then along came Stacy McLaughlin, who worked for an animation company in Universal City, a ten-minute drive from Malpaso Productions at Burbank. McLaughlin had to drop off a videotape at Eastwood's office. She did. She also parked in his spot. Now, parking spots at Hollywood Studios are like gold mines – when you get one you hang on to it. There was a story going back to the 1970s which features the sledgehammering of a car parked in the wrong spot.

A Malpaso worker recalls, 'What happened is a gentleman who used to work for Malpaso went out and beat in the windshield of a car that was parked in Clint's space.'

Depending on how the mood takes him, Eastwood has two methods for those who invade his space parking-wise. If the keys are in the ignition he will quietly drive the vehicle to the furthest point on the back lot of the studio, park it and walk away without saying a word.

If things are more hectic he has been known to nudge cars out of the way with his truck without damaging them. McLaughlin claimed she got the nudge. She said she left her car in Eastwood's spot while she went to visit another producer, Paul Maslansky, and in Maslansky's office she was told by a security guard to move her car. When she returned it had already been moved.

McLaughlin sued for $1,000 for damage to her car and $100,000 in punitive damages. When the case was heard in Burbank Municipal Court, Judge Marion Gubler ruled in Eastwood's favour. And she ordered McLaughlin to pay the star's legal costs. In turn, Eastwood, who said he was only trying to park his quarter-ton pick-up truck in its rightful place, paid $960 to repair the headlight and bumper of McLaughlin's car.

Eastwood was becoming a little teed off at the way things were going for him; suddenly he didn't appear to be in control.

In Africa, he was.

Writer Peter Viertel – who lived in Spain with his wife, the actress Deborah Kerr – went to Africa in 1951 to complete the script for *The African Queen* for director John Huston. He was hired after James Agee, who adapted the script from C.S. Forester's novel, died of a heart attack. Huston was a legend even then – the director of *The Maltese Falcon* and *The Treasure of the Sierra Madre* – and as formidable as his films. The image was the reality: he was a hard-drinking, self-indulgent and passionate man. The writer watched Huston descend close to madness, the victim of a crushing obsession.

Viertel wrote a novel based on his experience in which he fictionalised the names of himself, Huston and producer Sam Spiegel. He wrote about Huston's wild desire to kill an elephant and he believes today that Huston only took on *The African Queen* because it provided an opportunity to hunt big game. The director treated everyone who did not want to hunt as a traitor.

The writer believed Huston was squandering his talents and putting production of *The African Queen* – despite everything it still became an Oscar-winning classic – in jeopardy: 'John was a gifted film-maker but he was also a supreme egotist. He would get distracted by some personal whim and he would have his way no matter what.'

*White Hunter, Black Heart* was written in 1953 as a sort of anti-hunting open letter from Viertel to Huston. There had been great rows between the two men but Huston offered to sign a release for the book before he had even seen it and Viertel recalls: 'After he read the first draft he suggested a different ending which I used and he never mentioned the book to me again.'

Eastwood was intrigued by the idea of Huston taking the money to make a film and then going off seeking the big tusker while his stars Katharine Hepburn and Humphrey Bogart idly sat around. You can understand his questioning such action, for it goes so much against his own instincts.

He never met Huston. who died before *White Hunter, Black Heart* began filming. But in the film he played him in the guise of director John Wilson in both voice and manner. It was a stretch and although many critics applauded Eastwood the director, they believed he had cast the wrong actor in the lead role. But he explained: 'What's the point of doing it if you don't stretch yourself?' Which was also the creed of the sometimes macho, blustering eccentric Huston, who in moments Eastwood catches eerily well.

'There was a lot of tension over Huston's obsession with elephant hunting and even in his book he talks about going off on a three-week safari, leaving his crew just sitting around,' said Eastwood. 'He admits to being possessed though he claims he never shot an elephant and Peter Viertel backs that up. Of course, I am sort of anti-hunting. I don't put down what anyone wants to do but it seems to me that killing creatures for fun is not a progressive idea. It's probably one of the oldest things that mankind's done but by the same token there's a certain kind of obsolescence about it. And I guess I just like animals a lot.

'But I was kind of interested in Huston's obsessions because he always seemed to have one, but more so on this film. Though he managed to make really fine films, there was seemingly some distraction on all of them, whether it was racehorses on one or a woman on another. Most people envision a fine film-maker as someone who puts everything in the world into his picture, but in his case it didn't seem that necessary.

'There was an incident that was supposed to have happened during *The African Queen* which Katharine Hepburn talks about. She was doing this scene with Bogart in the back of the boat and Huston was up at the bow, fishing. And she said: "John, you're not watching me." And he replied: "I can hear you, darling. I can hear you." Maybe he'd seen the rehearsal and kind of knew what was going on; maybe just keeping that partial attention was what his great talent was – to never get too wrapped up, to know when something was right.

'Before going to Africa, I looked at most of the documentaries on him and listened to talks he'd made, public-service announcements, and *American Sportsman* shows. I sat next to Anjelica Huston at a party and talked to her. She wasn't that familiar with that era in his life, but she did say that Peter Viertel's book probably had a little more truth than poetry to it.

'I just looked at a lot of Huston's delivery and thought in terms like that. He had a certain patronising quality and a certain paternal quality, and I just thought about that and let it happen.

'His enunciation was a little bit conscious of the way he ... you know, when he's talking to you, he's commanding everyone to listen in. It's very difficult with that particular kind of character not to want to... I mean, I used to do an imitation of him, but I didn't want to do an impersonation. Huston himself would have probably been much more exacting. He would have highlighted the characteristics – I just sort of took on the feeling.

'I guess I could have played it completely differently, but I kinda liked the Huston character. Some of the philosophies he expounded... Huston in life could be an extremely personable person but at the same time he could be very cruel to his friends and neighbours, depending on the mood he was in.

'I think everybody has had something that they've been obsessed about in their lifetime. Maybe it's large, maybe it's small. In Huston's case it was large – everything he did in life was large. He was a sort of bigger-than-life character. It was interesting because the character was such a dichotomy. On the one hand, he tried to rough-house, and on the other hand he was a self-educated man, an incessant reader. When he was a kid he was misdiagnosed with a heart problem by his doctors, and it was thought he was going to die at 25. Maybe he thought: What the hell? I'm going to live beyond my expectations.'

You wonder what Peter Viertel's expectations were all these years after he first went into the jungle with John Huston. Deja vu? With Eastwood it was the opposite, of course. There was control. 'On the set I found him aloof,' Viertel observed. 'There was the feeling that he was the boss without any shouting or megaphones or tantrums. He withholds. I think he's a very shy man down deep.

'I think he is a man propelled by a terrific ambition. You have to make money for these bastards [the studios] otherwise they don't give you any more. But he doesn't want to be the richest man in the cemetery. He's a man with something to say.

'Love – that's the key to any man. I think in the last years of his life that has been one of his lesser productions. He probably has to beat women away with a club. But I'm not talking about sex. I'm talking about human emotions.'

It was more physical than emotional when Eastwood took *White Hunter, Black Heart* to compete at Cannes in 1990. Sylvester Stallone and Arnold Schwarzenegger were also there and the trio turned the town into muscle beach. The threesome were mobbed at the forty-third festival and Eastwood hugely enjoyed himself.

He also liked the topless blonde. Interestingly, she was Californian and not French. She made her points. During a break in St Tropez, the resort Bardot made famous, Eastwood and Bruce Willis and half a dozen other film-makers were having lunch when Michelle Gray jumped on their table and stripped off.

She danced for ten minutes while Eastwood forgot about his discreetly oiled *salade Nicoise* and concentrated on some other light dressing. Why was he paying so much attention?

'People's excessive behaviour fascinates me and Michelle put on a great performance. If you've got it, you should flaunt it.'

Of course, he didn't want to flaunt his private life. The palimony case was still lost somewhere in the spaghetti of paperwork at Los Angeles Superior Court. Eastwood was a little more vocal about it as time dragged on and he admitted: 'I felt so disappointed – and the disappointment was with myself. How could I spend so many years with Sondra? How could I have been such a bad judge of character? Everywhere I went I couldn't get away from it – it made me so uncomfortable.'

Eastwood felt the palimony lawsuit showed a double standard. He had helped her find work as an actress and also encouraged her to direct films. Of the lawsuit he said: 'It's not at all classy. At some point a person has to make up their minds whether they want to be a film director or an ex-girlfriend. I gather the people who advised her thought I would be brought to my knees by some public humiliation. Well, they didn't read me right. They misread me by thinking that making false statements would flush me into some giveaway programme.'

Valiant words, but discretionary tactics would follow.

Women! Women! Eastwood was also having to deal with personalities even closer to home. And, seemingly, always closer to him: 'I have always treated my kids as adults,' he said of Kyle and Alison. 'I have never talked down to them. I just let them be themselves, allow them to make their share of mistakes. If you train them well they won't make that many of them.' His children grew into their teens as the offspring of divorced parents but Clint and Maggie Eastwood have always been united, like any parents, in wanting to do the very best for their children.

Maggie says Alison – a Gemini like her father – takes after him: 'They are independent, sure of themselves. They are fast-moving people and they think fast. Now, Kyle's a Taurus, a bull, and of a completely different nature, he's steadier.'

Kyle, six foot two tall, a former film student, is lean and wiry, like his father, and says of being brought up by a superstar: 'I'm pretty much used to it. People do think that my father is the same as he appears in the movies, which he isn't really. It's almost like there are two people – sometimes it shows through in movies the way he really is but most of the time it's pretty much an act. Most of my close friends know. He's pretty much an ordinary guy in real life. As far back as I can remember I remember being on movie sets. I was born during the filming of *Where Eagles Dare*. I think the first set I was on was *Paint Your Wagon*.'

He says he always understood the need for his father to work and says: 'Maybe it was kind of hard – but there was a lot of good about being his son.' He played his own age, 14, in 1982 when he starred with his father in *Honkytonk Man* and was happy with the experience: 'The wonderful thing was I was just being myself. I can handle myself but I don't go around saying: "I'm Clint Eastwood's son." My dad's a good teacher and he helped me a lot. It was a time to be close to him and I loved that.'

Alison Eastwood said: 'I know my father has a lot of pressures but he never piles them on me or my brother. He always has time for us. He's so patient – he's not the man you see on the screen. He's gentle and caring.'

Eastwood's daughter has model looks. In 2005 she was an actress who had posed for *Playboy*, but when she was just starting out – a slinky size six on a five-foot-eight frame with long, blonde hair and blue-green eyes – she said: 'I have my dad's squint – all I need is a cowboy hat and a little stubble.'

But that was not how the tall and willowy girl graced the cover of *Town and Country* magazine in January 1990. Photographer Tom Hollyman says: 'She's not just a pretty girl – she's arresting.' After that magazine appeared another called her 'the prettiest moving picture Clint's ever made'.

Alison was just eleven years old in 1984 when she appeared with her father, who calls his children 'sawn-offs', in the sex-thriller *Tightrope*. And that led to a fan travelling halfway around the world to stalk her. In 1989 Mike Joynson, a drifter, who was then 20, left his mother's home in New Zealand to try to meet Alison. He had been obsessed with her since the film in which she played cop Eastwood's daughter Amanda, who is handcuffed and bound by a psycho killer.

Joynson found his way to Pebble Beach, near Carmel, where Alison was living with her mother Maggie Eastwood in their spectacular Pacific Ocean-view home on California's world-famous 17-mile scenic drive. The family went to court to get a restraining order against him and Alison told the Monterey County Court: 'In early 1989, he jumped the security fences and entered my mother's home where I lived without knocking, demanding to see me and give me presents, saying he'd madly wanted to see me since seeing me in the movie *Tightrope*. He left before security officers arrived.'

And then, just as suddenly, he returned a year later. Alison told the court of the 1990 incidents: 'He's come to the entrance gate to my mother's house three times insisting on seeing me and has repeatedly phoned and faxed messages on unlisted numbers. He spent hours at Robert Louis Stevenson School trying to see me and slipped past the Pebble Beach gate guards and apparently started to camp out.'

Joynson arrived in Carmel on 14 January that year and booked into a $60-a-night room at the Coachman's Inn. He stayed in room 102 and a motel worker said: 'I remember him. He was strange. He wore a Walkman all the time – even when people were speaking to him. He always used to lose his glasses and every day he would come to the manager's office looking for them. He always had a backpack on like he was ready to go somewhere.'

Officials at Robert Louis Stevenson School, from which Alison later graduated, had to chase Joynson away from the gates. Meanwhile flowers and gifts arrived at the house and Joynson at the security gates. On 17 January Monterey County police and Pebble Beach security officers became involved when they found Joynson had pitched a tent in a wooded area near the entrance to Alison's house. All that was in the tent was a locked suitcase. Police discovered Joynson riding a bicycle near the Eastwood home and a spokesman said: 'He admitted his interest in her and that he had sent her flowers and gifts although they didn't know each other.'

Later that day, Sergeant Bruce Palmer says, he served a restraining order on Joynson preventing him going within 500 yards of Alison. But Joynson was determined. Even Eastwood doing his Dirty Harry routine could not dissuade him, although when he confronted Joynson in a bar and told him to 'stay away' from Pebble Beach Joynson readily agreed. But within 24 hours he was in jail, having been arrested on a charge of disorderly conduct. His bail was set at $2,000 and when he could not meet it he was held for five days in Monterey County jail. Joynson pleaded guilty to the disorderly conduct charge and then left the country. It was another major worry for Eastwood.

And then Alison, who, during an interview in May 1990, had shocked her mother by announcing: 'I could see postponing school for a little while', dropped out of Santa Barbara City College without finishing one term. There were reports of her dating older men and she was a fan of the heavy metal band Johnny Monster and the Nightmares. Alison was constantly at the band's concerts. For Eastwood, it was all beginning to turn out like every father's nightmare.

Alison was using fake identification saying she was 20 – the legal age for drinking in California – to get into nightclubs. In October 1990 she went to see Johnny Monster and the Nightmares play at a club in Hollywood. One of her friends revealed: 'Once she was in the club she got loaded on booze right away. Then the band played one of her favourite songs and she jumped onstage with the band and started dancing like a madwoman. She was shaking and jumping so furiously that her breasts came out of her top.

'Alison was so drunk she didn't notice until some guys started to whistle and applaud. Then she laughed and put them back in her top.'

After the club Alison drove her friends to Westwood, the university area of Los Angeles, in the 1988 BMW given to her by her father. She took one corner at 50mph and skidded across three lanes, according to the Beverly Hills police report. Officer J. Sabbe's report says a breath test revealed her blood alcohol level was .17, which was well above California's legal limit of .08.

She was held in jail overnight. On 7 October 1990 Maggie Eastwood bailed her daughter out of jail. On 20 December that year Alison was fined $846 and sentenced to three years probation for drunk driving. Her licence was restricted, allowing her to drive only to and from work or school. Clint Eastwood 'fined' his daughter the BMW.

Unlike her father, Alison has an impulsive streak. In 1991 she was at a party in Hollywood when she met a striking 30-year-old man, Chad McQueen, the son of screen legend Steve McQueen. They were then seen out on dates and the gossip machine went into overdrive. By early 1992 they were 'planning marriage' and then Eastwood was supposedly begging them to live together rather than marry ... and then they had broken up.

There was also talk of Eastwood getting married – to Dani Janssen, the blonde widow of his friend from his army days David Janssen. Dani arranged a surprise sixtieth birthday party for him in 1990, but the wary Eastwood found out and trimmed the celebration down to dinner with a few friends. Blonde, beautifully turned out and manicured, Dani Janssen is a Hollywood ex-wife who divorced her fourth husband, stuntman turned director and Burt Reynolds's best friend, Hal Needham, in 1987. In 1992 she was 50-something. She was 16 when she married Frenchman Donalde Crayne; 20 when she wed singer Buddy Greco; 30-something when she lived with and then married David Janssen, who died suddenly in 1980; and in 1990 she was free again after marrying and divorcing Needham. Would Eastwood be husband number five?

# ELEVEN

# CASANOVA CLINT

'Try something new, always be open
to a new challenge.'

JACK GREEN, EASTWOOD'S VETERAN
CINEMATOGRAPHER

DANI Janssen's thoughts about someone rather than
something old, something new and something blue, were
rather premature. When Eastwood began filming *The
Rookie* in 1990 there was another lady around on the set of
the buddy-cop movie.

Red-haired Frances Fisher – something of a Sondra
Locke lookalike – has starred in two extremely popular
American daytime soaps, *Guiding Light* and *Edge of
Night*. She appeared in Eastwood's *Pink Cadillac* in 1989
and would later, in a career breakthrough, play
the legendary Lucille Ball in a television movie about

the late comic actress and her former husband, Desi Arnaz.

There had been stories that Eastwood and Locke's fierce disentanglement had been forced on by his interest in *Pink Cadillac* co-star Bernadette Peters, but in fact the one that didn't get away was Fisher. It was no surprise that she chose to be on the set of *The Rookie*. Eastwood was directing himself as veteran detective Nick Pulovski, who is a specialist in car-theft rings. Charlie Sheen was playing his young partner. The late Raul Julia was the Mafia-connected evil mastermind. And Brazilian actress Sonia Braga was Liesl, the cocaine-snorting, karate-chopping hit woman for the thieves.

Braga arrived on *The Rookie* with a very sexy reputation. She was personally chosen by Eastwood for the role. Previously she had been romantically linked to Robert Redford after they made *The Milagro Beanfield War* together. This was a different sort of film for her. Cops and robbers. Car chases.

The Brazilian actress was delighted with the change of pace. And she got to sexually assault Eastwood while, as Pulovski, he is strapped to a chair with his hands tied behind his back. It is the film's most erotic scene and a break in the relentless crash and bang of the car chases and constant carnage.

She rolled around the floor of a suite in the Beverly Hilton Hotel when she talked about working with Eastwood and it was easy to see why he was intrigued by the actress known as the Marilyn Monroe of South America. It has nothing whatsoever to do with her looks. Braga bombshelled in an age when such ladies had largely been replaced by bimbos.

There's a certain sexual explicitness that has little to do with titillation but more with bravado. In the land of coffee and dental-floss bikinis, she's been the nation's biggest star since Pele stopped scoring.

In *The Rookie* she is a kinky nymphomaniac and before she rapes Eastwood she plays around his chest with a razor blade, then gets into torrid action.

'How did I seduce him? He was the director. He knew what he wanted.'

Braga has her own goals. *Dona Flor and her Two Husbands* and *Kiss of the Spider Woman* put her on the international, if art-cinema, circuit. Robert Redford loved her and cast her in his mystical *The Milagro Beanfield War*. He had called her mystical and wonderful and all the other euphemisms which immediately make you believe he is sleeping with the leading lady, and she offers similar words. But also the admonishment: 'I never lie. It is not true. There is nothing wrong with affairs, but I never had it.'

With Eastwood, the sex goddess from Brazil got into major mainstream movies. He offered her a chance to revel in her sexuality in *The Rookie*. Now she had even more reason to give hope to Brazilian womanhood. As she said: 'They all wanted to be blonder and more blue-eyed. They hadn't accepted their identity. They wanted to be Doris Day. Through my success they realised they could be five feet three with frizzy hair, brown eyes, wide hips and be beautiful. The audiences are my accomplices because I am the representative of a collective desire.'

She had taken off her clothes for films and for magazines, but she is a serious person. Is this a serious person's performance? She talks in a sort of half-English by way of Garbo and Marlboro and bares all her uncapped teeth. (Brave stuff in Beverly Hills.) 'In Brazil it is not unusual to do that if you are a singer or an actress. If you are asked to do it, why not? I am not ashamed of my body.'

She enjoyed *The Rookie* and the stunt people: 'All the explosions and the pretending – it is my first action film and I've had a lot of fun doing it with all the kicking and running. It doesn't matter too much about the screenplay – you know what the plot is because it's always the same. But something happens with the action and the choreography, the big dance, the big ballet. People when they do action, they are very busy. Those are people who believe more in violence than in love. With the action everyone gets tense and the great lesson to me is that people are not too comfortable about love at these times. I want to do sex scenes as I do action.

Men? I can make them laugh. I tell them I love them and they laugh. They can't believe it. You tell them every time what they have to do to make you happy and they do the opposite because they don't want to be told. Which is good. If you do what they tell you then you will be together for ever and nobody wants that. All men are confused.'

What about Eastwood, to whom she makes love in *The Rookie*, in a scene involving bondage and sadomasochistic overtures? 'I cannot sit on the set of a film thinking nobody is going to see it, so I am lucky that Clint chose me for the character. He is one of the best in action because of his background and that's why people will see the film.

'The violence? When I was four years old I was watching

*Tom and Jerry* and when I'm up there with a gun and I have to shoot somebody I'm playing out my earliest fantasy. I'm either Tom or Jerry. We don't read cartoons as violence. It is like being a kid in the circus seeing all these stunt people. They're making great cartoons – but making it spectacularly.

'Yes, my feelings and my brain sometimes clash. We have a lot of discussions here with my brain because it's not everything I like that my brain agrees with. That's when you become repressive with yourself and you become prejudiced.

'People are saying we shouldn't have sex in our life – you know what I mean? It's so primitive a thing, right? This is like nature. Normal. You should talk about love, you cannot talk about sex. Look at love stories. They kiss wrong. And you know because you've been kissing before ... you know what a kiss is. A little one. A big one. It's good. It wouldn't hurt you. It's good. What's the problem?

'Do you remember *Last Tango in Paris*? Why was it this huge, huge event? Because it was so real. It was good, it was tense and it was open. It would be harder to make that film today. We continue walking backwards. We're becoming like to kiss is going to be difficult on screen.'

Frances Fisher's concerns were not about what was happening on screen. Sometimes she would wait for Eastwood into the early hours during night filming and they would take off for breakfast in his big red GMC truck. And, it seemed the Dani Janssen relationship was off despite Cupid efforts by Frank Sinatra, who was convinced Eastwood and Janssen should marry. 'They're perfect for each other,' he said.

Ladies? They were making life complicated. And Kimber,

his daughter by Roxanne Tunis, was also putting on pressure from long distance. Things had become extremely strained between Eastwood and the girl, born in 1964. By 1991 she had changed her name to Kimber Eastwood and had married for the second time, to Denver businessman Douglas McCartney. She claimed Eastwood wouldn't acknowledge her because she had talked about their father-daughter relationship: 'I'm out of the family. I guess we never had the greatest relationship. He says I cut myself short by my actions. I'm upset because of my son Clinton but on the other hand His Highness can't bother me any more.'

Eastwood remained publicly silent on that.

Despite all these romantic wanderings, Frances Fisher appeared to become a permanent part of Eastwood's life towards the end of 1990. They visited his home in Sun Valley, Idaho, and they were seen around Carmel and in Los Angeles. By early 1991 they went very public and went skiing together in Beaver Creek in Colorado's Rocky Mountains. 'I've known Clint for two years and we've been going out together for over a year. In love? Yes,' she said. 'He's a wonderful man and a special friend – it's nice to be together.'

As welcome as it must have been to resolve his palimony lawsuit with Sondra Locke. That was all concluded while he and Frances Fisher were on their Colorado skiing trip. Eastwood and his lawyers decided to settle with Locke five weeks before the case was scheduled to go to a jury trial in Los Angeles Superior Court, which would have been a very public showdown between the couple.

It was a difficult decision for Eastwood. He had fought long and hard not to give in to Locke's demands. But discretion won out as he imagined the headlines around the world as his intimate life was stripped bare. It was a compromise he had to make. The amount of money involved has been quoted as anywhere between $6 million and $40 million. Neither side can legally reveal the exact amount but sources say it is much closer to the lower figure. Locke also got the Bel Air home and the Crescent Heights property in Hollywood.

Locke's lawyer Norman Oberstein said the settlement followed a year of private negotiations: 'The matter has been settled and Miss Locke is very happy with the result,' he said.

Eastwood won some concessions. Locke cannot ever sue him for more money.

The actress went through a tragic time. On 12 September 1990 she had a lumpectomy at Cedars-Sinai Medical Center in Los Angeles. A week later she was readmitted for a mastectomy and reconstruction of the right breast. She spent five days in a private room on the eighth floor of the hospital before leaving the hospital on 25 September.

The breast cancer made her put her life in perspective. Until then she had thought the break-up with Eastwood was the most devastating thing that could have happened to her. Then, suddenly, her life was in jeopardy. After the operation doctors could assure her that the cancer had not spread to her lymph system. The American Cancer Society says that a woman whose cancer has not spread beyond the breast has a 90 per cent chance of survival. Locke decided on post-surgery counselling following her operation.

Eastwood was not around. Even given the then ongoing

palimony action, this seems strange, considering the years they had been together. Friends were quoted in American newspapers as saying Eastwood had 'blocked off Locke from his life'. He himself has made no further public comment.

He has talked about love, though: 'There are so many kinds of love. The love for one's children is hard to top. Sure, there's some battling that goes on. That's part of figuring out any relationship. Some people thrive on a violent kind of love – that's what works for them – and some want a serenity-tranquillity kind of love. As I've grown older, I've looked for more of the latter. It gets to be a kind of Zen thing, a plateau that you reach after you've been through everything else. The warrior ego gives way to something higher.

'The best kind of relationship is one where both people can express themselves freely and where there's mutual respect. I guess it's possible to love a woman and not respect her. But it wouldn't be anything that's gonna hang around for a while. Of course, everybody's in love in the sack. The question is: Are you in love five minutes afterward?

'I guess the line between love and infatuation is pretty slim. I always say if you can drive 200 miles with a gal and are still interested in talking with her, you know you're on the right track. But then again, you might drive ten miles and say: "God, I wish I left this girl home."' He's not left many at home.

With hindsight, it is interesting to see how those who were close to Eastwood over the years perceived him in their times with him. Eastwood is an icon and, like Bogart and Cagney and Gary Cooper and Cary Grant, people will be writing about him long after his final showdown. By then what people like Don Siegel and Sondra Locke have said will be archive material. Locke witnessed the man few have. She said: 'Without question, Clint has it – and the "it" in his case has a lot to do with good old-fashioned sexual magnetism. It's a certain magic that makes millions of people turn toward him like plants turning to light. When I see evidence of how popular Clint really is, it amazes me. Once when we were shooting a scene a huge crowd stood outside all day, waiting for him to appear at the door. And when he finally did, they sighed and oohed – they were enthralled. And the amazing thing is that Clint never thinks about his appeal. He never considers it.

'He remains something of an enigma, even to his intimates. People can know him for years and never be sure of what he's thinking. He's one of the warmest people in the world, but there's a certain distance, a certain mystery to him. He's always unapproachable to some degree… Clint is a rascal. The people I've enjoyed on the screen over the years have always had that element. No matter how dramatic the moment in the film might be, there's a twinkle in the eye that says: "I'm enjoying myself. I'm not taking myself too seriously, so sit back and enjoy yourself, too." All of them – Bogart, Cooper, Spencer Tracy – even at their most serious, always gave a subtle hint of slyness, of humour. Clint's a subtle actor, too. But because he seems so real, some people forget that he's acting. Yet to me, that's the ultimate in acting – when the character you play seems absolutely real.

'Versatility is another Eastwood strong point. We were dubbing a couple of lines on *The Gauntlet* and at the same time preparing *The Enforcer* for television release. They threw a reel from each up on the screen, and the difference in Clint was incredible. That's how to best appreciate an actor – take small clips from his films and see how he brings a totally different feel to each role. Even his face changes. He can control his facial muscles the way Stradivari could control a violin. He can look primitive and violent one minute and then, when he breaks into a smile, he looks just like a little boy.

'He's supersensitive, picks up on people's moods instantly – and he knows what's happening on every inch of the set. Never do anything you want Clint Eastwood to forget, because he remembers everything. He knows every single shot of every picture he's ever made. When he's making a movie, he's incredibly objective – about himself, the other actors, the way the story is coming together. He's got a kind of third eye open all the time. He knows about lighting and sound and editing, and he can run all the equipment himself – so he doesn't shoot disconnected scenes, he shoots with the whole picture in mind. People tend to trust him because of that, so the atmosphere on the set is friendly but controlled. He doesn't need to shout like a dictator from the director's chair. People naturally respect him, so he just circulates, acting and planning shots and standing back and then acting again. He's a strong presence on the set.

'I always saw something underneath those tough-guy roles that made him interesting – a hint of vulnerability, a certain boyishness and humour within the superman image. When we got to know each other, the boyishness became even more apparent. I've always been surprised that people don't pick up on it right away. That, and Clint's great sense of humour.'

The forceful director Don Siegel was one of the old school of Hollywood. Much like the director Sam Peckinpah, he had his own visions and could make the camera create ballets out of the most violent situations, by which he was able to stamp his work. He was Eastwood's film mentor and friend, and he died on 20 April 1991. Theirs started out as a head-butting relationship on *Coogan's Bluff* in 1968 but soon developed into one of mutual admiration.

Siegel, a merry man with his moustache usually partially framing a smile, said: '*Coogan's Bluff* was born out of chaos. I came on the picture after eight scripts had been written, and one director had quit. I found Clint very knowledgeable about making pictures, very good at knowing what to do with the camera. I also found that he's inclined to underestimate his range as an actor. I think he's a very underrated actor, partly because he is so successful.

'We started out with cautious, mutual admiration. He started to come up with ideas for camera set-ups. I started to call these "Clintus" shots and even if I decided not to use them they invariably gave me another idea, threw me into a "Siegelini" shot. We've developed this and it's become fun making pictures with him. We don't try to win points with each other. He doesn't try to impress on me that he is a big star and I don't try to impress on him that I'm a big director. If either one of us is really steadfast in an argument, whatever it is, the other has enough respect to realise there is something to it and give in.

'Clint is a very strong individual, on and off the screen. He doesn't require, and I don't give him, too much attention. A good rule with Clint is that when you give him a direction, be sure you're right about it. If you don't think you're right, don't say it. Clint knows what he's doing when he acts and when he picks material. That's why he's the number-one box-office star in the world. His character is usually bigger than life. I think people don't really want to see pictures about mundane things and ordinary people. Clint's character is far from mundane or ordinary. He is a tarnished super-hero, actually an anti-hero. You can poke at a character like that. He makes mistakes, does things in questionable taste, is vulnerable. He's not a white knight rescuing the girl: he seduces her.

'I particularly like the scene in *Two Mules for Sister Sara* in which Shirley MacLaine takes the arrow out of Clint's shoulder. It was done under difficult circumstances. The area was filled with ants. We used insecticides but they didn't do any good. Even without the ants it would have been a difficult sequence, particularly for Clint, who is supposed to get more and more drunk as the scene proceeds. At the same time he had to show that a closer relationship was growing between them. It's my favourite scene in the picture and I felt they were both very good.

'*The Beguiled* is my favourite film. I don't say it is necessarily my best film, but it's my favourite. This is a story about a huge, powerful, beautiful man, crippled in war, who's befriended and helped into a school, a sanctuary full of innocent, virginal girls – run by a headmistress whose virginity is caused by her frigidity. Behind the facade of innocent faces, when the chips are down, lurks just as much evil as in a group of hoodlums. Johnny McB[urney] is a beguiler. A man who thinks quickly on his feet. A con man. He sizes up every one of them… What happens is that Johnny McB unknowingly becomes a trapped man – helpless – by a bunch of sparrows.

'There's a careful unity about the film, starting with the first frame. We begin with black and white and end with black and white, we start with Clint and the mushrooms and end with them; we start with Clint practically dead. And end with him dead. The film is rounded, intentionally turned in on itself.

'The most important thing separating this from an ordinary picture, however, is not the rounding of the story, but the attitude of the females. For example, his murder, instead of filling the women with remorse, is followed by business as usual. Children are very cruel, and death doesn't have tremendous meaning. It doesn't happen to them. I tried to play that scene as if the women and girls were incapable of being touched. Women are capable of deceit, larceny, murder, anything… Any young girl who looks perfectly harmless is capable of murder.

'Case in point: *Play Misty for Me*, the first movie Clint directed [Siegel co-signed Eastwood's application to join the Directors' Guild]. He used my crew and persuaded me to take a small part in the film as the bartender. I wanted to be involved but I don't like being an actor. Clint tried to make me feel at ease but I felt so uncomfortable in front of my own crew. It was the first sequence he had ever directed in his life and it was the very first time I'd ever acted in a speaking role in a picture. I was extremely nervous and the only reason it apparently came off was because Clint was very kind to me and directed me very intelligently, so I calmed down and gave him what he wanted.

'Later that year Clint asked me to direct *Dirty Harry*. I saw Harry as a bigot ... a bitter man. He doesn't like people. He has no use for anyone who breaks the law, and he doesn't like the way the law is administered. The killer was a personification of evil. I like my villains not to be stupid. Gosh, I want my villains to be brilliant, and that makes my hero that much more brilliant. I loathe those anti-Nazi pictures where the Nazis are a bunch of dopes. I mean, what are you defeating? For *Dirty Harry* we actually printed only 60,000 feet of film. Of that we used about 10,000 feet in the finished picture. Now that is very little film for a Hollywood movie. Clint's famous for the way he hates waste.

'In *Escape from Alcatraz* there were no stuntmen or doubles. Everybody did their own stunts – and their own fights. If there was any such position as stunt co-ordinator on this film, it goes to Clint himself. Shooting in the cells was interesting. Each cell is five feet by eight feet. That's not much room to begin with and even less when you're shooting a six-foot-four actor. But, thanks to Clint's co-operation, it worked. Clint's very strong and he can contort himself into any position you want him to assume. He would crawl in and out of the cell, climb up through the hatch into the ceiling, climb down the roof to the roof below. And if he had missed by a step he would have been killed.'

From his early movie-making days Eastwood surrounded himself with 'the Team', a unit which for decades he has strived to keep together. And the loyalty has been mutual. You just need to listen to the people he has worked with. A Clint Eastwood film is always an event. Joe Cavalier, who worked on five Eastwood films as assistant director and second unit director, singled out *Coogan's Bluff*: 'We had to find 600 or 700 people for the disco scene. We used 150 extras from the Screen Extras' Guild but the rest of them were all people I'd picked up from the streets, real flower children. Actually they worked better than the extras, because they would do anything you might tell them to do, and the other ones wouldn't. We couldn't let them go out to lunch – we figured they wouldn't come back. So we had to feed them on the set. There was one flower child ... she wanted to go home at about 4.30 to feed her baby. I said: "Well, we're on our last show now, can you wait?"

'And she said: "No, look at me." And she opened up her robe and squirted milk. It went about four feet – she hit me right in the face with it.'

It was hot water rather than milk that Cavalier thought he and Eastwood were getting into with *Coogan's Bluff*. It contained one of Eastwood's earliest risque scenes and Cavalier explained: 'In the disco sequence Coogan comes across this high-wire girl who's partially nude. We had a discussion, Don Siegel and I, as to whether we should edit it out because of the censorship at the time. I thought it was the story's point, that she leads Coogan further on, and we should take a chance to leave it in, although in those days it was quite alarming. And, as it turned out, we asked the man in charge of censorship, and he felt it was important, too, story-wise; so we won that point with the censorship office. All I had to do as a trade-off was trim down the sequence where the nude woman is being decorated, later on, and the sequence where they are smoking marijuana.'

The perfectionist trio of Eastwood, Siegel and Cavalier teamed up again in 1970 for *The Beguiled*. Realism is all-important to them and Cavalier found the perfect solution to the sound Eastwood's character, the limping McBurney, would make when he walked. He brought in a one-legged extra.

All members of the team are involved in the decision-making and Carl Pingitore, who was film editor, said: 'I've never worked on a film with such values. And Clint was very involved; once the first cut was finished, there was a real close collaboration between Eastwood, Siegel and myself. They're just two of the most brilliant men in the business and we were all working toward the same goal. We thought alike. There were times we were seeing a sequence and Clint would go: "Huh?" and they didn't have to say what was wrong – just knew it. *The Beguiled*, *Play Misty for Me* and *Dirty Harry* were the most harmonious films I ever worked on.

'*Misty* was Clint's first directorial endeavour and, I must tell you, he did a brilliant job. He was such a professional and had such instinct – it all tallied. Siegel has a small part in the film – he was a bartender – and he had such stage fright, but there was such affection and respect between the two men that Don insisted on being involved, and this gave him the opportunity. So he just did what Clint said, and Clint was marvellous.'

Most people on Eastwood films do as the tall man says but he does let his crew enjoy freedom if things are going to plan. Bruce 'Spanky' Surtees, director of cinematography on *The Outlaw Josey Wales*, says: 'Clint's easy to work with because he lets his people alone. Whatever I wanted to do, I did. I've met a lot of directors and some of them think they know about photography and they hamper you more than help you. But if you get a good director who knows about staging and things like that, then it all fits together.'

That admiration is echoed by production designer Ted Haworth, who worked on *The Beguiled:* 'It was a great satisfaction to work with Clint Eastwood, a man who has done it the hard way up, by his own bootstraps – a fine, creative, dedicated, unique man.'

Costume supervisor Glenn Wright is a long-time Eastwood employee. He chooses his words as carefully as he chooses the actors' clothes: 'Cost is something you have to be concerned with, of course, so you try not to spend money needlessly. But with Clint it really isn't a problem – he just wants you to spend your money wisely. He has no objections to your doing it, as long as you make sure you've got your dollar's worth, and it works for the film as a whole. Clint wears clothes so well it's easy to make him look nice – it doesn't have to be expensive. The toughest thing is to make him look bad.'

Eastwood's penchant for keeping the team together led Wright to follow in Siegel's footprints as a nervous 'star' in

*Escape from Alcatraz*. It was another Eastwood-Siegel in-joke. Wright had to stand in the shower and hand out towels, using the same lines that he said in real life when he allocated clothes from the wardrobe. 'I didn't want to embarrass them or myself so I did my best,' says Wright. 'Then Don insisted I apply for membership of the Screen Authors' Guild and now I do a little acting as well. It's fun, but it's not easy. It's a challenge and it's hard work.'

Fun. Hard work. Perfection. These are the sort of words that you hear from the team. Steve Dorff, who has composed the music for a number of Malpaso films, says: 'They were all a lot of fun. Particularly *Every Which Way But Loose*. It was a ground-breaking film for Clint – it was really different. And it was at a time when country music was very popular. We had a very, very big hit record with it and it was the first movie that I'd ever done, so I look back on it as being my favourite. It was real unusual, too. I remember looking at a rough cut of it before we started even coming up with the music and to be honest I didn't know what to make of it. I just sat there and laughed and enjoyed it.

'Something that made an everlasting impression on me was that as we were watching it, Clint would say: "This is going to bring the house down" or "This is going to be great", and even though I might have doubted it at the time, when the picture was finished and released, he was right. Clint really knew his audience and knew what would work.

There was another in-joke – a fun scene mimicking the Man with No Name. 'That was Clint, says Dorff. 'He just threw it out as an idea – "Why don't we do a spaghetti

Western kind of take-off?" and so we did it. It's a cute gag.'

Eastwood, who seeks out talent rather than big names, gave David Worth his big Hollywood break as director of cinematography on *Bronco Billy* – it was his first Hollywood break and the first time he had worked with Eastwood.

'The crew was made up of people who had worked with Clint before. He works with basically the same crew year after year – Glenn Wright, who does wardrobe, goes all the way back to the Rawhide days. A lot of his people – his property people, his special-effects people, his costume people – go on and on and on with Clint.

'I worked with Clint exactly one year from the time I started to the time I finished – I did *Bronco Billy* and *Any Which Way You Can* back to back, with just a couple of weeks break in between. I considered it to be my PhD in film-making. He was a real pro; very well prepared, someone who hires talented people and trusts them to do their job. During the year I worked with him I never heard him raise his voice once. He's a guy who's in charge, knows what he wants and knows how to get it.

'Seventy-five per cent of the time he prints on rehearsal or the first take. Of course, that gives a certain pace and confidence to the crew. On *Bronco Billy* we actually finished two and a half weeks under schedule! I think that stands as a record to this day. It was valuable for me to realise that this was a man who has made hundreds of millions of dollars for the studios over the years; if he wanted to indulge himself, he could do it. No one would even bat an eye. But he was just the opposite. He absolutely detested the thought of wasting a penny that wasn't going on screen. This is the way I grew up working … and I found that all of the things I was doing out of necessity were being done by Clint Eastwood out of efficiency.

'It was very, very interesting. I'm in love with *Bronco Billy*. I think it's a very endearing film and, to this day, I believe it's one of Clint's favourite films. This is where I discovered what a generous actor Mr Eastwood is to his fellow performers. He went ahead and shot the master for the scene and then over his shoulder to the other actor, and then the medium shot, and then the close-up on the other actor before he ever turned the camera around on himself. His close-up was the last thing we ever did in the scene. He's not only an extremely well prepared director but also very generous to the other performers, saving his own shots for last when he's actually the best on the rehearsal or the first take.'

Eastwood covers all the corners, all aspects of the film-making process and Jack Garsha, a colour timer who has worked repeatedly with him, explained: 'Eastwood will use his editor, his cameraman, even his extras, over and over. You find out what he likes, and that's all there is to it. There's no sense in going through the same thing with a new timer for every picture. I mean, his people know what he wants and he knows they know what he wants, and you do your job, and he keeps out. You don't do your job – you're out.'

Eastwood veteran Jack Green endorses all this: 'You get what I call a "finger-wave" rehearsal, which is: Clint tells you what the scene will look like; he'll give the actors instructions as to where they should be; he'll talk to me about the camera angles. With the actors unrehearsed, with the lighting and camera moves only worked out on stand-ins, he'll bring the actors in and "roll on rehearsal". Seven out of ten times, it'll be printed and we'll move on.

'Film is like contemporary art. When you lose track of trying to find a new way to do something, when you become complacent, you become boring. I always want to have the Eastwood option, which is: "Try something new, always be open to a new challenge."'

Another long-time Eastwood collaborator, composer Lennie Niehaus, said: 'I've done quite a few movies for Clint. I know how he works; the great thing about him is that he recognises that each person he hires has his own creative ability and he doesn't want to thwart that. I see him do it with actors, too; he might give a few suggestions but it's almost like: "Let's see what you can do with it." He makes everybody at ease.'

*Bird* title star Forest Whitaker agrees: 'He's very cool, calm and very relaxed.' Whitaker's co-star actress Diane Venora felt the same: 'I feel he trusts his people, from the top to the bottom. He knows who he hires, he likes what they are, and he trusts that they will work according to what he liked in them. He wants an uninhibited response, so his feeling of not rehearsing is to create that off-balance for an actor. He exudes: "I enjoy making films, I'll make them my whole life, it's a great place to be, I'm so grateful to have this as work."

'And that kind of generosity and love bleeds into everything, so nobody gets that uptight. There's never a moment of doubt who is in control of the set. He is truly that kind of director where there's never a hazy or grey area and that's a powerful thing because if you have a strong head, the rest of the body looks great. He is a gentleman.'

Regular cinematographer Tom Stern said: 'To me it's almost like a repertory company. It is almost like when you get together for the spring play every year. I don't spend my time socially with Clint, though we are in constant touch on projects.'

He is the third person Eastwood has promoted to director of cinematography: 'He did the same thing with Bruce Surtees and Jack Green, said Stern, who began working as a gaffer on 1982's *Honkytonk Man*.

'Everybody has a rapport. It is pretty interesting because there is not a lot of talk on the sets, but he is able to communicate what the goal is. I think since *Honkytonk Man* we have maybe had eight hours of production meetings, and I am not sure I have ever had a meeting together with Clint.

'The two commandments working for Clint are the audience is a lot smarter than everybody thinks. That means you don't need to spell everything out for them. And the second axiom is that I am supposed to get as much of every dollar stuck on the screen as I can.

'It is real simple too. If you are going to build a log cabin, you just do it economically. Some people say that's cheap and I say frugal. It's got nothing to do with cheap.

'He is very frugal cinematically. It leaves so much to your imagination and own thought process.'

Even the usually critical author Norman Mailer, though not part of his team, is a major fan of Eastwood. He cites the moment in *Play Misty for Me* when Eastwood's character realises that the girl he's casually dating is a dangerous psychotic: 'As the camera moves in, his stare is as still as the eyes of a trapped animal. Yet his expression is luminous with horror. He is one actor who can put his soul into his eyes.'

And he had waited many years to unveil the very dark soul of William Munny in *Unforgiven*, which would go on to be nominated for nine Oscars and win four, including Best Picture and Best Director, at the 1993 ceremonies.

It was the first time production designer Henry Bumstead collaborated with Eastwood as the director, although he had worked on his movies *Joe Kidd* and *High Plains Drifter*. It was the beginning of a beautiful friendship embracing eight more movies.

'I wouldn't be working for anyone else at my age. Clint takes the b.s. out of making movies. Working with Clint is like the old studio days. When you were part of a major studio, you knew everyone and you worked with everyone. This is the same thing. Clint doesn't do anything for a couple of years and once you go back to work everybody you worked with before is there. It's like a reunion. Clint likes to have people around him that he knows and works with.'

'Bummy', who was diagnosed with prostate cancer before production began on *Million Dollar Baby*, was able to work on that film while receiving treatment because Eastwood supplied a wheelchair and a car with a driver to make it easier for him: 'I wouldn't have worked this long now if I hadn't gone back with Clint. He gives me great freedom, so it's fun working with him.'

On Eastwood's film sets no one makes much noise. Nobody yells, nobody calls out: 'Lights!' or 'Camera!' or 'Action!' Sometimes Clint says: '*Azione!*', like Sergio Leone, but usually it's just: 'Go ahead' or 'OK.' There are certainly no day-to-day histrionics.

Actress Marcia Gay Harden said working for Clint was 'like being on a Zen retreat – everything is so quiet and peaceful'.

Most of the of the usual suspects were also in Alberta, Canada, to tell the story of William Munny and create a cinema triumph. One of them was Joel Cox, 62 in 2005, who, for his film editing, would win one of the landmark Western's Oscars.

Cox began working with Eastwood as an assistant editor on *The Outlaw Josey Wales*. Ferris Webster, one of Cox's mentors, was the official editor on the Western: 'What happened is that Ferris got sick and I finished the last editing on the picture with Clint. That is when our relationship started. He just watched my work and he had a confidence in me. I was a young guy coming up. He is very savvy about film-making, and he understands just about everybody's job. He just watched me like a hawk. I think he realised I pretty much knew what I was doing. Obviously he saw something in me, and after that film he said: "I am hoping you don't have any plans. I would like you to be on our next film."'

Eastwood has developed a visual style that's stark, simple and often a little ragged around the edges, much like the characters that inhabit his films. His quick-and-cheap ethos, film historian Gary J. Prebula said in 2005, means that micro-management is not part of the director's vocabulary.

'Not at the speed he moves, so he has to macro-manage. He has to pick the people that he knows what they are going to do and let them do their jobs. It's all about getting the job done efficiently and quickly as possible.

'The big thing is that Clint Eastwood knows what he wants, and he makes the decisions. When you know what you want as a director, it is infectious to work with somebody like that. If someone is very up front and open, your job is wonderfully easy and, importantly, fun. I suspect that these people enjoy what they are doing. When he's working I think his goal is to go home.

'Age equals knowledge to him, and you do find that people who are in the business for that length have an extraordinary amount of knowledge and hence can do it faster.'

Prebula has worked exclusively for Eastwood since 1982: 'In all the years I worked for him, only one scene have I taken apart. It was a scene in *Sudden Impact*. Other than that, I have never recut a scene."

'They call it the University of Clint Eastwood,' said Prebula, completing his picture of a man of decision with: 'Clint Eastwood as a director is not afraid of saying you did a good job, just as he's not afraid of saying you did a bad job.'

Up in the wilds of Canada they all did a great job.

Especially the Boss.

# TWELVE

# NOTHING FANCY

'I like simple things, yet I'm obviously more
complex than I appear on the surface.'

CLINT EASTWOOD, 1992

WITH all the outside personal pressures and the time on
African location for *White Hunter, Black Heart*, 1991
became only the third year in the previous 15 that Warner
Brothers did not have a Clint Eastwood film on their
summer or Christmas schedule.

But, in September 1991, Eastwood's latest showdown was
starting. He and his loyal band of film-makers were in
Canada, about 60 miles south-west of Calgary, to make
*Unforgiven*. Eastwood had made the location intentionally
remote and, to add authenticity, wouldn't allow modern
vehicles on the set.

The period Western – his first since *Pale Rider* in 1985 – was also filmed in the hamlets of Brooks, Drumheller, Stealer and Longview and also at rodeos in Calgary and in Sonora, Arizona, on the Mexican border.

It began as vintage Eastwood and concluded as vintage cinema. The script for the film was called *The William Munny Killings* and had been going the rounds in Hollywood for 15 years. Writer David Peoples completed it in 1976. But although *Josey Wales* had been successful, other impressive Westerns, like *The Culpepper Cattle Co.* and *The Great Northfield Minnesota Raid*, both made in the early 1970s, had floundered at the box office.

The genre was in a slump and Peoples, whose first screen credit was director Ridley Scott's *Blade Runner*, said: 'Nobody wanted to see Westerns.' His script was originally called *The Cut-Whore Killings* and director Francis Ford Coppola bought an option on the rights in the early 1980s but no studios were interested. Eastwood picked up the rights when Coppola's option ran out and had planned to make the film before the multiple Oscar success of Kevin Costner's *Dances With Wolves*, which did prove to doubting Hollywood that there is a market for good Westerns. 'Everybody wants to pronounce genres dead then somebody comes along with a new twist and changes everything,' said Eastwood. 'The audience changes. There's a whole new generation out there.'

Until *Million Dollar Baby* and another Oscar bonanza, *Unforgiven* was generally agreed to be Eastwood's finest film and had been described by many critics as a 'masterpiece'. Set in Wyoming in the 1880s, it tells the story of William Munny, a former murderer who, transformed by the love of a good woman, gave up a life of killing to raise a family and try his hand at pig farming.

With his wife now dead and his farm a failure, Munny is lured back into his old ways by the 'Schofield Kid' (Jaimz Woolvett), an aspiring young gunfighter who brings the older man word of a bounty being offered in the town of Big Whiskey. Munny refuses the young man's offer of partnership but later reconsiders, teaming up with his old sidekick Ned Logan (Morgan Freeman) and setting off to join the Schofield Kid. The journey will bring him up against the sheriff of Big Whiskey, 'Little Bill' Daggett (Gene Hackman).

Hackman, who won the Oscar for Best Supporting Actor, had originally turned down Peoples's script and, later, Eastwood's first offer to appear in *Unforgiven*. He felt he'd already done too many violent films, but was persuaded that the film would make a powerful anti-violence statement. His performance certainly spelled that out.

Eastwood also had a marvellous role for the late Richard Harris. And chance had it that Harris was watching *High Plains Drifter* on television when Clint phoned him to offer the role of the hired gun, a particularly colourful piece of work by the name of 'English Bob'. Harris said yes immediately, before learning about the film's content, and had to be persuaded by Eastwood to read the script before contracting to make the movie. Harris said: 'I was just wanted to be in a Clint Eastwood film.'

And what a film to be in.

Eastwood's lover Frances Fisher was perfectly cast as 'Strawberry Alice', right down to her hair colour. As the leader of the prostitutes, 'Strawberry Alice' raises the bounty to avenge one of the girls, whose face has been cut up by a cowboy.

Eastwood had total involvement in the project; he had waited till he felt he was old enough too play William Munny – to grow into the part. And although the score was arranged by his long-time collaborator Lennie Niehaus, he wrote the main theme himself. And he dedicated the picture to 'Sergio and Don' – Sergio Leone and Don Siegel, his two greatest influences.

All the characters seem less like mythical heroes and villains than like real people. Eastwood acknowledges: 'I like showing people's strengths and vulnerabilities. The characters in *Unforgiven* have a lot of weaknesses along with the strengths. That's true to life. The Gene Hackman character was appealing because he was not just a villain, he was a guy with a sense of humour who just carried things too far, was somewhat obsessive and had a twisted view of law enforcement. But he had this house and his dreams as he sat on the porch and watched sunsets. He had all the things that villains are never really allowed to have. They're always sneering.

'I think all those characters in *Unforgiven* were driven by other things. But this fellow William Munny is a renegade.

'The script was unusual, because David Peoples had approached it from a whole different thing – the fact that this guy had reached his lowest depths as a person, his background was haunting him and even to the point where he was monogamous to a deceased wife and even in death, she continued to be a great influence on him.

'And here's this young guy, the "Schofield Kid", coming along, who represents everything he was at one time in his life long past – and that's what he realises when he says: "That's a hell of a thing you're carrying there." He probably didn't think so when he was that age, but this kid is learning it early, and just as well.

'The story is everything. Whether it's a book or a screenplay, the story drives everything. If you don't have the material, the characters and the things to overcome and conflicts that give life to drama, you don't have it.

'I knew it was time to do *Unforgiven* – for me, anyway – to do that picture. I never thought it would make money. I just thought that this was a story I wanted to tell, my conclusion as to what the Western mythology is. And if I was ever going to do a last Western, it was the perfect one.

'It's very, very difficult to do stories about the West that are not rehashes of a lot of things that have been seen before. I couldn't tell you why my Westerns work. If you have a pretty good eye for material, and you can instinctively say: "OK, I understand these characters. This is a good story" – that's a knack.

'You're only as good as your choice of material. A lot of great actors have slid down their careers by just picking junk. And a lot of mediocre actors have sustained careers by having a little bit of an eye, and some luck.

'You can get a certain audience enraptured by the gun thing. If a movie doesn't have a good plot and I don't really care about the people, I couldn't care less. Starting out in violent pictures and shoot-'em-ups, I suppose if somebody gave me a great action-oriented film now that at least had a good storyline, then I would entertain it, but I'm not looking for that sort of thing. I figure there are a lot of younger guys out there who can do that stuff.

'John Wayne an influence? Wayne always seemed vulnerable with women. I've never felt that brutality toward women was a sign of masculinity. Probably the opposite is true. A lot of people thought he was one-dimensional, he always played John Wayne. But he took some bold chances.

'He played very villainous in *Red River*. He wasn't afraid to play a guy much older than he was, and to play all the rough edges of that. Of course, he was magnificent in *The Searchers*, and he just went ahead and boldly played an out-and-out racist. People don't associate that with him, because, like Gary Cooper, his strong personality overrode his acting ability.'

And maybe that's what happened when Eastwood lost out on the Oscar for Best Actor (it went to Al Pacino for *Scent of a Woman*). But the movie he felt so obsessive and parental about won Best Picture and he took the honours for Best Director. He says he knew on 29 March 1993 that he had won the Academy Award as Best Director by the grin on presenter Barbra Streisand's face – something he'd see in similar circumstances again.

It was his friend Jack Nicholson who handed him the Best Picture Oscar that evening.

And later another example of Clint's loyalty was displayed. Nicky Blair had been a young actor with him and also a talented chef. He made meals for his hard-up friends. By 1993 Blair had one of the most famous restaurants in

Hollywood – and Clint wanted to celebrate there, for old time's sake.

He meant it to be a quiet evening at 'Nicky Blair's', friends and family. It was a mob scene; more camera crews than all the ones he'd ever worked with over the years.

Joel Cox had an Oscar. Gene Hackman had an Oscar. Clint had two, but it was *Unforgiven* that beat them all – it was responsible for all four Academy Awards.

It had been, as he said, for him, the right time to make that movie.

As was the timing for *In the Line of Fire*. For this he became a 'hired hand'; it was his first film away from Warner Brothers since 1979 and *Escape from Alcatraz*, and Malpaso had no involvement.

He worked well with the director, Wolfang (*Das Boot*) Petersen, and his co-stars, John Malkovich and Rene Russo, establishing with Russo a marvellous, romantic screen chemistry.

He made the film as glory after glory was being heaped on *Unforgiven* and this gave him the confidence to go along with the improvisations of sometimes maverick actor Malkovich. Petersen worked differently to him but they established a bravo partnership and the director said he left the movie an even greater fan than when he began.

To Petersen's surprise, Clint offered to do the scene where he hangs from a ledge above an alley for real, with only a harness and a wire set in the wall to protect him; there were no safety precautions in the alley below.

They made a fun movie. As Secret Service agent Frank Horrigan he has to hunt down Malkovich's Mitch Leary, a former government assassin turned renegade out to get the President. Horrigan was present at JFK's assassination in 1963 and is still haunted by his failure to protect President Kennedy by taking the fatal bullet.

*In the Line of Fire* was a hugely successful film, at the box office and for Clint. As Horrigan he describes himself as a 'white, piano-playing, heterosexual male over the age of fifty' and that, like several other lines, he had a grand time saying. He embraced the role like an old friend. And it worked.

He was swiftly back in action with Malpaso, in the director's chair once again – and as Kevin Costner's co-star in 1993's *A Perfect World*. This was the first film since *Where Eagles Dare* and *Paint Your Wagon* in 1969 for which Clint did not receive top billing, which went to flavour of the moment Costner.

Yet all involved knew who was in charge. That became abundantly clear following a true incident which has now become part of film lore on the internet and in scores of articles. The story originated in a 1996 biography by admired film critic Richard Schickel.

In the film, which won plaudits for Clint as director, Costner played escaped convict Butch Haynes, who takes hostage a seven-year-old boy played by T.J. Lowther. The relationship between the convict and the boy is the heart of the piece as Clint leads the manhunt as Texas Ranger Red Garnett. The pursuit through 1963 Texas – JFK's death in Dallas not far in the future – takes over the movie. It is relentless.

The production was pressured. In one scene Costner as the runaway convict has a moment's scene with an extra who simply has to wave a greeting at him. The extra kept getting the timing wrong. Costner walked off the set.

Clint looked around and saw Costner's stand-in – in costume. He filmed the scene using the stand-in. Then he did some more work with the stand-in running, the camera filming him from behind.

A calmer Costner reappeared and Schickel recounted the conversation between the two men.

Costner: 'What's up?'

Clint: 'Nothing. We shot everything.'

'What do you mean?'

'It's all done. I used a double here.'

'Whoa. Well, I mean, you shouldn't have. I mean, you didn't have to.'

'Daly and Semel [Warner Brothers executives] pay me to shoot film. If you walk off, I'll shoot close-ups of this double. Because I'm going to shoot film.'

'You wouldn't do that, would you?'

'You watch. This guy'll play the whole movie. It may not match anything, but you know, that's what I'm here for. I'm not here to jerk off.'

Costner reportedly gave a half smile and said: 'OK.'

Eastwood commented: 'Everything went pretty well after that.'

There was also much personal pressure. Frances Fisher was pregnant and after nearly a day's labour gave birth to Francesca Ruth Fisher-Eastwood – 'Frannie' – on 7 August 1993.

Clint devoted himself to mother and child; it was an ideal time for them following friction between the couple which mostly centred on Eastwood's selfless or not commitment. Professionally, he was being applauded, and in September that year was presented with membership of the British Film Institute by Prince Charles. His acclaim was widespread; he was asked and accepted the job of chairman of the Cannes Film Festival jury in 1994. His back-up, the vice-president of the jury, was the beautiful and legendary French actress Catherine Deneuve, whom, many years earlier, in the era of *A Fistful of Dollars*, he had known intimately while doing promotional work in Paris.

Despite the birth of Frannie, his relationship with Frances Fisher was fraught. She had her 'needs' personally and professionally. He, as always, simply wanted to get on. Without fuss. He had spent time with the television journalist Dina Ruiz, whom he'd met in the aftermath excitement of *Unforgiven* and encountered many months later at a town meeting in Carmel. It was, they insist several years later, a friendship rather than a romance at that stage.

Eastwood acknowledges his need to go about his personal and professional business without the trappings of success, without making fanfare out of the day. When told that Henry Bumstead said he took the bullshit out of film-making he replied: 'That's flattering coming from him. Bummy knows his stuff. As a designer, he's still the best, still putting out, at his age. The actual ages of these people, the ones who can do what he does at that level, don't mean a thing. He knows how it was with some of the special people I worked with too in what might be called the great era of movie-making. They were terrific people, like John Calley and Don Siegel. They read a lot. They knew a lot. If you asked one of them a question, you got an answer.

'Today, there are many differences. We have a lot more technology, a lot of toys to play with, but they don't necessarily do anything to make movies better. Unfortunately, today, when a movie is successful, they try to make 20 more like it.

'Billy Wilder was asked: "What's a modern screenplay?" and he said: "The modern screenplay is where you build a set and then you blow it up." That would sum it up. Nowadays you'd have many battles before you blow it up, but eventually you'd take it down. And that's OK, I don't heavily quarrel with that, but for me personally, having made films for years and directed for years, I long for people who want to see a story and see character development. Maybe there's not really an audience for that, but that's not for me to really worry about. So, we keep trying.

'Some people have wanted me to do *Dirty Harry* again. Harry or Josey Wales were just characters, and they came with a dramatic situation. They weren't like me, and the less they were like me, the more fun it was to do them. However, at some point in your life that kind of thing becomes less challenging. You have to start to grow within yourself, or else you'll start going backwards.

'I don't understand Sylvester Stallone. I hear he's going to do *Rocky* again. For me, it would look like you're doing it for the paycheck. I like to move on. I enjoyed making *The Bridges of Madison County*.'

He's brought several books to the screen, including *Midnight in the Garden of Good and Evil*, *Blood Work* and

*Absolute Power*, with differing success and admitted: 'It's hard to take a book and put it on the screen. You try to capture what the author captured, or your interpretation thereof. Really, when you do books, you're always open to some criticism. A lot of people didn't care for the book *The Bridges of Madison County*; they thought Robert James Waller was a second-rate writer. Some folks thought it was sappy, the paradigm of the last cowboy.

'And I didn't like that either. But I thought the idea of these people meeting – and neither one of them is dying of incurable diseases, but it still doesn't work out – was kind of hip. And so I just took out all of what I thought was drivel. By and large, it did well.

'I hadn't read the book when one day the producer Lili Zanuck called me and told me to read it. She said: "You're in it." I hung up. The phone rang again. It was Terry Semel, who was then co-head at Warner Brothers. He said: "There's a lot of you in the character."

'So, I read the book and fought my way through the fancy, pretentious writing. I could see the story. In my mind, however, I saw it as a woman's story. So that's what it became as a movie. What often has set me off in making a movie is a song. I did it once before in *Play Misty for Me*. In *Bridges* for the love scene in the kitchen where I dance with Meryl Streep, I used the song "I See Your Face Before Me" by Johnny Hartman. Music often leads me into the sequence.'

Eastwood also composed the theme 'Doe Eyes' for the movie and it's what telephone callers to his Mission Ranch at the mouth of Carmel River, which he bought and saved from less than historic development in 1986, hear when they are put on hold. It was there for a very telling reason.

*The Bridges of Madison County*, released in 1995, was a rare example of a movie improving on the book. Adapted from the huge bestseller by Robert James Waller, the film told the simple story of Meryl Streep's Iowa housewife Francesca – by happenstance the name Frances Fisher gave her and Clint's daughter – Johnson who meets Eastwood's travelling *National Geographic* photographer Robert Kincaid; he has arrived in Madison County to photograph its picturesque covered bridges.

It's *Brief Encounter*.

Consummated.

While Francesca's husband and children are out of town she and Kincaid begin a four-day affair they both know can never be more than that.

A framing story follows Francesca's children, after her death, as they discover their mother's secret and take stock of their own lives. Eastwood and Streep won plaudits – and Clint, in his first, full romantic leading man role, thrived in partnership with the accomplished Streep.

He was facing retirement age – 65. He had much to consider. Frances Fisher had asked for the role of Francesca's daughter in the back-up story of *Bridges* but Eastwood thought that was not a good idea. He was apparently feeling pressured. He was devoted to Francesca but the relationship with her mother was becoming more and more difficult.

And he was more and more intrigued by Dina Ruiz. Or 'Doe Eyes'.

Dina Ruiz was what that 'Love Theme from the Bridges

of Madison County' theme tune was all about: the inspiration for an older man who'd just made a movie about missing out on long-term love. A movie about missed opportunity.

And to spice it up even more there were rumours that he and Meryl Streep had been as enamoured and intense off screen as they were on. But they both said it was good acting and dismissed the reports of romantic involvement that had appeared in the *Los Angeles Times*, which, as Hollywood's local paper, is usually above reporting on such matters.

It was also at this time that Frances Fisher found out about what she called his 'other family', Jacelyn Reeves and her and Clint's kids, Scott and Katie. It was a difficult time for Eastwood. His close friend Jane Brolin, the one-time wife of actor James Brolin, who is now married to Barbra Streisand, was killed in a car accident. It followed the death of another friend, and in this case mentor, Frank Wells, a powerful Hollywood executive and, most of all, a buddy, 'one of the good guys'.

Eastwood was awash in a very complex time in his life. He'd never made the arithmetic simple. But this was a more than usually difficult time. It reflects his character, his way of thinking, that he was most single-minded about all these emotional meteors crashing in on him.

It was reported that Frances Fisher suggested they spent a quiet weekend together to get over all the trauma.

Eastwood said it might be easier for him to deal with everything, not dwell on all that had happened, by taking part in the Bob Hope Desert Classic Golf Tournament in Indian Wells, near Palm Springs. So in February 1995 he went off to the upmarket oasis in the Californian desert.

It was a couple of weeks later that Frances Fisher first saw the photographs of Clint and Dina Ruiz at the golf tournament. And they were looking very friendly; 'snuzzling', according to one American newspaper caption. That they were doing it publicly was what was important for Eastwood and his fraternity.

# THIRTEEN

# THE SECOND
# MRS EASTWOOD

'He's a philanthropist, not a philanderer.'
DINA RUIZ, AUGUST 1996

DINA Ruiz became Clint Eastwood's second wife on 31
March 1996. They married at the home of his friend Steve
Wynn, who owns much property and casinos in Las Vegas
and also the Shadow Creek golf club, near where the
wedding ceremony took place.

Kyle Eastwood was his father's best man; Alison
Eastwood was among the guests. Dina Ruiz was escorted
down the aisle by her father, a part African-American, part
Japanese, school teacher, for the ceremony, conducted by
the Reverend Judy from Las Vegas.

The bank played 'Doe Eyes' and 'Unforgettable' and later
the new Mrs Eastwood said: 'The fact that I am only the
second woman he has married really touches me.'

For there had been many relationships. That was emphasised on their honeymoon in Hawaii. On the island of Maui they met up with Clint's former lover Jacelyn Reeves and his and her two children.

It was reported and never denied that during the meeting between his present wife and former lover the two women talked babies; 'mommy advice' was given and accepted.

Apparently, it was during the Hawaiian honeymoon that Dina Ruiz Eastwood became pregnant with Eastwood's seventh known child. Others have approached Eastwood suggesting that he is their father but not been acknowledged. Sondra Locke made a caustic comment saying it was 'sad' that he had chosen to marry someone who was not the mother of one of his children when he had not married others who were.

Yet Eastwood was having a prime time. As always, he dwelled on the present, not the past. He received the American Film Institute's Life Achievement Award and a string of other honours; but he was back at work on location scouting for his next movie, *Absolute Power*. He certainly seemed to have that. It was during this time that it became certain that his new wife had become pregnant in Hawaii.

Washington lawyer David Baldacci's political thriller about superstar professional thief Luther Whitney, who witnesses a little too much, was crafted as a vehicle for Eastwood. The usual suspects were present, including Gene Hackman, giving a turn as a shallow, evil US President and Australian actress Judy Davis as his amoral Chief of Staff. Also in the cast was Laura Linney, and making appearances were Clint's daughters Alison and Kimber Eastwood.

Luther Whitney is an ageing master thief who, when we first see him, is sitting alone in an art gallery making sketches of one of the paintings. Later that night he breaks into a large country house, whose occupants are on holiday in Bermuda, defeating the complex security system with relative ease; he proceeds to remove the contents of the vault, situated off the master bedroom.

However, the mistress of the house returns unexpectedly with a man (who turns out to be President Allen Richmond), both drunk. Luther takes refuge in the vault, the door of which is a two-way mirror, and witnesses the scene which follows.

Events in the next room turn violent: the woman stabs Richmond in the arm with a letter opener and is about to wound him further, when two Secret Service agents burst in and shoot her dead. Gloria Russell, the President's Chief of Staff, then enters and swiftly organises a cover-up, making it look like she surprised a burglar, but in the confusion the letter opener (which has both sets of fingerprints and the President's blood on it) gets left behind. Luther picks it up when they have left. Realising they don't have it, the agents rush back and chase Luther, but he escapes.

And the intrigue and action begin in a movie which was a throwback to Eastwood's earlier work rather than a celebration of his success as both director and actor in *Unforgiven* and *The Bridges of Madison County*. This was 1980s Eastwood but it had a personal significance for him. Kimber, his daughter by actress Roxanne Tunis, appears as the White House tour guide. But it was his relationship with Alison which brought the story close to home for him.

It told of a troubled father-daughter relationship. 'I'd been there – I could relate to that.' He is referring to his once difficult relationship with Alison, who appears in the first scene of the film as an art student looking at Luther's sketching and telling him: 'Don't give up', his reply being: 'I never do.'

Alison was also with her father in 1997's *Midnight in the Garden of Good and Evil*, which revolves around the visit of a New York writer sent to Savannah, Georgia, to cover a very prestigious Christmas party. This elegant, lavish and stylish event is given each year by Jim Williams, one of Savannah's most prominent and colorful citizens.

Williams (Kevin Spacey) is an antiques dealer, collector and restoration specialist who has built his wealth through the reconstruction and sale of the numerous 18th- and 19th-century homes which elegantly frame the city's historic squares. His own home, Mercer House, is located on the corner of Monterey Square and was built in 1860 by General Hugh Mercer, whose great-grandson was popular songwriter Johnny Mercer. The house is an elegant, stately Southern mansion.

Writer John Kelso's (John Cusack) assignment seems straightforward. He will simply immerse himself in Savannah's gracious atmosphere and describe the colorful history of Mercer House. He will highlight the party preparations and Jim Williams's exclusive guest list. Finally, he will attend the elegant black-tie event and report on the festivities.

Things don't quite work out that way. In a sequence of events set in motion following his courtly Christmas party,

Williams is arrested for murder. Claiming self-defence, he has shot and killed his live-in lover, Billy Hanson (Jude Law), who seems to have had a history of irrational, often violent behaviour.

This was Eastwood's twentieth film as director and only the third in which he does not appear. Although not a bad film, it didn't enjoy anywhere near as much success as the book it was based on.

Nevertheless, the avid reader Eastwood was after another book, *Blood Work*, by another highly successful novelist, Michael Connelly. It was a perfect role for him – right age, right style. The hero is a retired FBI specialist on serial killers who has undergone a heart transplant. He is asked to go back to work by the sister of his murdered heart donor. It's a good plot and read. Eastwood worked with Connelly on the conclusion of the book before it was published.

But first he had to plan to go into space, and make *True Crime*, based on yet another bestseller. As always, he kept the production tight. *True Crime* was shot in just seven weeks, around the Bay area of San Francisco, where he grew up and where the five Dirty Harry movies were filmed.

Steve Everett (Eastwood) is an investigative reporter with a lot of problems. An alcoholic, he's only been sober for two months. An unrelenting womaniser, he's on the verge of being thrown out by his wife, Barbara (Diane Venora). Thanks to his messy personal life, he was fired from the *New York Times*. He has since relocated to the West Coast and the *Oakland Tribune*. If it wasn't for his friend Alan Mann (James Woods), the *Tribune*'s editor-in-chief, he wouldn't have a job at all.

The move to California and the last-chance job haven't really influenced Everett's style much, which angers the *Tribune*'s city editor, Bob Findley (Denis Leary). Everett's behaviour has personal consequences for Findley that make their work situation even more hostile. In fact, when Findley wants to send Everett on a particular assignment, he calls home and asks his own wife, who is in bed with Everett at the time, to please put him on the phone.

It seems that another reporter, covering the impending San Quentin execution of convicted murderer Frank Beachum (Isaiah Washington), has been killed in a car crash. The final interview with the condemned man has therefore been handed to Everett, who reluctantly begins to do a little research on the case, anticipating a routine story.

Everett's background check on Frank Beachum, connected to the details of the robbery and homicide, which took place in an Oakland convenience store, just doesn't add up. When he meets Beachum at the prison, he receives information that confirms his instincts. He quickly begins a manic search for information which will stay the condemned man's execution.

Eastwood enjoyed the film: 'It's half a character-study and half a mystery unravelling. It's not the kind of movie they're doing today, you know – it's hampered by having a story. But I think there's somebody out there who appreciates that, so I'll keep on trying.

'Most editors wouldn't have an old guy like that around. He's an obsessive personality. He believes that when he has a feeling for something, it's the right thing to do, but that's taken him down a bad path. He's chasing salvation and has never found it.

'It's fun to play people who are flawed, but have some redeeming features. This character's a womaniser, he's been an alcoholic, he smokes cigarettes. Everything that's politically incorrect. I love that. If it's incorrect, I'm going to find it interesting.'

Eastwood's daughter Francesca appears in *True Crime*, as does Frances Fisher.

'It was written originally that he had a son, and then I thought that maybe it would be better if it was the other gender, and also what a big risk using little Frannie would be, because at that time she was just turning five. Having worked with orang-utans and children before, I think I can keep their interest and try to shoot at the time when you have their interest-level the most.

'Frances Fisher? Absolutely. We're still friendly. Frances is a very good actress, so I might as well use her as someone else. I figured maybe the antagonism would come easier. She might enjoy it.'

Next he made *Space Cowboys*, co-starring with James Garner, Tommy Lee Jones and Donald Sutherland as geriatric astronauts who are brought back to complete one more mission for NASA.

The scenes filmed at the Johnson Space Center in Houston, Texas, included training sequences in which the entire team was put through virtually the same training phases used to prepare actual astronauts for space travel.

'I wanted to make the film as believable as possible. In order to do that we needed NASA's help to get as close as we could to the circumstances surrounding a launch. It's a complicated process and it requires careful planning and teamwork on all levels. Bringing a film crew in to simulate the whole thing was probably an even bigger headache for NASA, but the Agency really came through for us.

'I think we've been pretty good with it. We've used every trick possible, from where the actors are floating themselves and looking loose, or sitting on a special kind of bench that moves this way or a table gliding, or gliding across the floor.

'In previous space-set films, the cast and production crew would all fly up in a giant cargo plane to achieve weightlessness for a few seconds at a stretch. They used to call it the "Vomit Comet", which is an old G-3 that they would take up and get into a weightless situation and then you would try to play a scene. If you were in a small container, you could do that and build the set on the plane. But it got that nickname for a reason. It was a little harder this way, but it beat the alternative.'

He was now ready to tackle *Blood Work*. At one level it's vintage Eastwood; he plays hotshot FBI profiler Terry McCaleb, who until he suffers a massive heart attack was a can-do success. Now he must, moment by moment, look after his new heart – and try to catch a psycho killer. 'It's a detective story and a human relationship story. This project was an opportunity for me to take a different approach to detective work, which I've been associated with over the years. At this particular stage in my maturity, I felt it was time to take on characters that have different obstacles to face than they would if I were playing a younger man of 30 or 40.

'I especially like McCaleb's vulnerability, both physically and psychologically, which presents an interesting challenge for him to overcome. He's a guy who is very good at his job and committed to it; then, all of a sudden, he's forced into retirement. He's trying to enjoy it as best he can, given the situation, and live in peace on his boat in the San Pedro Harbour until a stranger comes to him for help.'

For the role of Graciella Rivers, the beautiful stranger who convinces McCaleb to come out of retirement and risk his tenuous recovery to help her solve her sister's inexplicable murder, Eastwood cast accomplished actress Wanda De Jesus. 'In the novel, Graciella was written as a Latino woman, and I wanted to stay true to the book in that regard. In the screenplay, the character is described as a woman strengthened by adversity, not beaten by it, and Wanda communicates this quality beautifully.

'We shot this film in 38 days, and that's quick by today's standards; shooting at that pace might make others uncomfortable, but I've been doing this a long time and I don't feel that I compromise anything by doing so. If somebody said: "Shoot it in 45 days", I don't know what I'd do any differently, besides having a couple of days off. Everybody works hard, we get it done and then we move on.'

Anjelica Huston – Clint played her father, John Huston, in *White Hunter, Black Heart* – appeared as McCaleb's heart doctor and said: '*Blood Work* was one of the more relaxed, extremely operational and good-humoured sets that I've ever been on, and I think that's due to the fact that most of the crew have worked with Clint for many years. There's a kind of shorthand between them, and a wonderful camaraderie and interest in the work.

'Also, Clint's a funny guy and he keeps everyone in a good mood. He makes it look simple. My father had an expression whenever I came to him with big questions, which was: "Just do it, honey." And Clint seems to just do it beautifully.

'I spent many years with my father in Intensive Care Units and watched him undergo a heart aneurysm operation. He was not well for the last 12 years of his life. So the combination of my experience with my father in hospital and Clint's having played him in *White Hunter, Black Heart* was strangely convergent.

'In terms of the man Clint is, his way of being, his ease and calm, reminds me a lot of my father. He has a wonderful way of slow talking and slow moving that just makes you feel right at home. His style really lends itself to a relaxation on set that is tremendously useful and calming for an actor, particularly when you come in nervous to work with Mr Eastwood.'

Co-star Jeff Daniels nearly made more impact on the movie than anyone else: 'It was my second or third day of filming, and I was driving, Clint was sitting in the passenger seat and the camera and operator were positioned in the back seat. The sun was going down, and I was manoeuvring the car along this curvy road as we're playing the scene and trying to nail the shot before losing the light. The car's side mirror was catching a reflection of the camera, so they asked me to adjust it.

'As I'm fixing the mirror, I see Clint reach across me, grab the wheel and turn it just slightly. I looked up and realised that he had very calmly avoided a head-on collision with a mini- van coming around the turn.

'I froze, thinking: I almost killed him! I almost killed Clint Eastwood!'

He's not going to go that easily. Clint acted in almost every scene of the film and performed his own stunts: 'I've been doing this a lot of years and it was particularly difficult on this picture but I enjoy the whole process and I want to give the audience their money's worth. It's a demanding job, both physically and mentally, and I wouldn't have it any other way. It's not supposed to be easy; it's supposed to be fun. Each step is involving and requires serious preparation. I don't care if it's the planning or design of a film, the execution or the editing: I'm there and I'm part of it.'

When Eastwood moved to south Boston to work on *Mystic River* in 2003 he joked that he did not even have to take a suitcase. 'You don't need to bring your own clothes when you work here,' he told visitors to his film set. He'd been given dozens of T-shirts by local organisations, unions, the police and firemen, and made a point of wearing a different one during each day of filming.

The film, always the story for Eastwood, this time by respected and impressively selling novelist Dennis Lehane, revolves around three blue-collar friends, Jimmy (Sean Penn), Dave (Tim Robbins) and Sean (Kevin Bacon); their demon is in the past and involves sexual abuse.

For Eastwood, it was an impressive line-up of talent. He said during filming: 'These actors are so good and so enthusiastic and they've all worked and prepared so hard, it's for me alone to screw-up. There are so many characters and the story weaves back and forth in time, so those are the only difficult aspects for me to deal with. I stay close to the impression of the story I got when I first read it. Sometimes embellishments just come. The actors bring them to me.'

He was the director of *Mystic River* and not a player in it: 'It feels great. This is just more fun. As an actor, I'm constantly being fiddled with. I'm being told: "You gotta do this, you gotta do that." Somebody is always fussing over my hair, someone else is tampering with my skin.

'Here I come to the set in my T-shirt, jeans and sneakers and nobody cares what I look like. I'm free, free of extra pressure, the constant worry of how I'm doing and what I'm doing. As the director I want to be watching my actors – it's fun to watch the emotions in actors unfold. If it weren't fun, I wouldn't be doing it.'

In one scene Sean Penn's Jimmy – Penn won the Oscar for Best Actor, Tim Robbins for Best Supporting Actor for *Mystic River* – discovers the body of his murdered teenaged daughter. It was painful and powerful acting and Penn's director said: 'I try to get what I have in mind but if an actor does what he has in his mind and it's anything like I just saw here with Sean, I'm very grateful to take it. It's like going to a store and seeing all the suits on the rack and seeing one that makes you feel: "That's exactly what I had in mind." He's a terrific actor – and that's all I was looking for.

'I never had to work with someone like a Marilyn Monroe, who, I've heard, made everybody wait for three hours before showing up, that sort of thing – that would drive me fruitcake.'

# FOURTEEN

## SELF-PERCEPTION

'It's a special film set when you're standing
there watching Clint Eastwood stride down the
middle of a California boulevard with a sawed-off
shotgun, blowing away a Ford.'

JEFF DANIELS, 2002

CLINT Eastwood has always had the reputation of not
being a talker but that is a misconception – a movie myth.

He had, until the late 1990s, been reluctant to talk at any
length about his private life. But he has always been willing
to talk about himself and his work, and his views on that and
on his public and politics give insight into his personality.
The world has changed dramatically since the late 1960s,
when he became an international superstar, but a decade
earlier he was already a television name worldwide.

Eastwood has been an influence for more than three decades but although he talks with assurance, he makes his points quietly: 'I'm at an age now where a lot of people have grown up with my films and gone through a lot of stages of their life with me. It means more sometimes when you look back. I don't wear make-up. I think it looks bad on men and sometimes on women and I don't wear it. If I look up on the screen one day and say: "OK, this is silly for the guy to be playing this kind of role," I'll step back and direct some films.'

Nevertheless, Eastwood maintains a rigid diet and exercise routine, although he insists: 'I'm not really a fitness fanatic. I just want to feel good. Some people think that when you're older you're supposed to sit down and watch TV reruns and squeeze beer cans. That isn't for me. I don't know if people want to meet me exactly. I get the feeling sometimes that people would rather have me pull out a .44 Magnum and say: "Do you feel lucky, punk?" They'd much rather meet the character than me.

'I've probably had as many profitable films as any actor around and maybe more. I just have to satisfy myself. Hopefully, I've made enough money for financiers in the business that I can afford myself a change of pace now and then. If you do a few small films you love and they're not commercial, they're sometimes better for you than doing a massive commercial thing that people take lightly. People may think more of you as an actor.

'Though I like Westerns and I like cop dramas, I'd hate to turn around 20 years from now and say: "Well, I did 900 cop dramas and 800 Westerns, and that was it." The truth is, I've done a lot of things. I just like certain movies. My performances vary a lot, a lot more than people think they do. Because I'm not an extroverted, extremely mobile type, I play things in reserve a lot of times, so people think my performances are similar. But if you place them side by side, you'll find they're quite a bit different. *The Outlaw Josey Wales* was really nice work – as good as I can do. *Dirty Harry* I thought was good, for a certain style that worked for me. It might have been harder for somebody else.

'Some actors try to show as much as they can. When you start in drama class, that's what you learn, to express as much as you can, express so much you tell the story without the dialogue. In your face. So, when you tell the story with the dialogue, it's a very expressive kind of thing. But if you look back through history, the people who have been the strongest in film were people who could express a lot by holding certain things in reserve, holding a certain amount in reserve so that the audience is curious to find what the reserve is. If you're reserved, the audience is constantly reaching forward to the character on the screen. If they sit back, they say: "OK, that was great, give 'em four stars for the news or something." But they're not interested in going back.

'I know I watch myself. I edit film of myself and I always have to look at him. Such as cut to him over there. I always think of "him" as another person on film. But in real life I'm not complicated. Yet I am complicated, I suppose. I like simple things, yet I'm obviously more complex than I appear on the surface.

'Learning and refining and growing, that is what is fun

about maturing in life. The downside is maturing, and the upside is maturing. Your tastes get broader and you appreciate things a lot more. You look back on things you overlooked as a youth and say: "My God, how could I have been that stupid?"

'They didn't have any schools in film when I started out, but they are quite popular now. I learned through hanging about. I have limitations, same as everybody. More than a lot of people. Certain things I do OK. Life is like a multiple-choice test. You can talk yourself out of the right answer most of the time if you think too hard and long about it. Most people have the ability to rely on their natural instincts, but too often they ignore them.

'I suppose I've regrets about a lot of things, but I don't think about those things. I look forward to what's going on now and tomorrow. If everybody dwelt in the past, you'd see them with tears in their eyes. Everyone's made certain mistakes they would have corrected if it had been possible, but it isn't possible, so you just go on.

'As an actor I'm a little hard to understand, if you try analysing it. The public seems to understand me on an instinctive basis. Sometimes when people can't break something down, they get bugged by it. But I guess I'm kind of an oddity.'

An oddity? Well certainly one who has made a fortune. But as we have seen, he is not one to flaunt it.

'Sure, money is nice. I wouldn't want to be broke, but it doesn't mean much to me really. I don't have a lot of needs; I spend a little; invest a little. I just try to take care of my family and the people close to me. I get periods of being obsessed by work but when I play I just 1-a-y back. I go through periods of just not wanting to do anything, maybe just sitting at home watching whatever's on TV. An actor's lament, of course, is you're always wondering where your next job's coming from and the plain truth of the matter is that the majority of the Screen Actors' Guild have a rough time making a living, just staying in that profession only. It's a tough profession. You have to really want it. If you're in it just for the dough, then you'll get a rude awakening. And if you're lucky – I use that word a lot – you can made a fine good living in the profession. I never begged for respectability. I never said: "Come, let me show you, come like me."

'I guess I can lie like anybody else, but I don't like it. I'd hate to exist constantly, day in, day out, having to come up with something. Having to come up with something whether it's the truth, a variation of the truth or whether it's an outright lie or variations on a lie. I don't really know myself. I don't think too much of myself.

'I remember going on interviews – cattle-call type – with 10, 15, maybe 20 guys all your size and colouring. Every interview you go to you see the same people. I was never very good at the presentation at the office for some reason. I always got somehow dim-witted. I met a lot of people that I suppose knew a lot, and I met a lot of people that didn't know a lot, so I'm always very careful when I interview actors not to put them through any undue stress. I don't like to read actors because I can't stand to do that. I'll look at film often while doing research before I'll ever meet them, so that way I never get their hopes up if I'm considering somebody else. It's more work, but it's just a matter of sensitivity. Once you've been sort of mentally kicked around you kind of become aware of that. There's an awful lot of other people that are really good that are overlooked. I like to try to reach out and grab them if I can.'

Eastwood's image is much more macho than mediator but he has always thought of himself as a daydreamer, right from his schooldays, making up stories and characters.

'I've always kind of meditated. I was a daydreamer as a kid. I just like being by myself and meditating. I think a certain kind of meditation is good for anybody for some sort of peace of mind. Some people find it looking at the ocean, some people find it in religion. It depends on the individual. I don't believe in the old adage that men shouldn't cry. If a person feels like crying it's probably the greatest catharsis in the world. I don't get as emotional as the next person, everybody reacts differently.'

But he's practical about what he describes as only 'the job'.

'I just figured I'd do the job. I remember when I was first starting out everyone used to sit around and argue about whether we wanted to be great actors or movie stars. Of course, everyone would say: "Well, I'd rather be a great actor" because that's the idealistic and noble thing to say. But then if you start analysing it, the movie star gets offered all the great roles. And it's nice to be in a position of power where you can generate the kind of roles you like to play.

'Everyone here wants to get side-tracked – get in a series, make a lot of money. Of course, British actors like to make a lot of money too, but they take their work seriously. And generally speaking, American actors don't have the versatility. They do one thing well and that's it. I suppose I have to put myself in that category. Certain things I do are OK, I guess, but I'm not the kind of actor who'll play a 25-year-old bank clerk one day and a 90-year-old derelict the next.

'I was never a discovery of the press. I never had a publicity build-up or any amazing covers. I had to have the success first. I don't try to be a parody of myself. After I had acted for a few years and was thrown out of Universal and voted least likely to succeed as a contract player, I did an awful Western. It was so bad they didn't even show it to the cast and crew, they just put it out. When I finally saw it, I just slid lower and lower in the seat. I thought: I've got to get out of this business, I've just got to get out. My wife at the time encouraged me, and I finally mustered up the sand and said: "I'm going to win this game." But I don't mind being pessimistic at times.

'Wherever I came from, I always came out of left field. I wasn't predicted to do anything. So it was easy to say that this guy was going nowhere. And then when he does try to do something, maybe that disappoints the soothsayers who've decided his type isn't supposed to do anything at all.

'I never second-guess audiences because many times they're just so much further ahead of you. And then sometimes they miss what you think you've been explaining so simply. So, you can't second-guess. All you do is build on your own instinctive reactions. That tells you what to do. You do it the best way you know how, and hope, of course, that somebody likes it.

'I can't be analytical about it, it's an animalistic kind of thing. Acting isn't a very intellectual art really; in fact it's not intellectual at all. People like to intellectualise about it and others like to make out it's a very misty thing but the basis for acting is very childlike; that's why children are brilliant actors – they can fantasise about anything. We just stack on the inhibitions as we grow up.

'There must be plenty of people a lot prettier than I am. I suppose somehow it is the combination of the way I sound, the way I think and somewhere in there I've managed to represent to people something that they like. They like an element of escapism and I evidently have been able to transmit some of the escapist thing. Men can probably identify more with me than the prettier actor. They might say: "I'd like to be able to do what this character is doing." And the female audiences – well maybe they'd say: "If I were involved in that story, I'd like to have this man on my side."

'Everybody has to play characters that suit them. Somebody else might try the same characters and it might not work. There are a lot of marvellous actors in the world with better training and schooling than me but if they'd played Dirty Harry it wouldn't suit them. Olivier would have looked ridiculous with a poncho and pistol.

'Everybody likes to draw a picture of you walking into a supermarket and a director coming up and saying: "Hey, you're the lead in my next movie," but that's a dream. Anyway, if that had happened I wouldn't have been prepared. It would have been a disaster.

'To some people I represent a dying individuality within our system. I feel there is a crying out for individuality. I feel that because of the intellect, the human race, we've bogged ourselves down in such bureaucratic nonsense, that it seems like we have made life much more complicated than it should be.'

He's been called complex. And complicated. Has he failings? Things he doesn't like about himself?

'I guess I am vain. I never thought about it. I don't look in the mirror and ask: "Who is the fairest of them all?" If you do that a voice comes out and says: "Snow White, baby, and don't you forget it!" I have never come to the point where I wish I was back a few years. I have always felt every year is always better than the last.

'I hate to be mauled. I don't like large crowds of people. I like people but I'm not that comfortable with them. I've been on film sets where after lunch, girls came up and asked for my dirty plate or empty beer bottle. It has a lot of downsides. You don't have a certain amount of privacy in your life and I am kind of a private person. Once in a while it has an upside. It can get a table down front or something.

'People like different things. Stardom enables you to get a front-row seat but it also means you are stared at, that you are constantly interrupted by people recognising you, you're always the observed rather than the observer. But then people have spent their time viewing you, so you've had some effect on them through your entertainment, probably brought something into their life. You must consider that and accept it.

'I tell people if you really want to do it, you must be willing to study it and stick with it through all opposition and having to deal with some of the most no-talent people in the world passing judgement on you. They're going to pick the worst aspects of you or of anybody else they cast. If you can't take all that and keep grinding until some part comes along that fits you and your feelings, then sometimes the odds will come up for you. But you have to have that kind of perseverance.'

Of course, he has often played that sort of role, the man against the odds, and talking about his movies he warms to the subject.

'A lot of my characters are sort of the lone guy struggling against some element in society. I never felt any moral problems with these pictures. I felt they're fantasy.

'I don't think my movies are that stimulating. People in the audience just sit there and say: "I admire the independence. I'd like to have the nerve to tell the boss off or have that control over my life." In the society we live in, everything is kind of controlled for us. We just grow up and everything's kind of done. A lot of people are drawn to an original like Dirty Harry. The general public interpreted it on that level, a man concerned with a victim he'd never met. Like everybody says: "Boy, if I were the victim of violent crime, I'd sure like to have someone expend that kind of effort on my behalf." And I think a lot of people believe that there isn't anybody who's willing to expend that kind of effort if they were in that situation.

'There may not be. That may be the fantasy – that there might be someone interested in my problem if I was ever in that spot. That preys on people's mind these days with crime in America, in the world. Jesus, is there somebody there, is there anybody there?'

Eastwood has looked after himself, which of course is his great screen appeal. But it wasn't always easy simply to believe in himself.

'Everything that has been successful for me was done against advice to the contrary, including the motion-picture business to begin with. There are two types of actors – those who reach out to their audience and say: "Come, caress me" and the others who say: "Here I am. Watch me if you want." I'll give you an example from old-time actors. Kirk Douglas and Burt Lancaster were more "reach out": "I'm coming down to the front row to see you. Sit back in your seats – pow!" A lot of power. Gary Cooper and Henry Fonda were more: "Lean forward, 'cause I'm going to be talking very quietly. You're gonna have to reach for what I'm gonna give you or you'd better just leave."

'If a character doesn't grow in each film, if he doesn't learn something about life as he goes along, there isn't any sense in doing the film. I think that women have changed, men have changed, too, and I hope for the better.'

Neither is it simple to explain his intimidating work ethic.

'I shoot fast. *Play Misty for Me* was wrapped in little over five weeks. *Breezy* was completed in less than five weeks. It's not just a matter of money; I like to have momentum, to keep the spirit and energy going. To me, directing is knowing the concept you want and getting it. Shooting on location is easier, because a crew gets wrapped up in the spirit of the film. I cast my crews as carefully as I cast my actors. That's why we have such happy, democratic crews. And we move – I try not to keep people on location too long.

'A director should change camera angles a lot. My theory is when you're looking at a film, you're looking at a flat piece projected on to a flat surface. The only way you can approach a 3-D feeling is to cross over and get the camera right in there so the audience can feel a part of a group rather than just observers of a group. Camera work is a lot like penmanship: the way you film a film says as much as the way it's written.

'Casting is one of the most important aspects in making a film. A film can live or die on it. The cast has to bring those characters to life. If you miscast a character, or one stands out strong, you can throw the whole picture out of whack. It's like having a pebble in your tyre.

'People say I know just what the public wants. I don't think that people themselves know what they want until they see it or hear about it. One should judge a property [a potential film] simply by whether or not one would like to go see it. There's a lot of gut instinct going when buying or rejecting a property.

'A lot of critics thought *Dirty Harry* was sort of a right-wing film. It wasn't at all. It portrayed the circumstances that one guy was put into, and showed the frustration with our courts and our judicial system. Which is all very timely even today. The film was just ahead of itself. I try to say something different in every film and this one is about that frustration. *Play Misty for Me* was a little statement on commitment and misinterpreting commitment in men and women. There is not a Clint Eastwood message. There are lots of different messages.

'You learn from everyone you work with. I'm surrounded

by the best crew around and we all like to move at the same tempo. I think if the director is slow and ponderous, it can hurt the final project. The movie might not be as satisfying and, besides I'd get bored. My sanity would not have lasted through *Heaven's Gate*. I'm a little more patient than I used to be, but not that patient.

'In recent years I have learned to look at films and I like films a lot better. There is something about the whole film-making process that has been more important to me. As a young actor, it was different because you only cared about the overall production. That is a different thing. I have dreams to do more films. More expansive roles. As I get older, I fit more roles. Hopefully, I will be able to broaden the spectrum.

'I have my own production company. I'll probably keep that going for a long time. I have been very, very lucky to have gotten into a position where I can sort of control my destiny, so to speak; to do the kind of things I want to do. That is a dream to me and that's more important than any monetary compensation. It's an old game to say you can make a picture for such and such when you know darned well you can't, and then your financiers are vulnerable. I don't play that game. I give the financiers respect – and I demand it in return. If they don't know it, they shouldn't be hiring me. I don't know all the answers. But I don't know anyone who does.

'You do need a great deal of patience to direct any sort of film. I'm sure I was less tolerant when I was younger, although I don't think I've ever been regarded as a difficult actor to work with. I always try to be reasonably sensitive to other people's needs.

'I'm never looking for any particular type of script – they just come about. I think I've been lucky. If I had sat down and planned it that way, I probably wouldn't have planned it any better. You do things as best you can. I've always had a philosophy, I guess. I try to get as much on the screen for the money as possible. I treat the audience as having the same IQ as myself.

'I was raised with films that had a lot of action, with Gary Cooper and John Wayne and stuff. And people are interested in action in films. Action and drama and conflict seem to be the motivating force for a lot of entertainment. I like romantic films but it's easier said than done. It's so hard to find material. There's a certain element of the public who like those Dirty Harry roles and it's a great male-fantasy kind of character, but I think you can only do that so much in life and then eventually you want to branch out and do other things, and I've done other things in between.

'I think Westerns are a great form of entertainment and maybe it's a chance doing one. I never know. I don't think so. I think the public will go for it if it's any good. That's the way I felt about it all along – just because I'm in it isn't going to help. If it's not a good film, then the public doesn't feel rewarded in some way when they leave the cinema.

'You try to treat people well because they're treating you well. They're going to your films. I don't have much respect for people who look down on the public as somebody that gets in the way. After all, you asked for it, you fought to get where you are – on the other hand, you want privacy too, because otherwise if people can use you up to a point, your central nervous system goes berserk. In fact, you just do the best you can. To me, I'm still only interested in work.'

But how do you do the best work? How does *he* do his best work?

'I think every actor has a different way of getting to the same result and there's no set formula. Some people like to go bang their head against the wall to cry, and other people sit there and think about their puppy that was run over when they were ten years old. Some people just think of the situation at hand, whatever it is. Whatever way it gets you is the way there. All you're trying to do is affect the audience and make them believe that you're believable. Acting is more than ranting and raving and rolling around on the floor. I've always felt that a full barrel makes a lot less noise than an empty one. Still waters run deep.

'I always feel a responsibility to do the best I can for the people who are putting money up. But at the same time, I have to do it the way I believe. You can't try to make your film based on what people may want. I don't think studio executives are always happy to hear what I want to do. You should have heard the arguments I made to get them to let me do *Play Misty for Me*. "Who the hell wants to see Clint Eastwood play a disc jockey?" I said: "Well, who the hell wants to see me do anything?" It's good for me, and it's good for them to try other things. If I'd stayed in the Western genre I don't think I'd still be around. I don't think I'd ever have been able to do *Escape from Alcatraz* or *Bronco Billy* or *Honkytonk Man*. I wouldn't have been able to branch out into directing. People get tired of seeing you do the same thing.

'Some people don't want you to take that big swing. It's just not what they expect or want from you. But I can't let that stop me. If you think about that, you're going to make decisions for all the wrong reasons. If you don't take some chances, why do it?

'When I was going over the material for *Sudden Impact* with the screenwriter I came to the line: "Go ahead, make my day." I said: "This is really good," I knew it would click. But how! One lady hired an airplane to tow a banner saying: "Clint, make my day," signed Kathy or whatever it was. It was just crazy. But it hasn't changed any. It's everywhere I go.

'If you start thinking about the end results and start anticipating what an audience might feel, you may be dead wrong. I just go ahead with my way and figure that at least I can have the satisfaction of having put it down. And if it works, it works, and if it doesn't, move on. You have to put personal relationships aside. You have to be selfish about who you use in a picture. You use people you think can do the job. You can't just let your mind be ruled by other feelings.'

Eastwood then emphasises his admiration for Action Women and Men: 'I've always felt that the more a woman is active in life, same as a man, the more interesting she is to be around. There's no reason women shouldn't try to attain everything they're capable of. During the 1970s we had to pigeonhole everybody in some category – either sexist or racist or chauvinist or whatever-you-call-ist. That was an unhealthy period, and I'm glad it's over. A lot of other films I've done appeal to fantasies. The romance of the individual who says and does the right thing at the right time is very strong. As women become more involved with careers, they understand better the kind of Mickey Mouse bureaucracies the characters I play are always fighting against. But I think women still find a man they can rely on appealing. I don't think the roles have changed that much.

'Most people who get to a certain stage in making movies usually are the best at what they do. In other words, they do things that nobody else can do. There's a lot of other actors that do more variety, but no specific thing that is them. You can say that about Cary Grant, John Wayne. Whatever they did, they did it and nobody else could do it. People would try to imitate them over the years and nobody could imitate them. Most actors don't work that way, don't work in reserve, because it's a hard thing to do.

'Gary Cooper, when he was asked to explain his acting technique, used to say that he was just thinking hard what his next line was. George Cukor used to get great results from Garbo by telling her to think of nothing in the close-ups. Obviously, her thinking of nothing was more interesting than another girl thinking of a lot of things.

'"Macho" is probably one of the most misused words in the language. Over the years, I think the most macho guys on the screen were also very sensitive people. I think Bogart and Cagney and Wayne could all portray great sensitivity. The truth is that strong men are sensitive and aren't afraid of showing it. It's the people that are insecure about their manliness, who are adverse about showing their feelings, who have to do that cock-of-the-walk, strut-your-stuff kind of thing. And it's the people who take man pills and have to go around kicking over furniture all the time who are usually insecure about their manliness. Just like a woman who has to go around acting twitty all the time, flirting and chirping like a canary. A woman like that may be insecure about her femininity. Femininity is an inner thing – it's that simple. A woman doesn't have to be a centrefold to be beautiful. She could even have a low voice like Katharine Hepburn's. This culture has too many clichés and stereotypes.'

But clichés and stereotypes aside, Eastwood has enjoyed magic moments, the good, the bad and the ugly of movie-making. 'This has been a great era for actors. Any actor who's doing well can have a certain amount of control. In the old days it was: "Here's your next picture, Mr Bogart." Today you're a free agent. So I pick things that jump off the page at me.

'Cary Grant never won the Academy Award. He was a brilliant comedian. People didn't understand how brilliant he was. One of the great entertainers of our lifetime. Not that he needed it, he probably didn't care.

'I remember going to a party when I was a young contract player at Universal. Someone introduced me to Cornel Wilde. I'd never met a movie star. I didn't know any celebrities. Cornel Wilde was in his heyday then. He said to me: "Save your money." I said: "I don't have any money." He said: "If you get any money, save it. That way you won't have to do projects just for the sake of existing." I gather he was talking about himself. Perhaps he felt he had done a lot of movies he shouldn't have done. I've always remembered that advice. A lot of it is luck, but if you manage yourself well, you can step back if things aren't right.'

Eastwood then argued about the violence of his films

against the reality of violence. His heart today certainly sounds as though it is hovering around the less commercial films he makes.

'Everybody's trying to break the bank or make a $100-million film. Everybody's looking for the road to commercial success. I've had a certain amount of commercial success along the way, so I'm just looking to make some good stories. Rigidity is death and flexibility is birth. God gave you a brain to think, and if you don't use it, it's going to get rigid, and it's going to get smaller, until it's just a tiny pea inside your skull. I think the directing personality is just being able to lead the platoon up the hill and the acting personality is, OK, what are we going to shoot at on the way to protect ourselves? It's a life of escapism. Maybe that's why so many actors get screwed up along the way. They tend to rely on the escapist part rather than the reality part. I think I've always been a realist. Your brain can go fast. After a while you forget that you once bagged groceries or worked in a gas station or dug ditches.

'When we were kids, we thought if you kill somebody, they electrocute you. Jimmy Cagney, the big house, the chair, zzzzz, you're dead. Nowadays, it's not that way. One guy gets 30 years for robbery, another gets six for murder. If there's irresponsibility in *Dirty Harry*, there's irresponsibility in Robin Hood, Tom Mix and the Old Testament. There is violence in all of them. I don't advocate violence, I never have. I don't enjoy arbitrary violence, and I think hunting animals is disgusting.

'Everybody has certain reservations about violence. I don't mind sexy movies and I don't mind violent movies, but I don't like sex and violence together. That bothers me. But what relationship violence has to society, I don't know. I don't know which is imitative of which. I think movie violence is a convenient fall guy. When you haven't got anything else to blame, blame it on that. My generation grew up watching Paul Muni, George Raft, Humphrey Bogart and James Cagney blowing people away, and it didn't make us criminals – I'm not sure it does today. People have to monitor what their kids see. I guess that's what the rating system's all about.

'I tell you, kids are amazing. Adults always have the greatest fears about kids and probably justifiably so, but kids know a lot more than most adults think they know and with the violence thing I've never had to explain much to them. We'll see a movie together and maybe the movie is in poor taste and then we'll discuss it.

'I'm against war – period. When I was in the army I was against the Korean War, and after that – although I wasn't a protester – I was against Vietnam. But people want to see reality in movies, and the world is a violent place. It's nothing new. Being killed with a gun is probably better than being hacked to death with a sword, the way they did it in medieval times. People want to see crooks being punished hard. They see the cops losing the battle for law and order. There is a wave of feeling in America among people who have had it up to here with violence on the streets. The trend in our country now is to weight the scales in favour of the criminal.

'My sympathy has always been with the victim. Not that I'm against the rights of the accused. Every effort must be made to see that a person is never prosecuted for something he didn't do. At the same time, I worry about people who are at risk.'

And there you have the dichotomy of the Eastwood image. Dirty Harry versus Zubin Mehta, Josey Wales versus Dave Brubeck – he's against injustice and pro the arts.

'I like art and I like music very much. I used to play flute, cornet and piano when I was a kid. In fact, I wanted to go to the University of Seattle Music School, but, unfortunately, I procrastinated and got inducted into the service, so I had to abandon that idea. I fiddle around on the piano – mostly writing things. I have composed music for three or four films. I am not a well-schooled musician, but I have loved music all my life. I am surprised that I never got into it.

'Any art enriches one's life, you bet. I don't collect any particular art or artist, but I have a lot of various pieces. I have Remington, Russell, some of the newer Western art people. I have Michael Coleman, people like that, but I also have Rockwell. I have all kinds of things; I'm not glued to one particular style. When I worked for a timber company in Springfield, near Eugene, Oregon, and all they played up there was country music – Hank Snow and all that kind of stuff – I never liked it. I always preferred jazz. I'd stay up all night so I could listen to Jimmy Lyons broadcasting from San Francisco at midnight, playing the hot stuff at the time – Brubeck and Mulligan and all that. My mother had a collection of Fats Waller records, and she played the piano and taught me. Later on I became interested in the self-destruct kind of country guys – Hank Williams, Red Foley – after I read *Honkytonk Man*. I appreciate it more now than

I did as a kid. I like rhythm and blues and pop. I thought rock 'n' roll by white guys was boring – sounded like guys trying to be black and didn't have it.

'There are two American art forms, the Western and jazz. It's funny how Americans don't support either of them any more. My Westerns are the way they are because of the point in history where I picked it up. John Wayne once wrote me a letter and he wasn't very pleased about *High Plains Drifter*. He said that isn't what the West was all about, that isn't the American people who settled this country. I said: "You're absolutely right." It's just an allegory, and it wasn't intended to be the West that's been told hundreds of times over by many players, about pioneers and covered wagons and conflict with the various Indian nations.

'*High Plains Drifter* was a speculation on what happens when they go ahead and kill the sheriff and somebody comes back and calls the town's conscience to bear.

'There's always retribution for your deeds.'

# FIFTEEN

# WALK TALL

'I don't think Clint will ever hang up
his guns. He'll go out blazing.'
SAM BOTTOMS

CLINT Eastwood entered 2005 on full firepower.

His *Million Dollar Baby* was fast establishing itself as one
of the favourites for the Academy Awards.

His actors Sean Penn and Tim Robbins had collected
acting Oscars the year before, but this looked like Clint's
year for acting and directing, for the Best Picture.

Again the Eastwood movie revolved around family ties.
Clint's Frankie Dunn has trained and managed some
incredible fighters during a lifetime spent in the ring. The
most important lesson he teaches his boxers is the one that
rules his life: above all, always protect yourself.

In the wake of a painful estrangement from his daughter, Frankie has been unwilling to let himself get close to anyone for a very long time. His only friend is Morgan Freeman's Scrap, an ex-boxer who looks after Frankie's gym and knows that beneath his gruff exterior is a man who has attended Mass almost every day for the past 23 years, seeking the forgiveness that somehow continues to elude him.

Then Hilary Swank's Maggie Fitzgerald walks into his gym.

Maggie's never had much, but there is one thing she does have that very few people in this world ever do: she knows what she wants and she's willing to do whatever it takes to get it. In a life of constant struggle, Maggie's got herself this far on raw talent, unshakeable focus and a tremendous force of will. But more than anything, what she wants is for someone to believe in her.

The last thing Frankie needs is that kind of responsibility – let alone that kind of risk. He tells Maggie the blunt hard truth: she's too old and he doesn't train girls. But 'no' has little meaning when you have no other choice. Unwilling or unable to give up on her life's ambition, Maggie wears herself to the bone at the gym every day, encouraged only by Scrap. Finally won over by Maggie's sheer determination, Frankie begrudgingly agrees to take her on.

In turns exasperating and inspiring each other, the two come to discover that they share a common spirit that transcends the pain and loss of their pasts, and find in each other a sense of family they lost long ago. What they don't know is that soon they will both face a battle that's going to demand more heart and courage than any they've ever known.

It was Eastwood's twenty-fifth film as a director, the twenty-first he had produced and the fifty-seventh he had acted in. Numbers?

His daughter Morgan, whom he calls 'Googles', appears in *Million Dollar Baby* as the little girl in the truck.

It was a family affair in many different ways.

Although he remains adamant he will not get into national politics, Eastwood has given his support to environmental causes. Environmental groups were delighted to recruit Eastwood, who showed he was a conservationist as well as a conservative. Yet he said: 'If I've got a presidential face I'm lacking in a lot of other areas.'

He's more interested in cinema showdowns.

He's arguably the Last Great Hollywood star. His involvement in any project doesn't automatically make it an all-round success but it gives it immediate authority. And that's what he is today. An authority figure. A serious man who likes his secrets to remain secret. There is a touch of fatalism about him and also much humour. In his films he can be a romantic albeit a guilty one.

The first sign of that was in 1973 when he directed the late William Holden and Kay Lenz in *Breezy*. The late Jo Heims, who also wrote *Play Misty for Me*, was an influential Eastwood friend and he says of her: 'She wrote the man and the woman's characters so well I thought: I don't know if I'm going to act in it but I'd sure like to make it. I liked the whole comment of the rejuvenation of a cynic living around Los Angeles, divorced, making good dough but hating it and then finding out about life through a 17-

year-old. She teaches him more about it than he teaches her. It's a mutual exchange but it doesn't go on for ever and she doesn't die of some exotic disease.'

He is enjoying his stature as an American icon.

Mature. Mellower. All those years of laying the foundations, from digging swimming pools to his roles in B Westerns, have paid off handsomely.

When he walks into the room he knows at least two people will say: 'Go on, make my day!' as they ask for an autograph. And at least one woman will slip him a phone number with a similar comment: something along the lines of how she could make his day. He has heard all the lines. But you would never know it. The fans usually get their autographs these days, the women get a friendly smile. If he likes what he's looking at the smile simply gets broader and warmer.

He has matured into a self-effacing but powerful force in Hollywood, in the cinema worldwide. Up on the screen he's larger than life. Off screen he walks about with similar confidence. Alan Murray, who has been the sound effects editor on a string of Eastwood films, found that image a problem: 'You can't have him hit somebody and make it sound like a slap – you've got to hear the bones break in the guy's jaw. You try to match the sound to the character. When he's mad, I will make the gunshot louder than when he's running down a street and shooting at somebody.

'The big challenge was always to give him a walk as impressive as his persona. It was difficult to get the right walk for Clint. I must have gone through ten pairs of shoes. Finally, I looked in a closet and found these shoes my father had worn in the 1940s. They had very hard leather soles with a bit of wood in between. And we tried these and it was Clint's walk. It had weight, it had manliness and strength to it.'

Actor George Dzundza, who worked for him on *White Hunter, Black Heart*, makes this point: 'You sense a sort of gentility, a sort of man's approach to things.' And that's one of the reasons why Eastwood rather than any other star – or celebrity image – is conjured up in messages from the White House to Gulf War campaigns to reflect a cool, calm but certainly effective way of taking care of business. Any sort of business.

For all the critics, all the bile over violence and *Dirty Harry*, Eastwood has emerged in the autumn of his career as an instant image. He's Mr Good. Mr Right. The Pale Rider. He has the major gift of *always* looking comfortable, no matter what role he is publicly playing. The difficult times have been as husband and lover; the times, we might say, when he was looking at the wrong end of a .44 Magnum.

He's a fascinating man. He's concerned about abused kids and the abused planet. He'll stop on the road driving through Arizona or Mexico to rescue an injured iguana. He bottle-feeds lambs on his ranch – even when he isn't running for political office – but until the past few years and Dina Ruiz he seemed strangely remote and unable to commit fully to human relationships. His second marriage changed that.

He could retire but that's not on the horizon, there's no crimson sunset he plans to ride into. He pulls a fact out of the air. Men don't live as long as women. Therefore? 'They have to take advantages faster.' He learned that growing up during the Depression. He was a loner then. And he remains one today. Content? Probably. Happy? Yes. Retiring? Never.

Recall actor Sam Bottoms talking about Eastwood on the set of *Bronco Billy*: 'I don't think Clint will ever hang up his guns. He'll go out blazing.'

Back then, Bottoms could never have known just how much 21st-century firepower his mentor and friend would have.

For nearly four decades Clint Eastwood has been the cinema embodiment of an all-American masculinity; the solitary gunslinger who rides into town to exact his unique brand of vengeance; the squinty-eyed cop who defies bureaucratic politesse to get his man; the ageing Secret Service agent who fights age and memory for his honour.

Lean. Lanky. Laconic.

He's always specialised in loners with a slyly ironic smile; men cut off by temperament and circumstances from the world around them.

He's the minimalist cowboy who could make you feel lucky.

Or unlucky.

Someone who could make your day.

# FILMOGRAPHY

CLINT Eastwood played Rowdy Yates in *Rawhide* from 1958 to 1966. The series began being shown on American television on 9 January 1959, with the episode *Incident of the Tumbleweed Wagon*. Frankie Laine, who sang the theme song, was a guest star in a 1960 episode entitled *Incident on the Road to Yesterday*.

Many remarkable names appeared in *Rawhide* over the years, including Nick Adams, Eddie Albert, Mary Astor, Claude Akins, Frankie Avalon, John Drew Barrymore, Richard Basehart, Ralph Bellamy, Robert Blake, Neville Brand, Charles Bronson, MacDonald Carey, John Cassavetes, James Coburn, Robert Coote, Linda Cristal, Robert Culp, Troy Donahue, Brian Donlevy, Dan Duryea, Buddy Ebsen, Steve Forrest, Charles Gray, Julie Harris, Louis Hayward, Pat Hingle, Martha Hyer, John Ireland,

Brian Keith, Julie London, Jack Lord, Peter Lorre, Mercedes McCambridge, Victor McLaglen, Jock Mahoney, Dean Martin, Patricia Medina, Burgess Meredith, Gary Merrill, Vera Miles, Agnes Moorehead, Leslie Nielsen, Warren Oates, Dan O'Herlihy, Walter Pidgeon, Denver Pyle, Claude Rains, Cesar Romero, Mickey Rooney, Zachary Scott, Barbara Stanwyck, Woody Strode, Bill Travers, Forrest Tucker, Lee Van Cleef, Efrem Zimbalist Jr. Many of the *Rawhide* guest stars would go on to appear in Eastwood films over the years. He had a memory. He was loyal.

Eastwood made ten films before the series began and during it made *A Fistful of Dollars* in 1964. Here are all the Eastwood movies:

### Revenge of the Creature
Universal-International, USA, 1955
Director: Jack Arnold
Producer: William Alland
Music: Henry Mancini, Herman Stein
John Agar (Clete Ferguson), Lori Nelson (Helen Dobson), Clint Eastwood (uncredited as Jennings, a lab technician)

### Tarantula
Universal-International, USA, 1955
Director: Jack Arnold
Producer: William Alland
Music: Henry Mancini, Herman Stein
John Agar (Dr Matt Hastings), Leo G. Carroll (Professor Deemer), Clint Eastwood (uncredited as a bomber pilot)

## Lady Godiva of Coventry
Universal-International, USA, 1955
Director: Arthur Lubin
Producer: Robert Arthur
Music: Hans J Salter
Maureen O'Hara (Lady Godiva), George Nader
(Lord Leofic), Clint Eastwood (First Saxon)

## Francis in the Navy
Universal-International, USA, 1955
Director: Arthur Lubin
Producer: Stanley Rubin
Music: Frank Skinner
Donald O'Connor (Lieutenant Peter Stirling), Martha Hyer
(Betsy Donevan), Jim Backus (Commander Hutch), Clint
Eastwood (Jonesy), Chill Wills (voice of Francis)

## Never Say Goodbye
Universal-International, USA, 1955
Director: Jerry Hopper
Producer: Albert J Cohen
Music: Frank Skinner
Rock Hudson (Dr Michael Parker), George Sanders (Victor),
Shelley Fabares (Suzy Parker), Clint Eastwood (Will)

### The First Travelling Saleslady

RKO-Radio, USA, 1956
Director: Arthur Lubin
Producer: Arthur Lubin
Music: Irving Gertz
Ginger Rogers (Rose Gillray), Carol Channing (Molly Wade),
James Arness (Joel Kingdom), Clint Eastwood (Jack Rice)

### Star in the Dust

Universal-International, USA, 1956
Director: Charles Haas
Producer: Albert Zugsmith
Music: Terry Gilkyson, Frank Skinner
John Agar (Bill Jordan), Mamie Van Doren (Ellen Ballard),
Richard Boone (Sam Hall), Leif Erickson (George Ballard),
Clint Eastwood (uncredited as a ranch hand)

### Away All Boats

Universal-International, USA, 1956
Director: Joseph Pevney
Producer: Howard Christie
Music: Frank Skinner
Jeff Chandler (Capt Jedediah Hawks, George Nadar
(Lt Dave MacDougell), Clint Eastwood (Lt Sherwood)

### Escapade in Japan
RKO-Radio, USA, 1957
Director: Arthur Lubin
Producer: Arthur Lubin
Music: Max Steiner
Teresa Wright (Mary Saunders), Cameron Mitchell
(Dick Saunders), Clint Eastwood (uncredited as rescue
pilot One Dumbo)

### Lafayette Escadrille
*(British title: Hell Bent for Glory)*
Warner Brothers, USA, 1957
Director: William A. Wellman
Producer: William A. Wellman
Music: Leonard Rosenman
Tab Hunter (Thad Walker), David Janssen (Duke
Sinclaire), Clint Eastwood (George Moseley)

### Ambush at Cimarron Pass
20th Century-Fox, USA, 1957
Director: Jodie Copelan
Producer: Herbert E Mendelson
Music: Paul Sawtell, Bert Shefter
Scott Brady (Sergeant Matt Blake), Clint Eastwood
(Keith Williams)

### A Fistful of Dollars

United Artists, Italy/West Germany/Spain, 1964
Director: Sergio Leone
Producer: Arrigo Colombo, Giorgio Papi
Music: Ennio Morricone
Clint Eastwood (The Stranger), John Welles [Gian Maria Volonte] (Ramon Rojo), Marianne Koch (Marisol)

### For a Few Dollars More

United Artists, Italy/Spain/West Germany, 1965
Director: Sergio Leone
Producer: Arturo González, Alberto Grimaldi
Music: Ennio Morricone
Clint Eastwood (The Stranger), Lee Van Cleef (Colonel Mortimer), Klaus Kinski (Hunchback)

### The Good, the Bad and the Ugly

United Artists, Italy, 1966
Director: Sergio Leone
Producer: Alberto Grimaldi
Music: Ennio Morricone
Clint Eastwood (Joe), Eli Wallach (Tuco), Lee Van Cleef (Setenza/'Angel Eyes')

### The Witches

United Artists, Italy/France, 1966
Directors: Luchino Visconti (Part 1); Mauro Bolognini (Part 2); Pier Paolo Pasolini (Part 3); Franco Rossi (Part 4); Vittorio De Sica (Part 5)
Producer: Dino De Laurentiis

Music: Ennio Morricone, Piero Piccioni
Silvana Mangano (Giovanna), Clint Eastwood
(Mario, Mangano's husband)

## Hang 'Em High
United Artists, USA, 1967
Director: Ted Post
Producer: Leonard Freeman
Music: Dominic Frontiere
Clint Eastwood (Jed Cooper), Inger Stevens (Rachel), Ed
Begley (Captain Wilson), Pat Hingle (Judge Adam Fenton),
James MacArthur (Priest)

## Coogan's Bluff
Universal, USA, 1968
Director: Don Siegel
Producer: Don Siegel
Music: Lalo Schifrin
Clint Eastwood (Walt Coogan), Lee J. Cobb (Sheriff
McElroy), Susan Clark (Julie), Don Stroud (Ringerman)

## Where Eagles Dare
MGM, Great Britain, 1968
Director: Brian G. Hutton
Producer: Elliott Kastner
Music: Ron Goodwin
Richard Burton (Major John Smith), Clint Eastwood
(Lieutenant Morris Schaffer), Mary Ure (Mary Ellison),
Patrick Wymark (Colonel Wyatt Turner), Michael Hordern
(Vice-Admiral Rolland), Donald Houston (Christiansen),

Peter Barkworth (Berkeley), Robert Beatty (Cartwright
Jones), Anton Diffring (Colonel Kramer), Ferdy Mayne
(Reichsmarschal Rosemeyer), Ingrid Pitt (Heidi)

### Paint your Wagon
Paramount, USA, 1969
Director: Joshua Logan
Producer: Alan J Lerner
Music: Frederick Loewe, André Previn, Nelson Riddle
Lee Marvin (Ben Rumson), Clint Eastwood (Pardner),
Jean Seberg (Elizabeth), Harve Presnell (Rotten Luck Willie)

### Two Mules for Sister Sara
Universal/Malpaso, USA, 1969
Director: Don Siegel
Producer: Carroll Case, Martin Rackin
Music: Ennio Morricone
Shirley MacLaine (Sara), Clint Eastwood (Hogan)

### Kelly's Heroes
MGM-EMI, USA/Yugoslavia, 1970
Director: Brian G. Hutton
Producer: Sidney Beckerman, Gabriel Katzka, Harold Loeb
Music: Lalo Schifrin
Clint Eastwood (Kelly), Telly Savalas (Big Joe), Don
Rickles (Crapgame), Donald Sutherland (Oddball),
Carroll O'Connor (General Colt)

### The Beguiled
Universal/Malpaso, USA, 1970
Director: Don Siegel
Producer: Don Siegel
Music: Lalo Schifrin
Clint Eastwood (John McBurney), Geraldine Page (Martha Farnsworth), Elizabeth Hartman (Edwina Dabney)

### Play Misty for Me
Universal/Malpaso, USA, 1971
Director: Clint Eastwood
Producer: Robert Daley, Jennings Lang
Music: Dee Barton, Ewan MacColl
Clint Eastwood (Dave Garver), Jessica Walter (Evelyn Draper), Donna Mills (Tobie Williams)

### Dirty Harry
Columbia-Warner, USA, 1971
Director: Don Siegel
Producer: Don Siegel
Music: Lalo Schifrin
Clint Eastwood (Harry Callahan), Harry Guardino (Lieutenant Bressler), Reni Santoni (Chico), John Vernon (The Mayor), Andy Robinson (Scorpio)

### Joe Kidd

Universal/Malpaso, USA, 1972
Director: John Sturges
Producer: Sidney Beckerman
Music: Lalo Schifrin
Clint Eastwood (Joe Kidd), Robert Duvall (Frank Harlan),
John Saxon (Luis Chama), Don Stroud (Lamarr)

### High Plains Drifter

Universal/Malpaso, USA, 1972
Director: Clint Eastwood
Producer: Robert Daley
Music: Dee Barton
Clint Eastwood (The Stranger), Verna Bloom (Sarah
Belding), Mariana Hill (Callie Travers), Mitchell Ryan
(Dave Drake)

### Breezy

Universal/Malpaso, USA, 1973
Director: Clint Eastwood
Producer: Robert Daley
Music: Michel Legrand
William Holden (Frank Harmon), Kay Lenz (Breezy)

### Magnum Force

Malpaso, USA, 1973
Director: Ted Post
Producer: Robert Daley
Music: Lalo Schifrin
Clint Eastwood (Inspector Harry Callahan), Hal Holbrook

(Lieutenant Neil Briggs), Mitchell Ryan (Charlie McCoy), David Soul (John Davis), Robert Urich (Mike Grimes)

## Thunderbolt and Lightfoot

Malpaso Company, USA, 1974
Director: Michael Cimino
Producer: Robert Daley
Music: Dee Barton, Paul Williams
Clint Eastwood (John 'Thunderbolt' Doherty), Jeff Bridges (Lightfoot), George Kennedy (Red Leary), Geoffrey Lewis (Goody), Catherine Bach (Melody), Gary Busey (Curly)

## The Eiger Sanction

Universal/Malpaso Company, USA, 1975
Director: Clint Eastwood
Producer: Robert Daley
Music: John Williams
Clint Eastwood (Jonathan Hemlock), George Kennedy (Ben Bowman), Vonetta McGee (Jemima Brown), Jack Cassidy (Miles Mellough), Brenda Venus (George)

## The Outlaw Josey Wales

Malpaso for Warner Brothers, USA, 1976
Director: Clint Eastwood
Producer: Robert Daley
Music: Jerry Fielding
Clint Eastwood (Josey Wales), Sondra Locke (Laura Lee), Chief Dan George (Lone Watie), Bill McKinney (Terrill), John Vernon (Fletcher), Sam Bottoms (Jamie)

### *The Enforcer*
Malpaso for Warner Brothers, USA, 1976
Director: James Fargo
Producer: Robert Daley
Music: Jerry Fielding
Clint Eastwood (Inspector Harry Callahan), Harry
Guardino (Lieutenant Bressler), Bradford Dillman (Captain
McKay), Tyne Daly (Kate Moore)

### *The Gauntlet*
Malpaso for Warner Brothers, USA, 1977
Director: Clint Eastwood
Producer: Robert Daley
Music: Jerry Fielding
Clint Eastwood (Ben Shockley), Sondra Locke (Gus
Mally), Pat Hingle (Josephson), William Prince (Blakelock)

### *Every Which Way But Loose*
Malpaso for Warner Brothers, USA, 1978
Director: James Fargo
Producer: Robert Daley
Music: Steve Dorff
Clint Eastwood (Philo Beddoe), Sondra Locke (Lynn
Halsey-Taylor), Ruth Gordon (Ma), Geoffrey Lewis
(Orville), Beverly D'Angelo (Echo)

### Escape from Alcatraz

Malpaso for Paramount, USA, 1979
Director: Don Siegel
Producer: Don Siegel
Music: Jerry Fielding, Gilbert Thomas Jr
Clint Eastwood (Frank Morris), Patrick McGoohan
(Warden)

### Bronco Billy

Warner Brothers, USA, 1980
Director: Clint Eastwood
Producer: Neal H Dobrofsky, Dennis Hackin
Music: Larry Bastion, Steve Dorff, Clint Eastwood, Snuff
Garrett, Larry Herbstritt
Clint Eastwood ('Bronco Billy' McCoy), Sondra Locke
(Antoinette Lily), Geoffrey Lewis (John Arlington),
Scatman Crothers ('Doc' Lynch), Sam Bottoms (Leonard
James), Sierra Pecheur (Lorraine Running Water)

### Any Which Way You Can

Malpaso for Warner Brothers, USA, 1980
Director: Buddy Van Horn
Producer: Fritz Manes
Clint Eastwood (Philo Beddoe), Sondra Locke (Lynn
Halsey-Taylor), Geoffrey Lewis (Orville Boggs), William
Smith (Jack Wilson), Harry Guardino (James Beekman),
Ruth Gordon (Ma Boggs)

### Honkytonk Man
Malpaso for Warner Brothers, USA, 1982
Director: Clint Eastwood
Producer: Clint Eastwood
Music: De Wayne Blackwell, Cliff Crofford, Steve Dorff,
Jimmy Durill, Snuff Garrett, Herb Remington
Clint Eastwood (Red Stovall), Kyle Eastwood (Whit),
John McIntire (Grandpa), Verna Bloom (Emmy)

### Firefox
Malpaso for Warner Brothers, USA, 1982
Director: Clint Eastwood
Producer: Clint Eastwood
Music: Maurice Jarre
Clint Eastwood (Mitchell Gant), Freddie Jones
(Kenneth Aubrey), Ronald Lacey (Semelovsky)

### Sudden Impact
Malpaso for Warner Brothers, USA, 1983
Director: Clint Eastwood
Producer: Clint Eastwood
Music: Lalo Schifrin
Clint Eastwood (Harry Callahan), Sondra Locke
(Jennifer Spencer), Pat Hingle (Chief Jannings),
Bradford Dillman (Captain Briggs)

### Tightrope
Warner Brothers, Malpaso, USA, 1984
Director: Richard Tuggle
Producer: Clint Eastwood, Fritz Manes
Music: Lennie Niehaus
Clint Eastwood (Wes Block), Genevieve Bujold (Beryl Thibodeaux), Dan Hedaya (Detective Molinari), Alison Eastwood (Amanda Block), Jennifer Beck (Penny Block)

### City Heat
Malpaso/Deliverance for Warner Brothers, USA, 1984
Director: Richard Benjamin
Producer: Fritz Manes
Music: Clint Eastwood, Lennie Niehaus
Clint Eastwood (Lieutenant Speer), Burt Reynolds (Mike Murphy), Jane Alexander (Addy), Madeline Kahn (Caroline Howley), Rip Torn (Primo Pitt), Irene Cara (Ginny Lee), Richard Roundtree (Dehl Swift), Tony Lo Bianco (Leon Coll)

### Pale Rider
Warner Brothers, Malpaso, USA, 1985
Director: Clint Eastwood
Producer: Clint Eastwood
Music: Lennie Niehaus
Clint Eastwood (Preacher), Michael Moriarty (Hull Barret), Carrie Snodgress (Sarah Wheeler), Christopher Penn (Josh LaHood), Richard Dysart (Coy LaHood), Richard Kiel (Club), John Russell (Marshal Stockburn)

### Vanessa in the Garden

(TV episode for Steven Spielberg's *Amazing Stories*),
USA, 1985
Director: Clint Eastwood
Producer: David E Vogel
Music: Lennie Niehaus
Sondra Locke (Vanessa), Harvey Keitel and Beau Bridges

### Heartbreak Ridge

Malpaso for Warner Brothers, USA, 1986
Director: Clint Eastwood
Producer: Clint Eastwood
Music: Clint Eastwood, Lennie Niehaus
Clint Eastwood (Sergeant Thomas Highway),
Marsha Mason (Aggie), Everett McGill (Major Powers),
Moses Gunn (Sergeant Webster), Mario Van Peebles
('Stitch' Jones)

### Bird

Warner Brothers, Malpaso, USA, 1988
Director: Clint Eastwood
Producer: Clint Eastwood
Music: Lennie Niehaus
Forest Whitaker (Charlie 'Yardbird' Parker), Diane Venora
(Chan Richardson), Michael Zelniker (Red Rodney),
Samuel E. Wright (Dizzy Gillespie)

### The Dead Pool
Warner Brothers, Malpaso, USA, 1988
Director: Buddy Van Horn
Producer: David Valdes
Music: Lalo Schifrin
Clint Eastwood (Inspector Harry Callahan), Patricia
Clarkson (Samantha Walker), Liam Neeson (Peter Swan)

### Pink Cadillac
Malpaso for Warner Brothers, USA, 1989
Director: Buddy Van Horn
Producer: David Valdes
Music: Bryan Adams, JC Crowley, Steve Dorff
Clint Eastwood (Tommy Nowak), Bernadette Peters
(Lou Ann McGuinn)

### White Hunter, Black Heart
Malpaso/Rastar for Warner Brothers, USA, 1990
Director: Clint Eastwood
Producer: Clint Eastwood
Music: Lennie Niehaus
Clint Eastwood (John Wilson), Jeff Fahey (Peter Verrill),
Charlotte Cornwell (Miss Wilding), Norman Lumsden
(Butler George), George Dzundza (Paul Landers)

### The Rookie
Malpaso for Warner Brothers, USA, 1990
Director: Clint Eastwood
Producer: Howard G Kazanjian, Steven Siebert,
David Valdes
Music: Kyle Eastwood, Jerome Kern, Lennie Niehaus
Clint Eastwood (Nick Pulovski), Charlie Sheen
(David Ackerman), Raul Julia (Strom), Sonia Braga (Liesl),
Tom Skerritt (Eugene Ackerman), Lara Flynn Boyle (Sarah)

### Unforgiven
Malpaso for Warner Brothers, USA, 1992
Director: Clint Eastwood
Producer: Clint Eastwood
Music: Lennie Niehaus, Clint Eastwood
Clint Eastwood (William 'Bill' Munny), Gene Hackman
(Little Bill Daggett), Morgan Freeman (Ned Logan),
Richard Harris (English Bob)

### A Perfect World
Malpaso for Warner Brothers, USA, 1993
Director: Clint Eastwood
Producer: Clint Eastwood, Mark Johnson, David Valdes
Music: Lennie Niehaus
Clint Eastwood (Chief Red Garnett), Kevin Costner
(Robert 'Butch' Haynes), Laura Dern (Sally Gerber)

### In the Line of Fire

Castle Rock Entertainment, Columbia Pictures, USA, 1993
Director: Wolfgang Petersen
Producer: Jeff Apple
Music: Ennio Morricone
Clint Eastwood (Secret Service Agent Frank Horrigan),
John Malkovich (Mitch Leary/John Booth/James Carney),
Rene Russo (Secret Service Agent Lilly Raines)

### The Bridges of Madison County

Malpaso, Amblin Entertainment, Warner Brothers,
USA 1995
Director: Clint Eastwood
Producer: Clint Eastwood, Kathleen Kennedy
Music: Clint Eastwood, Fletcher Henderson, Lennie
Niehaus
Clint Eastwood (Robert Kincaid), Meryl Streep
(Francesca Johnson), Annie Corley (Caroline), Victor
Slezak (Michael Johnson), Jim Haynie (Richard Johnson)

### Absolute Power

Malpaso, Castle Rock Entertainment, Columbia Pictures,
USA, 1997
Director: Clint Eastwood
Producer: Clint Eastwood, Karen Spiegel
Music: Clint Eastwood, Lennie Niehaus
Clint Eastwood (Luther Whitney), Gene Hackman
(President Allen Richmond), Ed Harris (Seth Frank),
Laura Linney (Kate Whitney), Alison Eastwood
(Art Student)

### True Crime
Malpaso, The Zanuck Company, USA, 1999
Director: Clint Eastwood
Producer: Clint Eastwood, Lili Fini Zanuck,
Richard D Zanuck
Music: Clint Eastwood, Lennie Niehaus
Clint Eastwood (Steve Everett), Isaiah Washington
(Frank Louis Beachum), Lisa Gay Hamilton (Bonnie
Beachum), James Woods (Alan Mann), Denis Leary
(Bob Findley), Francesca Ruth Eastwood (Kate Everett)

### Space Cowboys
Malpaso, Clipsal Films, Mad Chance, Village Roadshow
Pictures, USA, 2000
Director: Clint Eastwood
Producer: Clint Eastwood, Andrew Lazar, Tom Rooker
Music: JC Chasez, Clint Eastwood, Lennie Niehaus
Clint Eastwood (Dr Frank Corvin), Tommy Lee Jones
(Colonel William 'Hawk' Hawkins), Donald Sutherland
(Jerry O'Neill), James Garner (Tank Sullivan), Jay Leno
(Himself)

### Blood Work
Malpaso for Warner Brothers, USA, 2002
Director: Clint Eastwood
Producer: Clint Eastwood
Music: Lennie Niehaus
Clint Eastwood (Terry McCaleb), Jeff Daniels (Jasper
'Buddy' Noone), Anjelica Huston (Dr Bonnie Fox), Wanda
De Jesus (Graciella Rivers)

## *Mystic River*

Malpaso, NPV Entertainment, Village Roadshow Pictures,
Warner Brothers, USA, 2003
Director: Clint Eastwood
Producer: Clint Eastwood, Judie Hoyt, Robert Lorenz
Music: Clint Eastwood, Kyle Eastwood
Sean Penn (Jimmy Markum), Tim Robbins (Dave Boyle),
Kevin Bacon (Sean Devine)

## *Million Dollar Baby*

Malpaso, Lakeshore Entertainment, Albert S Ruddy
Productions, Warner Brothers, USA, 2004
Director: Clint Eastwood
Producer: Clint Eastwood, Paul Haggis, Tom Rosenberg,
Albert S Ruddy
Music: Clint Eastwood
Clint Eastwood (Frankie Dunn), Hilary Swank (Maggie
Fitzgerald), Morgan Freeman (Eddie 'Scrap-Iron' Dupris)